Contents

KU-646-962

Colour illustrations

Town Maps

Historic Towns of East Anglia

David W. Lloyd

Victor Gollancz Ltd
in association with
Peter Crawley
1989

First published in Great Britain 1989
in association with Peter Crawley
by Victor Gollancz Ltd
14 Henrietta Street, London WC2E 8QJ
© David W. Lloyd 1989
Photographs © Peter Crawley
British Library Cataloguing in Publication Data
Lloyd, David
  Historic Towns of East Anglia
   1. Historic buildings—East Anglia
   2. Cities and towns—East Anglia
  I. Title
   720'.9422 NA961
ISBN 0-575-04383-0
Designed by Harold Bartram
Filmset, in Great Britain by
Butler & Tanner Ltd, Frome and London
Printed and bound in Singapore by
Imago Publishing Ltd

More detailed maps of the individual counties showing all of the towns covered in them are shown at the beginning of each county section.

Previous page
North Brink, Wisbech, an unparalleled series of mainly Georgian houses along the embanked River Nene, although the nearest building, a bank, dates from 1928. Towards the end of the series, set back beside trees, is Peckover House, *c.*1725.

Historic Towns of East Anglia

Also by David W. Lloyd

Historic Towns of South-East England
The Making of English Towns
Buildings of Portsmouth and its Environs
Save the City: A Conservation Study of the City of London (General Editor)
with Nikolaus Pevsner: Hampshire (*Buildings of England*)
with Donald Insall: Railway Station Architecture.

Norfolk
Suffolk
Essex
Cambridgeshire

Preface

This book follows *The Making of English Towns*, published in 1984, and *Historic Towns of South-East England*, published in 1987 as the first of what is hoped to be a series covering England, region by region. East Anglia is the second region so covered. I know that many people will not be entirely happy with the title; East Anglia has never been precisely defined since it ceased to be an Anglo-Saxon kingdom. Purists in, say, Norwich or Eye may deny that it extends beyond the boundaries of Norfolk and Suffolk – let alone as far as Southend or Huntingdon. But what I call 'East Anglia' is at least a conveniently defined area including three ancient counties, and a fourth (Cambridgeshire) which dates in its present form only from 1974, when it absorbed the historic county of Huntingdonshire and the ancient Soke of Peterborough. Inevitably some towns have been omitted which might have been included and others described all too briefly – because of the constraints of book space. The places described range from great cities like Cambridge and Norwich to little places like Castle Acre, Cley-next-the-Sea and Dedham, which are now villages but which in the past were prosperous towns – when they were, respectively, an appendage to a castle and a priory; a port; and a weaving centre. I also include places of recent growth like Felixstowe, Thorpeness and Harlow; the latter however is based on an ancient small town.

The photographs, as in the previous books, by my publisher, Peter Crawley, are as splendid as those, with which many readers will be familiar, which he took for the late Alec Clifton-Taylor's *Buildings of Delight*. Many of them show that glorious skies, such as inspired Constable and the painters of the Norwich School, are still characteristic of East Anglia.

I should like to thank all the other people who have helped me personally, and the authors of all the books on local subjects which I have consulted, many of which are listed in the Bibliography.

The maps are reproduced with the permission of the British Library. They are taken from the early editions of the Ordnance Survey, dating from the end of the Victorian period – apart from that of Cambridge which is later. Their original scale was 25 inches to the mile, except those of Long Melford and Cambridge which were at six inches to the mile, but they are not necessarily reproduced to the original scales.

DAVID W. LLOYD
Old Harlow, 1988

Introduction

East Anglia as defined in this book is three, perhaps four, regions. East Anglia proper – Norfolk, Suffolk and something of Cambridgeshire – was an important kingdom in the dark ages between the sixth and ninth centuries. Its kings lived at first in the Woodbridge area, where one of them was associated with the ship burial at Sutton Hoo – from which the fantastic treasure is now in the British Museum. A later king invited St Felix from Burgundy to establish Christianity in the kingdom in 630; his first church was probably at Dunwich – a place now eroded by the sea. The last king of separate East Anglia was Edmund, slain by the Vikings in 870. But the region retained its special identity. Although the term 'East Anglia' is now used more widely – as in the title of this book – the East Anglian character is strongest and most specific in its heartland of Norfolk and Suffolk.

Essex was in origin a separate kingdom, of the east *Saxons* rather than the east *Angles*. Even today, submerged though much of its acreage is under London's outward spread, it retains a strong identity, subtly different from that of East Anglia proper.

The Fens have a special character of their own. They were a flooded or marshy wilderness, out of which rose a series of low but dry islands and peninsulas, some of which were attractive for early monasteries like Ely. Parts of the Fens were gradually drained in medieval times; most of the remainder became dry land as the result of the huge drainage schemes of the 17th century.

The western fringe of the area covered by this book – mainly the old county of Huntingdonshire – is different again, really a part of the Midlands, with a touch of the Home Counties. The spine of this district is the River Ouse, before it enters the Fens.

Among the major towns, Colchester and Cambridge have Roman ancestry; the latter grew into an important trading centre before the university was established in the 13th century. Ipswich was one of the first purely Saxon towns to develop. Norwich became important rather later, but from Norman times till the Industrial Revolution was one of the greatest cities in England, with a cathedral from 1094. Bury St Edmunds grew round the great monastery which enshrined the body of the slain king Edmund, but became important enough in its own right to survive the shock of the Reformation, when the abbey was shattered. Ely was more fortunate; the monastic church was made a cathedral in 1107, and as such survived the Reformation, although Ely never grew into a large town. The abbey church at Peterborough became a cathedral at the Reformation, but the town remained small until the 19th century. Huntingdon was once more important, but declined drastically in the later Middle Ages, and grew again significantly only in very recent times. The history of Thetford is fairly similar. On the other hand Chelmsford, although of Roman ancestry, was a small town until the 19th century; it became the county town of Essex because of its central position in the county.

Ports have always been very important to the area's economy. Some of the oldest were at the heads of estuaries: Ipswich on the Orwell; Colchester with its outport on the Colne; Woodbridge and Maldon on the Deben and Blackwater. Wisbech was originally on a very important estuary, where the combined waters of the main rivers flowing through the Fens – the Nene from Northamptonshire, and the Ouse, of which the Cam is a tributary – entered the Wash. About 1250 there was a drastic natural change when the main river flow was diverted to the east, and eventually entered the Wash near Lynn (later King's Lynn), where there had previously been the mouth only of a very small river. Despite this early limitation, Lynn was already an important port; it broadened its trade after the river diversion, through its water connections with a vast hinterland. Wisbech was virtually stranded for a time, but later the Nene flowed again through the town and its trade revived. Yarmouth started on a shingle bank across the once wide estuary of the Yare; in medieval times and later it was a great fishing port, particularly for herring – one of the most important items of food in the past. Lowestoft also shared in this trade, but on a much smaller scale until the 19th century. Harwich developed from the 13th century on a peninsula. Elsewhere, there were medieval ports on inlets or estuaries which had periods of great prosperity – notably Cley-next-the-Sea, Southwold, Aldeburgh and Orford. Cley and Southwold eventually ceased to be ports because of silting; Aldeburgh and Orford because their quays were cut off from the open sea by a shingle spit – Orford Ness – which the sea built up to an incredible length. But the most dramatic coastal changes were at Dunwich, an important medieval port which was steadily eroded away; now there is only a small village on what had been the landward approach to the town. Vessels sailed a long way up some of the rivers, such as the Yare and Wensum to Norwich, the Waveney to Beccles, and the Ouse with its tributary the Cam to Ely, St Ives and Cambridge.

Market towns were densely distributed over most of the area in the Middle Ages. Markets, usually held weekly, were places where surplus produce from surrounding villages could be sold and specialized goods bought. Some markets, especially in the principal towns, dated back to Saxon times; others developed in what had hitherto been important villages, like Swaffham, Dereham and North Walsham in Norfolk – in all of which weekly markets still flourish. It was an advantage for markets to be situated on important land routes, on navigable rivers, or at river crossings where routes converged. Medieval traffic was minuscule compared with today, but what there was – goods were sent by packhorse or primitive cart if they could not go by water – was slow-moving and dependent on local resources; towns on important routes could prosper through accommodating and feeding people and animals.

New markets could be established only by royal charter. Overlords of existing villages and towns could profit from markets, through rents for stalls and tolls for goods sold there. Some landlords founded entirely new towns on their territories, as did the Bishop of Ely on one of his distant manors at Needham in Suffolk in 1226; Needham's market flourished because it was on an important route. The Knights Templar laid out a new street at Witham (the present Newland Street) on the London to Colchester road in about 1212, to which the market was transferred from the less advantageously situated Chipping Hill nearby (69). Many towns developed beside castles, which were important features of medieval East Anglia. Some of the first castles were built by the Normans in already important towns, such as Colchester, Norwich, Huntingdon and Cambridge; others were built by powerful barons on strategic sites within their territories – the Bigods at Bungay and Framlingham (33), the Malets at Eye, the de Clares at Clare, the d'Albinis at Castle Rising (colour plate, page 23) and New Buckenham, the de Veres at Castle Hedingham, the Mandevilles at (Saffron) Walden, the Warennes at Castle Acre, and Henry of Essex at Rayleigh. Henry II built a castle at Orford (colour plate, page 88). Towns grew up beside all these (maps IV, VI) – though some declined to the status of villages after the abandonment of their castles (4). Other market towns grew beside monasteries, like Ramsey (86), Waltham Abbey (68), and Walsingham, famous for pilgrimages.

Medieval markets were sometimes held along wide streets, as in Colchester and Needham Market, but in East Anglia they more often took place in definite market places, which could be rectangular (as at St Neots), triangular (as at Wymondham), wedge-shaped (as at Romford), or of indeterminate form. Stalls were normally set up on market days only, after which they were dismantled till the following week. But in many places they were left from week to week, and became permanent fixtures. The next stage would be replacement by two-storeyed buildings with shops below. In this way many market places became considerably encroached on by islanded blocks of buildings. Evidence of such a process occurs again and again in East Anglia, as in Holt where an original, roughly rectangular market place has been encroached on by several blocks of buildings, threaded by a network of alleys; in North Walsham, where an originally large space has been reduced to two connecting triangles by encroachment round its edges; and at Swaffham where what had been a very large triangular space now has islanded blocks at its northern end. Evidence of similar encroachments, creating irregular and often picturesque effects, can be seen at Saffron Walden, Diss (map I), Eye, Beccles (22), Bungay (23), Ely, Dereham, Ramsey, Clare, Harlow, Braintree, Newport, St Ives (88) and, especially, Bury St Edmunds (map V), where the present open market occupies only part of the originally very large market place, the rest of which has been long since built over (although the town's other public square, Angel Hill (26), remains open and not encroached). At Norwich (13) the original market place was partly built on very early, but the encroaching buildings were mostly removed during the last century, returning the square to approximately its original extent; something similar happened at Cambridge. It must be emphasized that the existing buildings on market-place encroachments may not be particularly old; the first permanent buildings may have been replaced several times over. At Holt the islanded blocks were all rebuilt, probably to their previous ground plans, after most of the town had been devastated by fire in 1708 (map III).

Even in the later Middle Ages some markets were declining or ceased to operate. Trade became concentrated in fewer centres, and by the 19th century several former market towns had declined to the status of villages; examples are Newport, Kimbolton (83), Horndon-on-the-Hill, Hingham (map II), Hatfield Broad Oak, and the castle towns of Hedingham, Acre and Rising.

Much of the late medieval prosperity of East Anglia derived from the weaving trade. This developed in the 14th century or before (*not* significantly through Flemish immigration, as is so often repeated), and reached its first peak in the late 15th and early 16th centuries. Contrary to what many people suppose, it was largely confined to two limited areas. First there was the Suffolk–Essex border, from Clare in the west to Colchester in the east. The trade here was largely in the hands of master clothiers or merchants employing weavers, spinners and others who worked in their own homes, or in small workshops nearby. Most of these people were in effect piecework wage-earners, though some, especially weavers, were their own masters. The richest clothiers were the Springs of Lavenham, who made that small town one of the wealthiest in England for a few decades; there were others in Long Melford, Hadleigh, Coggeshall, Bocking and adjacent villages, all of which enjoyed great prosperity. The chief town of this area was Sudbury, well established as a trading centre before the wool industry developed. Saffron Walden benefited indirectly from the cloth trade, as it was the main centre for the production of saffron, obtained from a plant, which was used, among other purposes, as a dye.

The chief product of the Suffolk–Essex border was, till Tudor times, thick broadcloth, much of which was exported – either through Ipswich or, probably more often, through merchants in London, to which the cloth was sent by packhorse, or by water from Colchester quay. There was a second, quite separate, weaving area in Norfolk. The speciality here was worsted, a fine cloth woven with long, combed wool. It originated in the village of Worstead, but its production came to be centred on Norwich. The whole East Anglian weaving trade slumped in the 16th century, but was reinvigorated by an influx of Flemish refugees, mainly in the 1570s, escaping Spanish persecution. Many settled in Norwich and Colchester, and a few in smaller Essex towns. They brought skills in weaving light cloths, something like worsted, called 'New Draperies'. Norwich and Colchester became great centres for this type of cloth, the production of which spread to Coggeshall and Bocking – but not to old Suffolk weaving towns like Lavenham and Hadleigh, which simply stagnated or declined. Weaving in Norwich remained very important till the 19th century when it succumbed to competition from Yorkshire; it declined rather earlier in Colchester and the Essex towns. But there was a final development in textile production in East Anglia. From the 1790s the silk industry, hitherto based in Spitalfields, London, spread eastwards – to Sudbury (where silk is still woven), and also to Bocking and Halstead where the famous Courtauld firm flourished till recently (55).

Apart from weaving and port trade, the prosperity of East Anglia depended mainly on farming. Landowners like the Cokes of Holkham and the Townshends of Raynham, both in Norfolk, pioneered advances in agriculture in the 18th century, which obviously benefited local market towns and ports: much of the local produce was, in Georgian times, exported to Europe or sent by sea to London. The Fens throve too in the aftermath of the great drainage schemes; Wisbech was the principal beneficiary.

In the 19th century East Anglia was, for the first time for many centuries, off the main stream of the country's economic development. But agriculture continued to flourish until the 1870s and 80s when cheap imports, first of grain and then of frozen meat, affected its prosperity, except in areas like the north Fenland which specialized in vegetables and fruit. Important industries developed in some towns – notably engineering, as in Ipswich, Colchester and the small town of Leiston; printing in Bungay and Beccles; shoemaking in Norwich; malting in many places, notably Mistley (from which the malt was shipped to London); brewing in most towns. Peterborough and March developed as railway centres. Lowestoft and Yarmouth flourished as fishing ports, Harwich with Continental traffic. One of the most important 19th-century developments was that of the seaside resorts. Southend was the oldest of any size, starting in the 1790s; Yarmouth turned towards its beach as well as the harbour and became a popular resort; Southwold, Aldeburgh and later Cromer developed more discreetly out of ancient but decayed ports. Felixstowe, like other towns not included in this book, was a new Victorian and Edwardian resort.

East Anglia proper – Norfolk and Suffolk – has a highly individual tradition of building. There is almost no stone – only carstone, a coarse sandstone which occurs near King's Lynn, and septaria, a rough conglomerate found on the coast near Felixstowe. The one hard material which was plentiful was flint, used either in whole pieces – roughly round – or, in more sophisticated work, split or 'knapped'. Flint walls have to be bound on their edges, at corners, and round window and door openings with stone or, alternatively, brick. Only circular structures need no binding if built of flint – hence the large number of round flint church towers in the area, mostly in smaller villages. Fine stone for binding flint walls, especially on churches, for framing Gothic windows and doors, and for building arches within churches, had to be brought from elsewhere. Most came from the limestone quarries of Northamptonshire and neighbouring counties, brought down the Nene and then up the Ouse, or round the coast.

Norfolk and Suffolk are famous for their fine churches – in former weaving towns like Lavenham and Long Melford (39); in old ports like Lowestoft and Southwold (page 97); in prosperous market towns like Swaffham (19) and Beccles; in feudal castle-towns like Framlingham, and in many other places where there may have been benefactors willing to pay for rebuilding and enrichment in the golden age of church building from about 1370 to the Reformation. Outside, these churches generally have flinty walls and delicate stone dressings – especially on porches, which are sometimes elaborately treated; along parapets; and on towers, which are frequently crowned with elaborate stone tops with pinnacles (though some, as at Lavenham and Beccles, have notably flat tops). The outlines and proportions of towers are conditioned by the forms of the buttresses, which are usually stepped back upwards in several stages, though sometimes they are more substantial and end as corner turrets, as at Bungay (23). The decorative speciality of East Anglia is flushwork – or stonework embedded with flintwork, forming together a flush surface. This might be in the form of vertical strips, as on the tower at Eye; of Gothic tracery patterns like blank windows; of small squares or medallions containing geometrical or heraldic patterns; or even of letters spelling words as at Long Melford (**39**). Flushwork could be on wall surfaces, as on St Michael Coslany in Norwich; on parapets, stringcourses or bands near ground level, as at Woodbridge; on buttresses; or on the tops of towers. There are very few proper spires in Norfolk and Suffolk (despite the example of the cathedral) – the lead-covered one at Hadleigh is a regional rarity. But some churches have, or had, pleasant decorative miniature steeples, often of Georgian date, as at Diss and Aylsham (and also Chelmsford and Wivenhoe in Essex). Inside the larger churches the arcades were necessarily of good stone, but economically slender; the slenderness became an architectural virtue, as in the graceful arcades of Mildenhall, Lowestoft, Bury St Edmunds (both churches), Cromer and St Peter Mancroft in Norwich; the last two achieve an effect of soaring height.

The wooden roofs of East Anglian churches are often spectacular. Hammerbeams, like fan vaulting in stone, were a peculiarly English achievement, and most of the finest examples are in East Anglia, as at Swaffham, Wymondham (two), St Margaret's at Ipswich, and also March in Cambridgeshire. Sometimes, as in St Mary's, Bury St Edmunds and at Mildenhall, hammerbeams alternate with roof trusses of different form. The extraordinary roof at Needham Market is in a class of its own. All these roofs had, and have (though often renewed), winged angels affixed to the beams and elsewhere, which in the Middle Ages were coloured and gilt. It must be remembered that medieval churches were aglow with colour, with their great screens (often surviving to different degrees) which were painted, and with their original stained glass which, because of the ravages of the puritans, seldom remains; the best in East Anglia is at Long Melford. Some churches retain medieval figure paintings in panels along the bases of their screens, as at Southwold, Eye and North Walsham.

Essex has two grand churches, at Saffron Walden and Thaxted (**67**), and another, slightly smaller, at Dedham. Thaxted, a splendid amalgam of many periods, has, extraordinarily for the area, a stone spire (actually renewed in the early 19th century, but apparently a copy of the original). Otherwise Essex is notable for its timber towers – all on village churches – and for the early use of brickwork. Churches near the Thames used Kentish ragstone, as in the fine tower at Prittlewell (Southend); Rayleigh has a ragstone tower and an old brick porch.

Cambridgeshire, with Huntingdonshire, is a distinct region for building materials. From near Cambridge came clunch, a hard form of chalk used for building – excellent for internal work but weathering badly outside. Many of the early Cambridge colleges were built of it; most of the clunch walls that survive have been refaced. Cambridge used brick in the 15th century at Queens' and in the 16th at St John's (page 164) and elsewhere, but for their grander buildings the colleges usually relied on fine limestone from the Midlands, brought by water – the lovely Ketton stone from Rutland with its pinkish and orange tints seems almost indigenous to the city. The country west of the Cam was near enough to the Northamptonshire quarries for stone from them to be used for spires – the finest is at Whittlesey (**92**), one of the most beautiful spires in England. Huntingdonshire has many spires, but mostly in villages; there is one at Kimbolton (page 187) and a particularly slender one at St Ives – thrice rebuilt in the last two hundred years, but presumably in the original form. (The Victorians built another spire in St Ives, on to the Congregational church; the two punctuate opposite ends of the town.) St. Neots has a tower worthy of Somerset.

Nearly all the buildings mentioned so far have been churches. What of the houses? Bury St Edmunds has an early medieval stone-built house, and King's Lynn and Norwich have the remains of others. But most medieval houses in East Anglian towns were timber-framed. They followed the normal plan-forms, based on central open halls, until the late 15th or early 16th centuries, usually with solar and service wings, which generally ended in gables – though there are examples of the 'Wealden' type with continuous roofs (Saffron Walden, Newport). From about 1500, or a little later, houses were usually built from the start in two (or three) storeys throughout, with integral chimneys of brick – while nearly all older hall-houses became subdivided into two floors, with inserted fireplaces and chimneys. Upper floors were usually jettied (overhung), at least on the main frontages. Glazing was rare and expensive for all but the largest houses until a little before 1600; up to then windows were usually shuttered. Carpentry was a highly sophisticated craft, but the timber-framed houses of East Anglia seldom made elaborate displays on their frontages beyond structural needs – apart from the occasional diagonal or curved braces which may not have been structurally essential, or, sometimes, the use of more vertical timber members (studs) than was strictly necessary. External decorative carving was some-times found on bressumer beams (the horizontal beams at the angles of jetties) (47), window sills, or shafts and brackets at the corners of buildings where both sides were jettied. The relative plainness of East Anglian timber-framed buildings, apart from such details, contrasts with the tendency towards elaborate patterns in timber-framing which became characteristic of the western side of the country – as in Cheshire, Shropshire and the Welsh borderland.

The infilling between members of timber-framed buildings was, of course, normally wattle-and-daub – a woven pattern of tough sticks, usually of hazel, daubed over with plaster, flush with the timbering. The plaster finish was often coloured in varieties of deep red or brown, buff or ochre, not necessarily white. And exposed timbering was *never* blackened. Brick-nogging – the use of brick, instead of wattle-and-daub, as infilling between the timbering – is now known to have been practised as early as the 15th century.

After about 1600 it became normal on the eastern side of England to plaster over timber-framed buildings. This was partly because timber was getting scarce; poorer structural members were used, often slightly twisted or distorted, and these tended to be more widely spaced than before. The fashion spread to older buildings where timbering had previously been exposed, but was now plastered over. The plastering was normally plain, and rendered in the same range of colours – reds, browns, buffs and ochres as well as white – as had been used earlier on the surfaces between exposed timbers. These historical facts give rise to questioning when timber-framed buildings are restored or adapted. If the timbering was originally exposed, and later plastered over, should the plastering be stripped? If it is clear that the building was designed from the start for the timbering to be plastered over – as was usually the case in eastern England after about 1600 – the timbering should never be exposed nor blackened.

Pargetting was a tradition of forming patterns in plaster – either incised or, in most of the more elaborate examples, in relief. It seems to have developed in the 17th century and was particularly associated with East Anglia, though there are examples elsewhere (as in Kent). The two finest examples of pargetting are on the Ancient House in Ipswich (**35**) and the former Sun Inn in Saffron Walden (**64**), where there are lively representations of men, animals and objects in relief, as well as abstract patterns. There are others at Clare (**27**) and Wivenhoe.

By 1600 glass was becoming cheaper – though still only in small panes, needing lead framework for whole windows. Windows became generally larger. Oriels – flat-fronted bay windows, often with elaborated sills – were characteristic of this period, though there are examples going back as early as the 15th century (**43**).

Medieval to 17th-century timber-framed houses were almost invariably of oak, the supply of which started to become scarce in the latter century, when brick superseded timber as the normal building material. Surviving timber-framed houses are not evenly distributed in the area covered by this book. They are abundant in central and northern Essex, in most of Suffolk, and in parts of the fringes of Norfolk – the area where oak was plentiful till the 17th century. In most of Norfolk there were far fewer, since the county was less wooded. Some of the early houses in Norwich are largely of flint, perhaps with partly timber-framed upper floors; there are other examples in Walsingham. There are hardly any timber-framed houses in the Fens, but they are relatively common in parts of Huntingdonshire – though not in most of the towns.

The towns with the best collections of timber-framed houses are; in Essex: – Saffron Walden, Bocking, Thaxted, Newport, Coggeshall, Colchester and to a lesser extent Witham (Chipping Hill) and Billericay; in Suffolk: – Lavenham, Sudbury, Hadleigh, Long Melford, Clare, Debenham and Ipswich. King's Lynn and Cambridge have several, and so has Godmanchester.

Many East Anglian towns and villages have Guildhalls – though the name itself is sometimes a recent one applied to an old building. Guilds were medieval religious associations – 'clubs' would not be an inappropriate word – which were all abolished as a result of the Reformation. Only in the largest cities and towns, like London, Norwich and King's Lynn, did guilds have significant control over trade. King's Lynn retains two big guildhalls; at Norwich the more complex Guildhall was the civic hall. Elsewhere, guildhalls were simply places where the guild members met, like the large one at Lavenham, essentially a medieval house, and the small one at Eye. At Hadleigh the three-storeyed 15th-century Guildhall accommodated local guilds as well as the administration of the market. This overlaps with another distinct type of building, the town house, market house or market hall (the terms vary). Typically these had one or more upper-floor rooms, used for public meetings and sometimes courts, with open-sided ground floors where a few market stalls could be placed in shelter. A well-restored early example is at Horndon-on-the-Hill; that at Aldeburgh (page 69) is more elaborate but the ground storey has been walled in; the one at Wymondham (21) is small and octagonal. Thaxted has the finest example of the type (67), with two upper floors, both jettied – the name 'Guildhall' by which it is known is fairly recent and may not be correct. Woodbridge has an early brick building of the type, its ground floor now walled in; Peterborough's of 1671 is of stone, classical and delightful (84). The Custom House at King's Lynn, built in 1683 by an exceptional local architect, Henry Bell, as a Merchants' Exchange, is a superior example of the type (page 33); it too originally had an open-arched ground floor. Also very exceptional is the confusingly called 'Market Cross' at Bury St Edmunds by Robert Adam (24); the top floor was designed as a theatre but the originally open-sided ground storey sheltered marketing, just like the humbler market halls. Huntingdon's Town Hall of 1745 and later accommodated the county courts as well as an Assembly Room (82). Chelmsford's Shire Hall of 1791 combined the same functions on a grander scale. Assembly Rooms were more often privately provided, sometimes in special buildings, as at Norwich; at Bury St Edmunds the Assembly Room is part of the Athenaeum.

Mention must also be made of the simple 'Market Crosses' in some towns, consisting of roofs over pillars, providing limited shelter in the middle of market places. That at Whittlesey has stone columns below a square hipped roof (92); those at Bungay (1689) (23) and Swaffham (1783) (19) are sophisticated structures with domes over classical columns.

The change from timber to brick as the normal building material more or less corresponded with the adaptation of classical principles in the design of ordinary buildings. The 'Georgian house' originated in the later 17th century; the sash window, one of its most characteristic features, became universal after about 1700. Space is too short to analyse the evolution of the Georgian style in East Anglian towns; its course was no different in general from that elsewhere except in the use of materials. Brick was almost invariably made locally in earlier Georgian times, and there are infinite variations in the colours of old bricks in different areas, from deep dark reds to glowing lighter colours or, as in parts of the Fenland area, reddish buffs. Buff brick, miscalled white, became fashionable towards the end of the 18th century and was generally used all over the area, rather than red brick, after about 1800. Bricks of this colour are often called 'Suffolk whites' or 'Woolpit bricks' after a village near Bury St Edmunds where many were made, but there must have been plenty of other places from which they came. Flint was still used for quite substantial houses in some areas through the Georgian period, as in Swaffham – but even there most of the buildings of the period are of red or buff brick. Many timber-framed houses were given new classical fronts in Georgian times; houses which look Georgian outside are very often far older behind their facades; Long Melford, Bocking, Bury St Edmunds and King's Lynn have many such examples. Other timber-framed houses were simply plastered over (if they had not been before) and given new-style sash windows. Too many buildings altered in this way have been misguidedly treated by removing sash windows and other Georgian accretions, and substituting supposed reconstructions of earlier features such as windows, so giving them a 'restored' look. Later modifications to buildings, in the Georgian or any other period up to modern times, are as much part of the buildings' history as what remains of their original structures.

Mention must be made of the continuing tradition of timber-framing, using softwood, in parts of the area. Oak had become very expensive by 1700, but large quantities of deal, or softwood, were imported into London and the eastern ports in the 18th and 19th centuries. This was used instead of hardwood for internal joinery in ordinary buildings, and also for framed structures, especially in Essex and south-east Suffolk, right into the 19th century. Softwood-framed buildings are lighter in construction than those of oak, and never have jetties. Often they are finished externally in plaster, but a common cladding was weatherboarding – overlapping boards, themselves usually on softwood. Weatherboarding was also sometimes applied to older hardwood-framed buildings. The town with the most weatherboarded buildings is Rochford; they are also found in Harwich, Harlow (Churchgate Street) and Billericay. Weatherboarding was particularly used on barns and also on mills – the recently restored tide mill at Woodbridge is a splendid example (page 84–5).

There are some fine Georgian, or Georgian-fronted, houses in nearly every place described in this book. The places with the best collections are; in Essex: – Colchester (in various streets), Dedham, Maldon, and to a smaller extent Billericay; in Suffolk: – Beccles, Bungay, Woodbridge and especially Bury St Edmunds; in Norfolk: – Swaffham, Dereham, Aylsham, Holt, Yarmouth (facing the Quays), Norwich (especially St Giles Street, the Close, and Colegate) and King's Lynn; in Cambridgeshire with Huntingdonshire: – Wisbech (the finest largely Georgian town in the area), Huntingdon and Godmanchester.

The seaside towns are, on the whole, architecturally disappointing, apart from Southwold, whose delight derives from the informal ways in which the buildings are related to streets, greens and the sea rather than, with some exceptions, the buildings themselves. The best seaside architecture is at Southend – the Royal Terrace has one of the most memorable sequences of late Georgian balconies and verandahs in England. Yarmouth has a small amount of impressive Victorian development in the Camperdown area, part of a largely unrealized grander scheme.

The Georgian domestic tradition survived well into the Victorian period in East Anglia, as can be seen, for instance, in Ipswich (Museum Street) and parts of Bury St Edmunds. It also survived in the design of public buildings, as in some of the Corn Exchanges built in the agricultural boom years up to 1870. The one at Bury St Edmunds is the grandest; there are others at Diss and Rochford; some, as at Swaffham, are more blatantly Victorian. At Saffron Walden and Sudbury, impressive facades have been kept while the buildings behind have been transformed into libraries.

Apart from Cambridge, the town with the most interesting collection of Victorian buildings is Ipswich, the seedbed for several remarkable architects.

The Town Hall was designed by a man from Lincoln, but the remarkable classical Custom House (1844) was by a local architect, J. M. Clarke, who sadly died young. Very different in his works was T. W. Cotman, related to the famous artist, who, around the end of the century, enlivened Ipswich and also Felixstowe with buildings of picturesque outline and varied colour. Another Ipswich-based architect, at the beginning of the present century, was Munro Cautley, best remembered for his very detailed book *Suffolk Churches* and his shorter *Norfolk Churches*; he designed fairly convincing new half-timbered houses, and restored old ones rather too convincingly. Better than any of these was George Skipper of Norwich, one of the best and most inventive architects in England around the turn of the century; his Royal Arcade (page 49) with its Art-Nouveau back entrance, and *palazzo* for the Norwich Union insurance company (18) are masterpieces. Colchester has two Victorian landmarks, the extraordinary water tower, always called 'Jumbo', of neo-Roman grandeur (52), and the superb Town Hall of *c.* 1900 with its baroque steeple, by John Belcher. It makes an interesting comparison with Norwich's City Hall of the 1930s in the then fashionable Swedish-Dutch modern style. Apart from the University Library at Cambridge this is the most striking inter-war building in the area, though mention should be made of the excellent classical Town Hall at Peterborough.

East Anglia as a whole is not notable for Victorian churches; the finest is the Roman Catholic cathedral at Norwich by the second Scott, and the strangest the parish church at Leiston, by E. B. Lamb, with its extraordinary roof. One very remarkable inter-war church is St Andrew's at Felixstowe, built in reinforced concrete in a modernized version of East Anglian Perpendicular; the architect was the otherwise unknown Hilda Mason, who began as assistant to Munro Cautley. She was assisted by Raymond Erith, who later lived in a Georgian house of his own design at Dedham. The last great Gothic Revivalist is Stephen Dykes Bower, designer of the very effective 1960s enlargement of the medieval St James' at Bury St Edmunds as an Anglican cathedral, and restorer of the war-damaged St Nicholas at Yarmouth.

East Anglia remained something of a backwater right up to the 1960s, except for the parts near London. Harlow new town started about 1950 with excellent early housing schemes, carrying on the traditions of the earlier garden cities. Bury St Edmunds, Sudbury, Huntingdon, Thetford, Witham and King's Lynn were expanded in the 1950s and 60s to rehouse people from London, including new industries; in the first two cases (though not the others) the historic character of the older areas was scarcely affected. Peterborough became a 'new town' in the 1960s, and the old city, not particularly distinguished outside the cathedral close, has been expanded rather effectively. More recently the pressures of development have been private, not planned. The limits of London commuting which, not very long ago, scarcely extended beyond the borders of Essex, now stretch along the hugely improved railways and roads to Diss and Norwich, Cambridge and Ely, Huntingdon and Peterborough. The port of Felixstowe has expanded from a small near-derelict dock to the largest container terminal in Britain (while affecting the town strangely little). The economies of Ipswich,

Colchester, Chelmsford, Bury St Edmunds and, especially, Cambridge, as well as several smaller towns, are booming. The new college and university buildings in Cambridge provide the most varied examples of post-war architecture in the area, but the two most remarkable recent buildings are the Willis Faber offices in Ipswich and the Sainsbury Centre in Norwich.

Urban conservation – the preservation of the historic character of smaller towns, or parts of larger cities, often associated with the regeneration of decaying areas – has had many successes in the area. The earliest scheme was at Elm Hill, Norwich, started in the 1920s. Much more recently Norwich has set splendid examples in the reinvigoration of the once decaying Colegate district and other smaller areas in the city, as has Colchester in its 'Dutch Quarter'. The listing of buildings of historic interest and the designation of Conservation Areas in towns and villages have helped to save many an old building, street and town scene which might otherwise have disappeared or been mutilated. But legislation and designation alone do not save historic buildings in towns. Much has depended on the quality of planning administration and control by local authorities, and especially on the expertise of some of the planning officers, architects, conservation officers and historic buildings experts who advise them. There are, and have been, many devoted people in these categories in the service of some of the county and district authorities. But, most of all, the future appearance of historic towns depends on the good sense and taste of the owners and occupiers of individual buildings, and how sympathetically they use, repair and treat them, in relation to their surroundings. One aim of this book is to help such people understand better the character, history and importance of some of the historic places of the area.

Norfolk

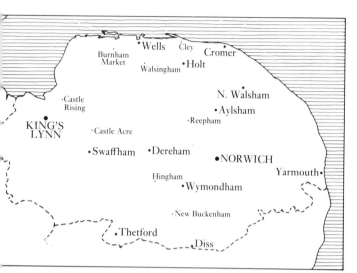

Aylsham

Like so many country towns, Aylsham is largely Georgian to look at but medieval in its layout. A market was recorded in 1296; there was some late medieval worsted weaving, but the 18th-century prosperity must have been based on agriculture, especially after the River Bure was made navigable up to the town in 1779. There is a fine market place, not quite rectangular, with interest concentrated in the corners. To the south-west is the Black Boys Hotel, early Georgian but stuccoed in Regency times and now brightly painted. North-westwards an alley leads through to the church, 14th and 15th centuries, whose slender tower, capped by a spirelet, rises above the buildings when seen from the market place. The north-east corner forms a sharp angle, where a lane leads out to the street beyond, between an ebullient town hall of 1857 and a fine early 18th-century house with carved brick cornice and pilasters, into which, incongruously but charmingly, an Edwardian shop front has been set.

Outside the market place, interesting Georgian or slightly earlier houses are scattered around a complicated network of streets and lanes – best understood with the help of the booklet *Aylsham, A Guided Walk*. On Norwich Road is Old Bank House, with a 17th-century Dutch gable and an early Georgian frontispiece; it housed a local bank till 1859. Bayfield House, also Georgian, closes the view along narrow Red Lion Street, while round the corner in White Hart Street are more pleasant houses in the warm local red brick. One of the most interesting streets is Millgate, leading north-east to the mill and river, passing Victorian houses with rounded flints, and several brick Georgian ones, including Bure House with a fine doorway, and Bridge House, making a nice picture as one looks along the street, with its adjoining old garden wall. The mill, seen from the bridge along a stretch of the Bure, was rebuilt in 1798; it ceased production in 1969 and is now converted into houses. One of the most surprising buildings in Aylsham is on the opposite side of the town, towards Cawston – the old workhouse of 1849,

1 *Below* **House in Millgate, Aylsham**, *c.*1840–5, using rounded flints, not split.

2 *Below left* **Aylsham Mill**, over the River Bure, 1798, now converted into houses.

now a hospital, designed by W. J. Donthorne, with a huge centrepiece, flanked by octagonal turrets topped by bulbous domes, a kind of parody of Blickling Hall.

Blickling Hall, the Jacobean mansion now National Trust showpiece, is two miles north-west of the town. On the way there is Aylsham Old Hall, much more modest than Blickling and built seventy years later (c1690). It is 'a perfect specimen of its date' (Pevsner),

in deep red brick, with white-painted eaves, round-arched doorway in carved brickwork, and sash windows – which are probably early substitutes for the original windows. It is well seen from the road through iron gates, and provides the link, stylistically as well as geographically, between pre-classical Blickling and the comfortable 18th-century houses of a town like Aylsham.

Burnham Market

Burnham, like New Buckenham and Hingham, is an old market town which has receded to the status of a village. Its market place is now a long and very pleasant green, spoiled only by the road that splits it lengthwise. House after house is Georgian; the majority of them are modest, with a few grander ones in deep red brick, especially one on the south side with a Doric porch. Roofs are dominantly in red pantiles, occasionally in the darker variety. At the far western end is Burnham Westgate church, fairly unpretentious but with remarkable carvings in stone of biblical scenes on the battlements of the 14th-century tower. Beyond the eastern end of the green are two continuing parallel streets, lined with pleasant houses in low key, with some flint as well as brick and stucco. They lead to Burnham

Ulph church, small and towerless, with a fine late Norman chancel arch. Westgate and Ulph are two of the seven churches beginning with Burnham; two more are only just outside the town – Burnham Norton with a round Norman tower and Burnham Overy with a massive central one of the same date. (The latter is in Burnham Overy proper, well inland from Burnham Overy Staithe on its marshbound creek, once the commercial outlet for the area, now a busy boating haven.)

3 Burnham Market. The long market place is now a village green, lined with pleasant, occasionally grand, houses in flint and warm brick, roofed in pantiles.

Castle Acre

Castle Acre was a tiny medieval town between a great castle and a rich priory. It was a stronghold of the Warennes, earls of Surrey for several generations after

the Norman Conquest, whose main base was at Lewes, Sussex. The castle began as a manor house, but in the twelfth century was reconstructed as a fortress with a

Opposite
Castle Acre Priory, founded
*c.*1090 by William de Warenne,
builder of Lewes Castle,
Sussex, and founder of the
priory there.

Above
Castle Rising: the Norman
keep seen through the castle
gateway. (5)

4 Castle Acre. This was the town gate, leading into the very small walled town which filled what was virtually an additional bailey of the castle. Most of the present village is outside the gate, behind where the photograph was taken.

detail. The town originally occupied a very small space west of the castle, defended by further earthworks and town gates, of which the north gate survives, with traffic passing through at the end of the narrow street which was the original main thoroughfare. At some early date houses spread beyond the gate, and the centre of the present village (which is the status of Castle Acre today) is a long and pleasant green with the gateway at one corner. The best of the old houses are in dark red brick with pantiles, and there is much use of flint. The church, in a large churchyard where the tombstones have been partly rearranged in regimented rows, has a pleasing tower with buttresses that broaden assertively downwards. Inside, amid much else, there is a glorious 15th-century font cover with delicate carved woodwork, a pulpit of similar date with paintings of the Doctors of the Church, and the base of a former screen with representations of saints in the panels. At the far end of the village is the ruin of the Cluniac priory founded by the second Earl Warenne about 1090. The magnificent west front is nearly intact in its lower part, with rows of rounded arches enveloping the main doorway, while much of the southern tower survives. The one building which is partly intact and roofed is the former prior's house, enlarged and altered repeatedly up to and after the Reformation. Among its special features are two first-floor windows, one a Tudor oriel, the other a boldly rounded bay window with nine lights separated by stone mullions. This has been said to date from just before the dissolution of the priory; if so it is most remarkable, but the official guide book is not very clear on this point.

keep on a large artificial mound, and a considerable outer bailey, all surrounded by massive earthworks originally topped by stone walls. Except for the earthworks the castle is now fragmentary, but archaeological excavations have revealed its complicated history in

Castle Rising

Castle Rising has shrunk from a town to a small village, but the castle remains and the church are magnificent. The castle was built by William d'Albini (William of Albany) in the 1130s as his chief residence, at about the same time as he built Buckenham Castle (map IV). Later in the century the surrounding earthworks were extended and heightened so that the original keep appears to be in a hollow – which makes it all the more dramatic when one suddenly sees it through the entrance arch. The main rooms were on the first floor of the keep (now a shell), approached up a splendid staircase and through richly treated Norman doorways. Albini laid out a town to the north of the castle with a grid of streets, a market place and a very

5 Castle Rising. The castle was built c.1138 by the powerful William d'Albini. The photograph shows the approach to the first-floor entrance to the keep. (Colour Plate, page 23)

fine church. Two major Victorian architects, Salvin and Street, successively restored the church but much is original, including most of the west front with its lavish ornamentation and the western crossing arch; the southern arch is impressive Early English, as is the exquisite threefold east window with foliage capitals and dogtooth carving; an etching by Cotman, reproduced in the church guide, testifies to its authenticity. The not very satisfactory gable top is an addition to the original tower. West of the church is the one-time market place, now a village green like those of New Buckenham and Hingham, though with more trees than either. In such a sylvan setting the stone 15th-century market cross, on five steps and tapering to a thin pinnacle, is an odd and remarkable survival. On the other side of the church is the delightful brick quadrangle of the Howard Hospital, an almshouse founded by an Earl of Northampton who died in 1614. For the rest Rising is now a small village, with no suggestion of urbanity. Yet it was once a port, reached by small vessels up the Babingley River which must have been wider than now, and a 'rotten' borough with two members of Parliament until 1832; one was Samuel Pepys and another Sir Robert Walpole the first prime minister, who lived in nearby Houghton.

Cley-next-the-Sea

Cley (pronounced to rhyme with cry) was a medieval port of some importance. The small river Glaven flowed into an estuary which extended nearly two miles in – the best haven between Lynn and Yarmouth. The original town was east of the estuary head, where the church stands. By the early 17th century at the latest (and possibly well before) the main town and quays had developed further north, where the present village is. The shift was due to silting and to the increasing size of ships; the silting was hastened by reclamation works. A landowner built embankments in the 1630s, primarily to enclose and drain the adjoining marshes. Although these had to be modified by court order in 1639, they irrevocably affected the flow and depth of the tidal water. Further drainage works took place in 1824, after which there was a very narrow river, accessible only by small vessels. In its heyday Cley traded with the Continent, but in the 18th and early 19th century its shipping was nearly all coastal – like nearby Blakeney and Wells, Cley was an outlet for the agricultural produce of the area, most of which went to London, though vessels still crossed to Holland. The coastal trade finally ended in the 1880s when the railway at nearby Holt provided a better outlet.

Cley has a long, narrow, twisty and, in summer, roaringly congested street with many attractive houses in brick and flint, many clearly of early 17th-century origin – probably replacing those destroyed in a fire that swept the town in 1612; some have 'Dutch' gables, but one retains a medieval doorway. Most are roofed in red or blue-grey pantiles, which are said to have been imported from Holland; it is not clear to what extent this was so and how many were made locally. Near the north end of the street there is an opening to the narrow, banked river filled with small pleasure boats, bordering marshland which extends for nearly a mile to the sea. A windmill, right on the river bank, ground some of the grain before it was shipped away. Part of the marshland is renowned as a bird sanctuary.

The church – a building of tremendous, varied quality, part 14th- and part 15th-century, adjoins a big green which may once have been a market place and was later a fairground. The south transept has been ruinous since the 17th century, but keeps the wilfully florid tracery of its main window, all the more dramatic as it is unglazed. The two-storeyed porch has filigree decoration in the parapet which Pevsner likened to Spanish work. Through the twisting ogee arch of the south doorway one enters a splendid, unencumbered space with arcades of whitish stone, embellished by lively little figures of engaging variety between the arches, and by small canopies with rich details above; there are more figures and foliage carvings on the corbels supporting the aisle roofs. This is a church that both impresses and entertains the visitor with its scale and details. Across what was the estuary is the sister church of Wiveton, smaller than Cley, which served what was originally another small maritime community.

Cromer

Cromer is a resort with a late Victorian atmosphere. It began as the landward end of Shipden, a medieval port which was probably built on low-lying land around where the pier is now. The main part of Shipden was eroded by the 15th century, when the people had re-settled on higher land to the south in the area called Crowmere – the crow's pond. Some sort of jetty or breakwater was built on the coast, and Cromer prospered for a time – to judge from the splendour of the church – but further erosion ruined the jetty and berthing facilities by late Tudor times. Cromer declined to a fishing village, where small sailing ships were occasionally beached at low tide. It was 'discovered' from about 1785 by a few rich families, especially Quakers from Norwich. A new jetty was built, only to be destroyed in a storm of 1845 and replaced, together with a sea wall and narrow promenade which has prevented further erosion. From about 1890, with two railway termini, Cromer briefly became one of the most fashionable resorts in England. Several big hotels were built (nearly all have been demolished), and the Norfolk Coast Express, the flag-train of the Great Eastern Railway, brought visitors in considerable comfort up to the First World War. The area became known through the writings of Clement Scott, a journalist and theatre critic, at first in *Daily Telegraph* articles and then in a sentimental poem called *The Garden of Sleep* about a clifftop churchyard in nearby Sidestrand (since eroded away), which was set to music and became a popular song. He called the area 'Poppyland' because of the flowers that grew among the crops at harvest time. Cromer's age of elegance ended with the First World War.

By far the finest thing in Cromer is the parish church, set amid narrow streets in the heart of the town as few are in East Anglia – they are more often in retired churchyards off the main streets and squares. It was built in the late 14th century to replace the eroded church of Shipden; it decayed later with the town, losing its chancel in the 17th century. A thorough, but authentic, Victorian restoration under Sir Arthur Blomfield gave it a new chancel and nave roof. The western part, with the superb tower, is nearly all original; there is fine flushwork around the tower base and the three grand porches, and a filigree parapet crowns the tower. Inside, the lofty arcades and tall aisle windows give an effect of tremendous height; the former are original, the latter have renewed Perpendicular tracery in the medieval window frames. Narrow streets, including High Street and Jetty Street, with flat-fronted Victorian bay windows, lead to the sea front with its tiered sea walls and pier, overlooked by the turreted red-brick front of a hotel, designed by George Skipper of Norwich (page 44). The local museum, close to the church, is a good one. At low tide the beach is spreading and sandy, giving good views back to the old town huddled on its hillock, crowned by the church tower - which has a specially graceful outline, with paired buttresses set back progressively to leave the top part clear and vertical.

Dereham

Dereham – strictly East Dereham in distinction from the much smaller West Dereham, some way away – is the busiest town in thinly populated central Norfolk. It was clearly prosperous in Georgian times, and continued so in the 19th century when an engineering industry developed. But its origins were far more distant. By tradition St Withburga, daughter of an East Anglian king and sister of St Etheldreda, foundress of Ely, established a nunnery here in the seventh century. When the church was being built, so a legend runs, there was a local food shortage, but the Virgin Mary appeared to Withburga in a dream telling her that two does, with a plentiful supply of milk, would appear in a certain place each day. They did, but the local bailiff, hearing the story, tried one day to kill them; he stumbled and died. Withburga was buried in what is now Dereham churchyard. Much later an abbot of Ely took away her body to be reburied at Ely alongside her sister. Immediately the body was removed – the legend continues – a spring issued from the spot; this, it is claimed, now fills St Withburga's Well, west of the parish church. The church is like a small cathedral, although the present building was never monastic (the nunnery did not recover from the Vikings). Unusually for Norfolk it dates mainly from the 13th and 14th centuries, and has a central tower which opens into the church below like a lantern, to tremendous internal effect. A separate bell tower was built alongside the church from about 1510; it was not quite finished at the Reformation and, like the older tower, has a flat top. The two towers counterpoise each other marvellously from different angles all around. By the entrance to the churchyard is Bishop Bonner's Cottage, a tiny 16th-century building, roofed in thatch, having a band of pargetting with a floral and foliage pattern under the eaves; it is now a museum. It is named after Edmund Bonner, a bishop of London who persecuted Protestants under Queen Mary and who was previously rector of Dereham. A more appealing local resident was the poet and hymn writer William Cowper, commemorated by Flaxman in the church; he died in the town in 1800.

The Market Place is a nicely irregular space, encroached by islanded blocks of buildings which divide the narrow Quebec Street from the main space. These include the Assembly Rooms, internally impressive, said to date from 1756 but looking later Georgian. On the opposite side is an intriguing Georgian building in red brick, with a pediment over a double classical entrance, flanked now by banks. Georgian buildings, roofed with a mixture of red and blue-black pantiles, curve round to a re-entrant of the market place, where the view is closed by Hill House, early 18th-century in warm red brick with a pediment over white-framed windows – the *beau ideal* of a country-town house. In it lived, in the later 18th century, Sir James Fenn, who studied and edited the medieval Paston letters, written not far away.

Diss

The name Diss derives from a Saxon word meaning a stretch of water – referring to the mere or large pond beside which the town grew. For an introduction to Diss it is a good idea to go to the southern, open, fringe of the mere, reached from the A1066 which bypasses the town proper. The buildings of the town centre rise beyond the tree-fringed mere, culminating in the church tower, crowned by cupola and vane. One can walk across to the bottom of Mere Street, busy with shops, which broadens into the irregular market place. The church is dominant, standing high beyond the end of the space, set off by odd small buildings in front, including the single-storeyed Shambles with open-columned front, once the butchers' stalls. The buildings around the market place are typical of the town; some are timber-framed, variedly altered or re-fronted; others are severely Victorian, in buff brick or stucco. This is a reflection of Diss's history; it prospered in the 17th century as a market for linen thread and cloth, spun and woven from flax grown in the neighbourhood, and in the mid 19th century as a corn market. It was not notably rich in the 18th century, so has fewer fine Georgian houses than, say, Beccles or Bungay.

The most fascinating part of the town lies west from the market place and church, along Market Hill, St Nicholas Street and the alleys in between. This was perhaps at first an extension of the market place, which was encroached over early, resulting in the present, very irregular, building pattern. Market Hill climbs gently as it opens into a succession of tiny squares, with the typical mixture of Victorian and altered timber-framed buildings. One of the latter, no. 23 in the last of the little squares, has a 15th-century corner post

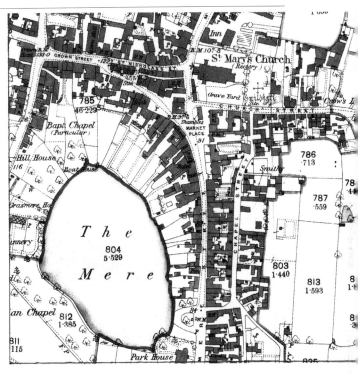

Map 1, Diss. This map of 1890 shows how Diss is related to its Mere. North-west of the Market Place is a series of tiny squares connected by narrowed spaces. This effect may have been partly caused by infilling as at Holt (map III) – the Market Place may originally have extended north-westwards in a roughly triangular form but was encroached on by the islanded blocks west of the church.

with carvings of the Annunciation and Nativity. This square opens into St Nicholas Street, near the Corn Hall of 1854 with its proud portico supported by Ionic columns. St Nicholas Street leads back from here as a narrow lane, ending opposite the church.

Hingham

Hingham is one of the many former market towns which have declined to the status of villages. This is seen, most delightfully, in what were once the market place and fairground, east and west of the church respectively. Both are now green spaces, shaded by trees, though intersected by roads. Round the former market place, especially on the eastern side, are several fine Georgian houses which certainly suggest a town. One of the best, in deep red brick with pilasters and keystones, stands at the south-east corner of the green. Another interesting house is in Bond Street, leading north, built of 17th-century red and grey chequer brick,

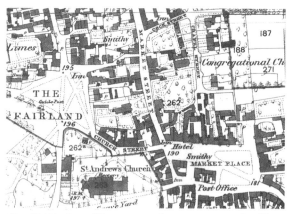

Map II, Hingham. Was once a market town, now a quiet village. Both the Fairland, where an annual fair was held, and the Market Place are now village greens. The latter, once nearly rectangular, has two small encroachments. Market Street leading north is now called Bond Street (6). The map dates from 1890.

6 *Above left* **House in Bond Street, Hingham.** An interesting mid 17th century house of red and grey chequer brick with 'Dutch' gables; the windows were altered in Georgian times, but traces of some of the original windows survive. (Map II)

7 *Left* **Hingham.** By contrast with (6), a simple rustic house, showing traces of its timber-framed origin.

with striking Dutch-style gables and later sash windows. The church is of dark flint with thin stone dressings, with a graceful plain tower and elaborate window tracery in the chancel. It is known to have been built by Remigius of Hethersett, rector from 1319 to 1359.

A better-known rector, Robert Peck, held the post from 1605. He was an ardent puritan, and had several followers in the town. He came increasingly into conflict with the prevailing high-church tendencies in the Anglican church. Matters came to a head in 1636 when Matthew Wren (uncle of the architect) became bishop of Norwich; Peck was then excommunicated at a diocesan consistory court. In 1638 he migrated, with others from Hingham, to Massachusetts where he settled in a town already called Hingham – founded a few years before by emigrants partly from the Norfolk town. Peck returned during the Civil War; he died in England in 1656. The town of Hingham, Massachusetts, is something of a showpiece, as attractive as its English namesake. Both Hinghams have another claim to American fame. Samuel Lincoln, who was born in Hingham, Norfolk, though he later became a Norwich weaver's apprentice, migrated to America in 1637; he too found his way to the younger Hingham. He was the ancestor of Abraham Lincoln.

Holt

Holt is one of three places in Norfolk where a market was recorded in Domesday Book – the other two, Dunham and Litcham, are now fairly small villages. The town was almost entirely destroyed by a fire of 1708, and what we see today is mostly Georgian. Instead of being replanned – which would have been very difficult given the multiplicity of ownerships – it was, like London a few decades before, rebuilt piecemeal, evidently to the old plan. Looking at a detailed map (III) it is obvious that there was originally a roughly rectangular market place, but at some time, as in many market towns, stalls became permanent and were replaced by solid buildings, forming islanded blocks often with narrow alleys and little spaces between them. In Holt this pattern was 'fossilized' in the 18th-century rebuilding. The present market place is only the southern part of the originally open area, with a smooth curve of mainly Georgian buildings on the south side and irregular blocks to the north, representing the encroachments; there are lanes and alleys threading through. Particularly intriguing is an alley roughly parallel with the market place, narrow and brick-paved, its buildings roofed in pantiles. Pantiles are the traditional roofing material in Holt as all over north Norfolk – either brilliant red or else in darker blue-grey, often mottled and with a slight glazed effect, the result of using salt water in manufacture (page 25). The other old building materials in Holt are simple – either flint (necessarily bonded in brick) or deep red local brick. One of the best buildings in the latter material is Hanworth House at the east end of Bull Street, dated 1744, with keystones over the windows and a roof of dark pantiles. A focal feature in the town is the old schoolhouse of Gresham's School at the east end of the market place. This was founded in 1562 through a bequest from Sir John Gresham, City magnate and sometime government adviser, uncle of Sir Thomas Gresham who founded the Royal Exchange in London. At first the school was in a Tudor house already owned by the family, but this was replaced in 1862 by the present old schoolhouse.

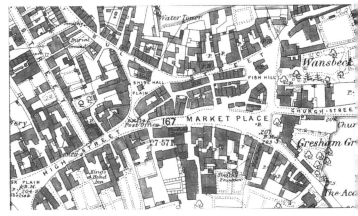

Map III, Holt. This map of 1891 shows clearly how an originally large market place – a rectangle stretched at the four corners – has been infilled by islanded blocks, creating a network of alleys and small irregular spaces. This pattern was 'fossilized' when the town was rebuilt, perhaps exactly to the old pattern, after a great fire of 1708.

Although well endowed, the school was small until 1900 when it was reorganized as a residential public school, with new buildings on the edge of the town; the old building was extended to become a boarding house. At the opposite end of Holt is a curiosity, the so-called Pineapple Obelisk, originally a gatepost from Melton Constable Hall a few miles away; it is inscribed with mileages to several places which are correct from Melton Constable but inaccurate for Holt.

King's Lynn

The name Lynn probably derives from a Celtic word, the equivalent of the Welsh *llyn*, meaning a pool or a stretch of water. The site was a patchwork of dry land, pools and creeks, marshy riverside, and sandbanks. The historic heart of the present town, Saturday Market, was first developed around 1095 when Bishop Herbert de Losinga, builder of Norwich cathedral, obtained a charter for the market. At about the same time he founded the adjoining church of St Margaret, with a related small priory which was a branch of the cathedral priory at Norwich. The town flourished and extended northward, beyond a small creek called the Purfleet, to where a second market place, Tuesday Market, was laid out by a later bishop about 1250; he also founded a second church, St Nicholas.

Until the middle of the 13th century most of the Fenland rivers, including the Nene and the Ouse, of which the Cam is a tributary, merged to enter the Wash through a single estuary near Wisbech. Only a few small streams flowed into the inlet on which Lynn was situated. Despite this Lynn developed into one of the richest ports in England by the early part of the 13th century. Like its even bigger rival, Boston across the Wash, it was an outlet for agricultural produce, especially wool; it imported cloth from Flanders, wine from France, timber and furs from the Baltic, and fish from

Norway. Around the middle of the century – the precise date is unknown –
the Ouse changed its course above Wisbech, possibly because the original
outlet there became silted, and flowed instead to enter the sea at Lynn. Later
large-scale artificial changes in the rivers' courses, especially in the 17th
century, have resulted in the present system in which the Ouse, having
picked up the Cam and smaller tributaries, enters the sea below Lynn, while
the Nene again flows through Wisbech. It must be emphasized that Lynn
first became an important port *before* the great river diversion of the 13th
century. After this diversion it had access by water to a huge hinterland
including Ely, Cambridge, and, very importantly, St Ives, where the great
international fair which flourished around 1300 was fed by river traffic to
and from Lynn. There was also access, via the Nene, from Northamptonshire
with its stone quarries.

Political considerations affected the prosperity of Lynn in the later Middle
Ages. The Hanseatic cities came to dominate the Baltic and Scandinavian
trade and, for a time, excluded English ships from trading with them,
though their own ships often called at Lynn. After 1475 they established a
steelyard or depot there, of which part survives. During this period, both the

8/9 *Below*
**Tuesday Market, King's
Lynn** was laid out *c.*1250 as
part of a major extension to the
town; it looks better on Tuesday
(or Friday) when the stalls are
there than when full of cars. It
has lacked a centrepiece since
the superb Market Cross by
Henry Bell, recorded in
illustrations, was demolished in
1830. The spire is that of St.
Nicholas, the town's second
church. The Duke's Head hotel,
1683–9, was designed by Henry
Bell, an outstanding local
architect whose *tour-de-force* is
the Custom House. (Colour
illustration, page 33)

export of raw wool and the import of Flemish cloth declined drastically, and Lynn was not well placed to benefit from the enormous growth of weaving in other parts of East Anglia. At the reformation the king took over the bishop's local interests; the town became *King's* Lynn. But by then it had ceased to be an international port of major significance; London had come to dominate overwhelmingly the external trade of most of England, except that from the western ports. However King's Lynn flourished, through to the 19th century, on river and coastal trade. Produce, especially corn, was brought down the rivers and sent round to London or the north-east; coal was brought in return from Newcastle and luxury goods from London, partly for distribution up-river. There was still some trade with Holland, the Baltic and Scandinavia, and also long-distance fishing, including whaling.

Today King's Lynn is still a busy port. The population increased in the 1950s and 60s, partly through 'overspill' from London; industries developed, and the shopping centre was re-shaped. Luckily, not much of architectural note was destroyed but the new shopping areas have little character and give a bad first impression of the town. The town now displays a strong contrast between the insipid, largely modern shopping area and the vividly historic

streets and buildings which extend, close to the riverside, from Tuesday Market in the north to Saturday Market and Nelson Street in the south.

Tuesday Market is potentially one of the finest market places in England. It is not quite a rectangle – the north-west corner takes more than ninety degrees. The buildings fronting it are almost all classical, varying in date from the Duke's Head Hotel, with its splendid baroque front of 1686 by the local architect Henry Bell, to the florid Corn Exchange of 1854. In between, chronologically, are numerous dignified classical fronts either in the older local red brick, which is dark and almost tannish in tint, or in the later buff brick. On Tuesdays, and also Fridays, when it fulfils its original purpose, the market place is vibrant, but on other days it is used as a car park. The buildings around are, collectively, not quite big enough to contain the great space, and something distinctive is needed in the centre. Such a feature did exist, a splendid Market Cross of 1710, with dome and cupola, designed by Henry Bell. It was demolished in 1830. If a suitable benefactor came forward, the design of a new centrepiece for the square would provide a wonderful challenge to architects.

The docks are to the north of Tuesday Market. Near their entrance, amid some narrow streets with a few well-restored old houses, is St Nicholas, the church founded about 1150 when the Tuesday Market area was first laid out. The present tower is 13th-century; the rest was rebuilt grandly in the early 15th and is the *beau ideal* of a great town church of the period – a huge rectangle with tall, slender arcades, high clerestory, and elaborated roof with tracery between the braces and beams. It now seems enormously spacious and perhaps a little drab, but in the Middle Ages there would have been elaborate screens, rich colouring on the timberwork and some of the stone-work, and vivid stained glass (of which none remains from the medieval period) in the large windows with their intricate tracery patterns.

The area of dense historical interest extends southward from Tuesday Market along King and Queen Streets to Saturday Market and Nelson Street. King Street is splendid; it has a gentle bend, and many of the best buildings are on the outside of the bend, backing on to the river. Most are, at least outwardly, Georgian, in dark red or buff brick, but they follow the medieval pattern, each standing at the front of a plot perhaps twenty to thirty feet wide, extending back to the riverside. Many had storehouses on the back parts of the plots, others had, and some retain, domestic gardens. Some of the houses are flanked by passageways entered through arches, running the length of the plots, giving access to the buildings behind and, originally, the river. Despite the prevailing Georgian character, the two most interesting buildings in King Street are medieval. One is St George's Guildhall, built in 1410–20 for one of the town's two chief guilds; it passed to the town council at the Reformation, after which it was put to various uses, including theatrical performances. It was fitted as a theatre in 1766, but became a warehouse in the 19th century. It was restored in 1951 and is now equipped again as a theatre and public hall, with restaurant in the undercroft and art gallery and arts centre in adjoining buildings. It is the centrepiece of the annual King's Lynn Festival. Nearly opposite is an extraordinary building, no. 28–32. This had an uninteresting front, but work

Opposite
Purfleet and Custom House, King's Lynn. The Purfleet is an inlet of the Ouse, enlivened by an old sailing ship, moored temporarily. The Custom House, built 1683 as a merchants' exchange, is a minor masterpiece by the local architect Henry Bell.

carried out for the King's Lynn Preservation Trust, which bought the building in 1975, revealed that it was a medieval house partly of stone, originally of the 12th century, altered in the 14th and 15th, and much changed and subdivided since. After repair and conversion it is now used for offices, with restored timber-framed frontage, and internal features displayed.

King Street leads on to the Purfleet, the tidal inlet which divided the original 11th-century town from the 12th century extension to the north. Most is now culverted, but the mouth is still open, with mooring for small vessels. The dominant feature is the Custom House, a minor masterpiece of the local architect Henry Bell, built in 1683 as the Merchants' Exchange. Originally, like many similar buildings, including less sophisticated market halls, it had an open, arched ground floor. In 1718 it was converted as the Custom House, and the arches were blocked. With its transomed windows and steep roof rising to a two-tiered lantern and cupola it looks very Dutch, except for the brown Northamptonshire stone of which it is built.

One can walk from the Purfleet round to the open quay, but it is better to go first along Queen Street, narrow, winding and traffic-ridden. Queen Street follows the line of the original shore, which, through reclamation, had receded about a hundred yards by the end of the Middle Ages, enabling buildings to be erected on the river side of the street. These included Clifton House, a complicated amalgam of several dates. The street façade is in dark red brick of 1708, possibly by Bell, with a rich doorcase flanked by twisted columns, leading into a courtyard garden flanked by early 18th-century ranges, all very Dutch. One of the ranges contains a 14th-century brick undercroft, showing how early this site had been reclaimed from the river. But the most striking feature is a five-storey brick tower rising from a corner of the courtyard, built by a 16th-century occupant; from it he could survey the river and quays and, no doubt, the ships carrying his merchandise. Towers like this were once fairly common in old merchants' premises, but this is now a rare, almost unique survival, at least in England. Behind the tower, and flanking the narrow King's Staithe Street, are old brick warehouses which were attached to Clifton House, themselves converted to houses.

The next remarkable group of buildings is Thoresby College. This was founded by a merchant, Thomas Thoresby, who died in 1510, as a college of priests, who served the Trinity Guild and also sang masses for his soul and those of his relatives. It lasted for only a short while before being dissolved at the Reformation, after which it was converted into a house, occupied by a succession of merchants, until subdivided in the 18th century; the original courtyard plan has been preserved. The front to Queen Street was remodelled c. 1590 in brick, with five little 'Dutch' gables, but the arched entrance and panelled door are original. The courtyard now has a repaired, Georgian domestic look, following the conversion work carried out by the admirable King's Lynn Preservation Trust after they received the then dilapidated buildings from a benefactor in 1963. The range nearest the river is still largely medieval; it contains the original hall, for long subdivided but recently reopened to its well-preserved medieval roof.

Queen Street opens into Saturday Market, small and irregular, where an open market is still held on the day appointed by Bishop Herbert. On one

Above right
Franciscan Friary, King's Lynn. Only the central arches and tower, of stone and brick, remain – in contrast to Norwich where a whole friary church survives, except the tower.

Above
The Hanseatic Warehouse, St Margaret's Lane, King's Lynn. This timber-framed range, with brick infill, was part of the Steelyard, or local depot for the merchants of the Hanseatic cities (Bremen, Hamburg, Danzig and others) which traded with Lynn; it probably dates from the late 15th century.

side is St Margaret's church; on the other, curving round from the market place back into Queen Street, is a complex of buildings including the Trinity Guildhall. This was built, like St George's Guildhall, for an important guild – that of the Holy Trinity, to which Thoresby College was attached – in 1421. It became the civic hall after the Reformation. It has a fine chequered facade of flint and stone. Round the curve is an Elizabethan addition, also chequered but with fancy detailing, and then there is an annexe in an attractive free style of 1895. All this formed the town hall until the local government reorganization of the 1970s added a huge area to King's Lynn and the administration moved elsewhere.

St Margaret's church is like a small cathedral because of its twin west towers, basically Norman, though later in their upper parts. The southern tower used to have a tall lead-covered wooden spire. Unfortunately this was blown down in 1741, wrecking the nave, and also damaging a central octagonal lantern which was the church's nearly unique feature, a simpler version of that at Ely. Nave and crossing were rebuilt in 1745 by Matthew Brettingham in a Perpendicular style – remarkable for its date but not inspiring. Far finer is the eastern part of the church, with richly carved details on the 13th-century arcades.

St Margaret's House, opposite the church, is outwardly another 18th-century house. But it too is the frontispiece of a complex of buildings round a courtyard, extending back towards the river. Here was the Steelyard, established in or soon after 1485 by the Hanseatic merchants as their Lynn base. The range on the long south side of the courtyard, fronting St Margaret's Lane, with overhung timber-and-brick upper storey, is part of the original, used by the Hanse merchants for storage. The lane continues to the open quay, which now extends for about seventy yards beyond the line of the late medieval river bank. There is not a great deal to see now on the quay apart from the river itself, and parts of old warehouses that used to stand nearer to the water. Going back along St Margaret's Lane, the buildings on the right belong to Hampton Court, yet another building group of medieval origin with later alterations.

Hampton Court fronts on to Nelson Street, which leads south from St Margaret's. The street frontage is a late 15th-century range with overhung upper storey, plastered now and painted red, probably a traditional colour. This part was added to a 14th-century range now forming the southern side of the courtyard which, though thoroughly altered, has traces of original doors and windows. The block at the far end of the courtyard was built in the 15th century as a storehouse; the lower storey was originally open and arched on the side facing the quay. The fourth range to the north, completing the courtyard, was not added till the 17th century. Like Thoresby College, Hampton Court declined and was finally divided into several tenements. Part was restored in 1951, the rest after 1958 by the King's Lynn Preservation Trust, and the whole now forms several attractive residences.

The narrow, slightly writhing Nelson Street is perhaps the most attractive street in the town, with its plastered timber-framed houses, especially the one on the corner of Priory Lane with a particularly bold overhang, and several fine Georgian frontages, some concealing older structures behind;

10 *Above*
Clifton House, Queen Street, King's Lynn is an amalgam of building from medieval to Georgian; the early 18th century entrance may have been designed by Henry Bell.

11 *Opposite*
The Guildhall, King's Lynn, built for the Holy Trinity Guild, 1421; since the Reformation the civic hall; the lower windows light a vaulted undercroft. The annexe is Elizabethan, hovering between the Gothic and the Classical in its inspiration.

Opposite
Elm Hill, Norwich was largely a slum early this century; in 1926 the city council started to buy properties and restore them and by 1939 it became a show street. Many of the buildings date from after a fire of 1507, variously altered since.

no. 9 has a medieval doorway. At the far end of Nelson Street the intensely interesting part of King's Lynn ends. Elsewhere there are scattered individual buildings of interest. Only two can be mentioned. The central part of the Franciscan friars' church survives in a green space on St James' Street, ending in a graceful 14th-century octagonal tower of brick and stone. This is a rare survival; other friars' churches that partly survive have lost their central towers, as at Norwich. Finally there is the Red Mount chapel on the eastern fringes, standing on what had been part of the town's earthen ramparts, now part of a park. It was built in 1485 by St Margaret's priory, supposedly as a shrine to be visited on the way to Walsingham; it is octagonal, of brick, in three storeys, the lowest an undercroft. The principal chapel is on the first floor, cross-shaped within, with a fan vault, and there is another chapel on the top floor. The whole has been rededicated for Catholic worship.

New Buckenham

New Buckenham was a feudal foundation. William d'Albini, or William of Albany, builder also of Castle Rising (see colour illus. p. 23) and son of the founder of Wymondham Abbey (page 60) built a new castle in about 1145–6, on a site to the east of his earlier castle in what is now Old Buckenham. The new castle had a circular bailey, artificially raised, whose earthen sides are now densely covered in trees. On the top is the base of a circular stone keep, which must have risen to a considerable height. It has been called the earliest known circular keep in England (previous ones were

square or rectangular), but there is another in Arundel Castle, Sussex, which may have been built at about the same time – William had been granted the lordship of Arundel by Henry I, whose widow, Adeliza, he married in 1138.

William d'Albini laid out New Buckenham as an

12 **New Buckenham.** The former market place of the town laid out by William d'Albini in the 1140s (map IV), now the green of a quiet village. The church suggests late 15th century prosperity, and on the right is a small 17th century former market hall with open ground storey.

Above
Elm Hill, Norwich, with St
Peter Hangate, now a museum.

Above right
**Erpingham Gate,
Tombland, Norwich,** the
entrance to the cathedral close,
1420; full of statues and
naturalistic carving in its deeply
recessed arch.

Map IV, New Buckenham. The small town with its grid plan was laid out by William d'Albini alongside the castle he built *c.*1145, with a round keep on a tremendous circular mound. The rectangular market place has been partly encroached on, but the rest is now a green (**12**), little changed since the date of this map, 1891.

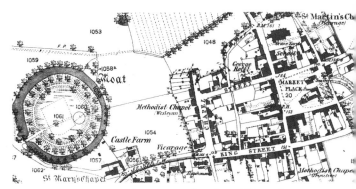

entirely new town, a short distance to the east of the castle. It has a grid plan, with two main east-west streets, four from north to south and subsidiary lanes, all originally enclosed within a defensive ditch. A large rectangular space within the grid became the market place. New Buckenham prospered modestly for a time, but by the 18th century was in relative decline and by the 19th had the status of a village. The market place, reduced a little by encroaching buildings at its south-east corner, became a village green. Its focal feature is a small, restored 17th-century market hall supported on pillars with an open ground storey. Other buildings round the green and along the streets are modest and of cottage scale, except for one grander late Georgian inn facing the green. The church rises beyond the buildings on the north side of the green, a rebuilding

of about 1480, suggesting prosperity then. There is flushwork decoration along the south aisle and porch, round the base of the tower and on its parapet.

Old Buckenham makes an interesting contrast. It is disposed loosely round an enormous village green, as many villages on the Norfolk–Suffolk border are. This was a true green, used for grazing, not a former market place as in New Buckenham.

North Walsham

North Walsham is a lively market town, especially on Thursdays when stalls fill the market place – which is in effect two elongated triangles, the corner of the base of one abutting to the apex of the other. The western triangle is dominated by the Market Cross, an intriguing open-sided structure with a three-tiered roof rather like a Chinese lantern; it was built in 1600 but restored and probably embellished in the 19th century. The buildings round the Market Place have austere and dignified fronts over the shops, in red or buff brick, though some are painted over. Clearly the market place was originally larger, but reduced through encroachment, especially by the predecessors of the buildings backing on to the churchyard. Three alleys called The Butchery, Pope's Passage and Marjoram's Opening lead through to the church, the last in front of the porch, with its flushwork depicting the arms of Edward III and his son John of Gaunt. The church is enormous, a rectangle with 14th-century arcades, now

a bit bare with its medieval screen reduced to its base; this has nearly twenty paintings of saints and apostles in finely carved panels. The font cover is lovely, a tall slender pinnacle becoming more elaborate in each tier upward. The once tall tower crashed in 1724, leaving a romantically jagged stump still reaching to more than three storeys on one side, and looking like a keep when seen above the rooftops from the market place. There are intricate alleys west of the church, opening into Market Street, from the far end of which there is a view back to the ruined tower rising above the trees behind a range of gables. There are interesting Georgian houses in various streets, including Scarborough House in Market Street, now the High School; Aylsham House in Aylsham Road; and Paston School, the oldest part of which dates from 1765 – the school was founded by Sir William Paston of the famous Norfolk family, who died in 1608; his monument is in the church. Nelson went to this school in 1768/71.

Norwich

Norwich has for centuries been one of the great cities of England. From Norman times until the 18th century it was always among the five or six largest, and at times was the second after London. It had no significant, Roman ancestry – the Roman town was at Caistor St Edmund, now a small village five miles to the south. The name *Northwic* first appears in records in the tenth century. *Wic* meant a trading centre (it could have had other meanings, but they are unlikely here); *North* might refer to its location in

East Anglia, or might even – although people in Norwich would not admit this readily – have been given in relation to Ipswich, which was a significant town over two centuries before. Late Saxon Norwich was important, and was probably centred where the cathedral is now, adjoining a crossing of the River Wensum, then navigable for seagoing ships. It extended in several directions; there was Saxon settlement in Pottergate and near the Castle site, as archaeologists have shown, and there is a Saxon tower to St Mary Coslany, north of the river. Street names ending in *gate* suggest Viking influence.

The Normans imposed drastic changes on Norwich. An earth-and-timber castle was thrown up, displacing many houses and soon to be rebuilt in stone; a new market place was laid out to the west, where it is still. In 1094 the East Anglian bishop's see was moved from Thetford (page 57) to Norwich. A new cathedral – essentially the one standing today – was built over what had been a central part of the Saxon town (which however may have been devastated following a rebellion a few years before).

From the 14th century Norwich was a major weaving centre. Its speciality was worsted – named from a village twelve miles away – a fine light cloth which did not require fulling and was therefore a suitable product for a city with limited water supply. The industry fluctuated and was in decline in the mid 16th century. Fortunately for Norwich there was an inflow of refugees from religious persecution in Flanders and Wallonia in the 1560s and 70s, bringing skills in weaving light cloths which were fairly similar to worsted – the 'New Draperies'. In 1579 it was reckoned that no less than 6000 out of the city's total population of about 16,000 were refugees or their children. After two or three generations their descendants were absorbed into the community.

In the mid 18th century 'Norwich stuffs' – light, often brightly coloured fabrics of several varieties – were famous and widely exported. Georgian Norwich was a regional capital, with shops, a huge market, professional services, assembly rooms and theatre serving the well-to-do of an important corner of England. At first the developing textile industries of the North did not seriously affect Norwich, which continued to produce fine fabrics by hand. But after 1800 Yorkshire developed its own mechanized worsted industry, with increasingly better products, with which Norwich was less able to compete. Furthermore the Napoleonic wars disrupted the city's overseas markets. Norwich tried to come to terms with the Industrial Revolution, but too late. In the 1830s a steam-powered factory was built, with floor space let to different manufacturers, but Yorkshire had irrevocably gained the initiative, and by 1900 the Norwich worsted industry was extinct.

The city developed other industries, notably shoemaking and food processing (especially mustard), and was prosperous through the Victorian period, but did not grow hugely in proportion to its previous size. Modern Norwich, with its newly founded university, its newspapers, its television studios, its major shops and its theatres is as much as ever a regional metropolis. Its official population of about 120,000 makes it sound deceptively small, as the city boundaries exclude several suburbs which, if added, would bring the population to nearer 200,000. It is a complex, infinitely interesting place, with a central street pattern that is still largely medieval; buildings of many periods; and an ambience which varies from the vibrantly modern to the quiet and picturesque. The following descriptions can only suggest, briefly and selectively, its astonishing wealth of interest.

There are three itineraries: (1) Market Place to Cathedral, (2) Colegate and Coslany: Norwich over the Water, (3) Maddermarket to St Giles, and across the southern fringes.

(1) Market Place to Cathedral

Norwich has the market place *par excellence*. It is a rectangle on a slight slope with stalls always in situ; the City Hall is on the higher side; a church and the medieval Guildhall stand on opposite flanks; shops front the lower side. It was not always the same shape. Originally, when laid out in the late 11th century, it was probably about as big as now. In time, buildings encroached on the square, reducing the market space to about half the original. The encroachments were cleared, in stages, by 1939, restoring the square to roughly its Norman extent. One should stand on the terrace in front of the modern City Hall, looking over the stalls to the lower-lying buildings on the further side, with the castle looming on the hill behind. The first wooden keep, on its artificial motte, was replaced in the early 12th century by a great stone keep which survives, though refaced with new stone in *c.* 1835; the pattern of small arches between broad buttresses is a copy of the original treatment. The keep is all that is left, apart from some earthworks; outer walls, gates and other buildings have all gone. It is now the centrepiece of a very good museum and art gallery, with *inter alia* works of the Norwich School of artists, of whom John Crome and the incomparable watercolourist J. S. Cotman were the greatest.

Back to the Market Place; the City Hall of 1932–8 is a remarkable building in a modernized classical style which was characteristic of Sweden and Holland; the slender, slightly tapering tower is very effective. It rather overshadows the medieval Guildhall, a complex building in dark flint with

13 Market Place and Castle, Norwich. The Normans built the first castle on a natural eminence heightened by earthworks, and laid out the market place underneath. The early 12th century keep, refaced *c*.1835, is now an art gallery.

stone dressings, much restored outside, though the east-facing elevation, with its chequer pattern, is largely original (see colour illus. p. 49). More splendid is the church of St Peter Mancroft at the south end of the square, with a row of buildings in front. This is the largest of Norwich's numerous parish churches and one of the few still in use; a rebuilding of 1430–55 where the interior seems to combine the effects of great expanse and great height in balance, with a hammerbeam roof coved at the sides.

Behind a plain frontage on the eastern side is the astonishing Royal Arcade of 1899, a work of George Skipper, one of the best architects in England of the period, whose practice was based on Norwich (see colour illus. p. 49). It curves gently, with slender arches supporting the continuous glazed roof; its fantasy is at the far end, where the external elevation to Castle Street has decorative tiles and faience in Art-Nouveau style, and a pattern of trees in stained glass over the entrance. Castle Street, a back street, leads north, across Davey Place with a glimpse of the castle up steps, to merge with London Street, a thoroughfare of character with some of the city's smartest shops. Once busy with traffic, it was one of the first streets in the country to be 'pedestrianized', in 1969, and is still one of the most successful – its twists and turns and relative narrowness make it ideally suited for such treatment (unlike some wider streets). Most of the buildings are solidly Victorian above the shop fronts, but a few are earlier, and there is a striking view back at the west end of the street, framing the Guildhall with its chequered end elevation, with the City Hall tower soaring behind. A sumptuous classical bank of 1924, with a cupola, punctuates the fork into narrow Bedford Street – a lively, low-key street with a mixture of timber-framed, Georgian and Victorian fronts over small shops. Narrower Bridewell Alley leads off, with more little shops, one containing a mustard museum, ending with the tall tower of St Andrew's church. The tower is typical of Norwich and Norfolk – tall, fairly slender, built in flint with a little flushwork, for instance, on the buttresses; the top is flat and has no pinnacles. Nearby is the Bridewell Museum, in origin a 14th-century house but very much altered; it was bought in the 16th century by the city council to be a 'bridewell' or house of correction, not quite a prison but a place where people such as beggars and small-scale offenders were kept and given supposedly beneficial work. It was opened as a museum for crafts and industries in 1925. Outside there is a fine wall of knapped flint facing the church.

Across noisy St Andrew's Street is St Andrew's Hall, the best-preserved friars' church in England, built by Dominicans in 1327 and reconstructed after a fire in 1413. At the Dissolution the city council bought the buildings; they converted the nave into an assembly hall, as it is today; the chancel had various uses and is now another hall. The tower in between collapsed in 1712. (In interesting contrast, at King's Lynn only the tower of the friary church survives, (see colour illus. p. 35.) Although much restored in Victorian times, the building is typically East Anglian with its slender arcades and plain hammerbeam roof. Parts of the other friars' buildings survive behind, including a cloister walk and a brick-vaulted undercroft.

Elm Hill, Norwich's show street, is reached from St Andrew's along

14 Norwich Cathedral from
the Close. The Norman tower
is part of the original cathedral;
the spire dates from *c*.1480–90;
the south transept facade is a
restoration of the 1830s – in the
Middle Ages monastic buildings
abutted on to this transept.

15 Hook Walk, The Close, Norwich, a little known and delightful backwater at the far end of the cathedral close; the buildings are of various dates with a mixture of external treatment. A path leads from the far end to give a stunning eastern view of the cathedral.

Prince's Street, where a gabled house, plastered to resemble stone, faces St Peter Hungate church – one of the first Norwich churches to become redundant, used as an ecclesiastical museum since 1936 (see colour illus. pp. 38, 40). Elm Hill descends from here; the first building on it is the oldest – the Briton's Arms (a restaurant), a recently restored double-jettied 15th-century house with, surprisingly in a city, a thatched roof. A fire in 1507 destroyed most of the other buildings in Elm Hill, and many of the present houses date basically from the subsequent rebuilding, some with timber-framed upper floors over flint-faced ground floors (this combination was typical of Tudor Norwich), others Georgianized or refronted. The street declined, till in the 1920s it was largely a slum, condemned for clearance by the city council. In 1926 the newly formed Norwich Society carried out a survey and recommended that most of the buildings on the street should be restored, but that poor property which crowded into what were formerly yards behind should be cleared. The city council accepted the report –

reputedly by one vote – and started to buy and improve the properties. Before the Second World War Elm Hill was already a show street; even more so is it now with its cobbles, its meticulously maintained buildings with window boxes, and its lantern lamps. Never in the past did Elm Hill look like that. The cobbles would have been covered in dirt; the houses would have been in different stages of repair or disrepair, and more varied commercial activities would have taken place than now. Nevertheless the street's rehabilitation – long before the conservation heyday of the late 1960s and 70s – is a triumph, infinitely preferable to total destruction or bit-by-bit erosion.

Elm Hill joins Wensum Street, close to the river (left) and to Tombland (right). Tombland was the Saxon market place, before the cathedral was built beside it; afterwards it became, like Angel Hill in Bury St Edmunds, a fairground outside the monastic precinct. Traffic now prevents it achieving its potential as a space, with an interesting shape (a rectangle with a narrower prolongation) and fine buildings. Two gateways lead into the cathedral precinct. Erpingham Gate of 1420 is an ornate arch with statues and carving set in its recessions, under a simple gable (see colour illus. p. 40).

The cathedral is essentially that started by Bishop Losinga, even retaining its Norman apse (as at Peterborough). The main later additions include the vaulted roofs, the stone spire added to the Norman tower *c.* 1475–1500 (the previous spire, of wood, collapsed in 1362) and, especially, the cloister which is the finest of its kind remaining in England, built in stages *c.* 1300–1430. The carvings in the oldest, north-eastern, part of the cloister are of superlative quality, particularly on the bosses. Norwich was a monastic cathedral but, apart from the cloister, few of the monastic buildings survive except for fragments, often incorporated into later buildings. But the monastic precinct has become a superb cathedral close, the largest in England except perhaps at Salisbury. There are two main parts, Upper and Lower Close, both centred on green spaces, linked by a precinctual road. At the southern end of Upper Close is St Ethelbert's Gate of 1316, very different from Erpingham Gate, with intricate flushwork, nearly all renewed. Adjoining the gate is a group of buildings that epitomize the close. First there is an austere Georgian house (the date 1702 given by Pevsner seems too early) in deep red brick; then at right angles, set back behind Almary Green, is a pre-Georgian range with gables and transomed windows of the type that preceded sashes; then there is an irregular house with 'Dutch' gables. The Lower Close has a more formal row of Georgian houses on its south side. This was originally the servicing area of the monastery, and some of the houses fronting the green were converted from the granary, brewery and other such buildings. Two lanes lead on, still within the Close. One, Ferry Lane, reaches the river; it follows the line of a filled-in canal coming into the precinct – convenient for bringing supplies and, specially, building materials. The other lane, Hook Walk, is exceedingly picturesque, curving past tree-hung garden walls, and then a series of houses, gabled or eaved in brick, flint or rough stone, and roofed in pantiles, with some unfortunate painting of old brickwork. From the far end a path leads off to cross an area of playing fields, with a magnificent view of the cathedral, east-end-on, displaying the full effect of the flying buttresses set against the clerestory of the choir, and of the spire springing between tall pinnacles from the Norman tower – the whole a soaring, dynamic composition. The path reaches Bishopgate, a winding street, opposite the extraordinary Great Hospital, founded by a bishop in 1249 for poor retired clergy and others; now it is a very large, frequently extended, home for old people, with a medieval core. From here an intriguing path leads back past the cathedral, or one can walk along Bishopgate, going first north then west, past old flint walls with new sheltered housing built behind them, to Palace Plain. This is an informal space, regenerated since a gasworks was closed, with a small church (St Martin's), the gateway of the former bishop's palace, and Georgian-fronted houses, one displaying a 15th-century oriel window on its side. From the too-busy road leading to Whitefriars Bridge over the River Wensum there is a view of one of the most incongruously impressive buildings in Norwich – the factory built in the 1830s to provide steam-powered space for spinning and weaving, eventually unsuccessful. It is paradoxically one of the finest early textile mills surviving, with five stark stories in dark brick, and a rounded end topped by a low dome. From Palace Plain it is a short distance to Tombland – or, more interestingly, one can find a path to the Quayside, now a riverside walk, where ships once tied up. Beyond is Fye Bridge, where the next itinerary begins.

(2) Colegate and Coslany–Norwich over the Water
Colegate is the street parallel to the Wensum on its opposite side from the city centre. Till the 18th century merchants lived there, many but not all in the worsted trade. The weavers and other clothworkers, often employed by the merchants, would have lived in some of the lesser houses, especially along the streets leading north. With the 19th-century collapse of local weaving, the shoe industry developed – first in small workshops and later in bigger factories. Numerous other trades flourished, especially near the river. The area became dominantly commercial, but many old buildings survived, often subdivided and in poor condition. By the 1960s many of the old businesses had closed or moved outwards, and the remaining historic buildings had deteriorated further. Regeneration of the area was then initiated by the city council. In 1971 they bought former commercial land near the river and set up a company in partnership with a local builder, which developed the site, called Friars' Quay, with private houses. They are of brick of varied colours, red predominating, with steep pantiled roofs, to an informal layout, especially where they border the river; the architects were the locally based and nationally known Feilden and Mawson. In the early 1970s this was a pioneering scheme – bringing people back to live in what was till then a decaying inner area. At the same time two fine early 18th-century houses, nos. 18–20 Colegate, and an adjoining older row, nos. 22–4, were bought and rehabilitated as offices, shops and flats. Since then many other old houses in Colegate and the streets leading off have been repaired and refurbished, either by the city council directly, or with the help of grants or loans available through housing and historic buildings legislation.

The itinerary begins at Fye Bridge, a short distance from the end of Elm Hill, from Tombland, and from the Quayside, described in the previous

Above
Royal Arcade, Norwich, a
minor masterpiece by the local
architect George Skipper, 1899,
with thin-arched glazed roof
and, at the far end, a fantastic
Art-Nouveau entrance facade.

Above right
Guildhall, Norwich, a
complex building of 1407
onwards, much restored in the
19th century, in typical local
dark flint with stone dressings.

16 *Above*
Colegate, Norwich, a
marvellous street, with
buildings rehabilitated after
decay, including the flint and
timber-framed Bacon House.
Two towers of Norwich's
numerous medieval churches
can be seen.

Opposite
Walsingham was a pilgrims'
town that grew outside the gate
of the priory which contained a
supposed replica of the Holy
House at Nazareth, built
following a dream by a medieval
lady of the manor. Many of the
houses are flint-faced below and
timber-framed above – a
combination also found in
Norwich. **(20)**

itinerary. Friars' Quay is seen on the left. Colegate itself leads off Magdalen
Street just north of the bridge. It is a superb street, one of the most interesting
in East Anglia, with five historic churches (two are nonconformist) as
well as numerous old houses. One of the churches is the medieval St
Clement's at the corner. The street begins narrowly with a slight twist, past
several Georgian house fronts, culminating in nos. 18–20, already mentioned,
on the left. Just before these, set back in a yard on the opposite side of the
street, is one of the two nonconformist chapels, the Old Meeting of 1693,
in glowing red brick with stone Corinthian capitals, hipped roof of grey
pantiles, and what are claimed to be the earliest sash windows in the city.
The classical interior is untouched. The second chapel, the Octagon of
1754–6 by Thomas Ivory, a leading local architect, is set back in another
yard a little further on. Again it has a marvellous interior with eight giant
Corinthian capitals and galleries between, recalling the work of Hawksmoor.
The houses opposite have Georgian-looking upper storeys but their first-
floor jetties give them away; they are timber-framed houses Georgianized.

    The heart of the rehabilitated area is where St George's Street and

17 Octagon Chapel, Colegate, Norwich, originally Presbyterian, later Unitarian, a perfectly preserved chapel of 1754–6 by the local architect Thomas Ivory.

Colegate intersect. Bacon House, on the corner, is a symbol of the regeneration – a 16th-century merchant's house round a three-sided courtyard, mainly of flint but with a timbered first floor on the main frontage (a typical Norwich combination), restored by the council as flats and for other purposes. St George Colegate, beyond the churchyard, still lives as a church, but the same is not true of the old factory opposite, where Norvic shoes were made until it closed a few years ago. This big late Victorian building of strong red brick, which must have seemed an intruder at first but is now regarded as a focal feature of the area, has been transformed into shops, offices, workshops, restaurants and flats. Opposite is another former shoe factory, less visible because it is built behind a row of Georgian houses fronting the street, which the firm retained as offices; they have been well restored.

From here one can continue to the far end of Colegate, but, with time, it is worth diverting northwards along Muspole Street – past restored old houses, new houses filling former gaps, and remaining industrial premises to a remarkable renovated block on the corner of Muspole and Duke Streets. For long unappreciated because of the dull way in which the outside had been treated, this group of 15/16th-century houses round a small courtyard was rescued and rehabilitated in 1975, and is now a colourful landmark. Opposite is St Mary Coslany whose late Saxon round tower is, with part of St Julian's (page 54), one of the two oldest standing structures in Norwich. The church has been well converted into a crafts centre, freely accessible. It has an interesting roof with intersecting timbers at the crossing.

Narrow Rosemary Lane leads back, past the thatched 15/16th-century Pykereli's House, to the church of St *Michael* Coslany (not to be confused with St *Mary* Coslany), at the western end of Colegate. This is a big building with the proudest display of medieval flushwork in Norwich at its southeast corner, imitated by the Victorians in the chancel. Round the church old houses have been restored by the Norwich Preservation Trust; the corner building with Colegate is a commendable new insertion where there had been a gap. On a grander scale is Barnard's Yard opposite St Michael's, a complex of flats built by the council from 1978 on the site of a foundry, extending back to the river. A series of massive, well-managed 'vernacular' facades follows the slight curve of Coslany Street, more Germanic than East Anglian but none the worse for that, while the internal courtyard focuses on St Michael's tower, seen rising above the end block. This scheme and Friars' Quay (public and private respectively), together with rehabilitation of fine old buildings in Colegate, Muspole Street and elsewhere, and infilling of new houses on what had been small vacant sites, set examples of how historic but declining areas can be rescued, revived and repeopled, reversing the (till recently) nearly universal trend of people moving out of the central parts of cities to the suburbs or beyond. Finally, by the river across St Miles Bridge, is a remarkable recent conversion. The rambling former Bullard's Brewery, grand in parts and mainly dating from the 1870s, has been transformed into a complex of houses, offices and other uses and activities, retaining the Victorian grandeur of the frontage.

(3) Maddermarket to St Giles, and across the southern fringes

This itinerary begins at St Miles Bridge across the River Wensum, where the last itinerary ended. It takes an intricate route to the City Hall, then up to the Roman Catholic cathedral, and finally across the southern part of the city centre looking at widely spaced individual buildings.

South of the bridge, with the converted Bullard's brewery on one side and new private housing on the other, St Lawrence's looms on the hillside – another redundant church. It has a fine interior and ought to be preserved so that it is possible for the public to visit it and appreciate it as a building. St Peter at Sudbury (converted into a meeting place), Holy Trinity, Colchester (now a museum), and St Mary, Bungay (simply kept as a consecrated building, generally open) provide precedents, as well as St Mary Coslany in Norwich. Steps climb into St Benedict's Street, a long and fascinating street, passing more churches. One is St Gregory's, up a slope to the south-east. This has been kindly treated after long disuse. It is now an arts centre – which means that the interior has been kept clear, not subdivided, and its splendid proportions, with tall airy arches, can be fully appreciated, perhaps more than when it was filled with pews and other fittings. St Benedict's Street continues east into Charing Cross – and Strangers' Hall, a most fascinating amalgam of building work from the 13th century onwards, now a domestic museum, which ought to be high on a visitor's priorities. Beyond and southward is one of Norwich's most atmospheric backwaters, centred on the church of St John Maddermarket. An alley leads past the Maddermarket Theatre, with an interior supposedly based on an Elizabethan model, and continues under the tower of the church (which is now Greek Orthodox) into Pottergate, yet another interesting street. A short distance up Pottergate is a focal point where several streets and paths meet in a tangle, with the small green churchyard of St Gregory's to the north. Just to the east of the church is Strangers' Court, a little group of houses, partly new, partly conversions, formed on the site of a factory in 1976 – one of an encouraging number of recent 'infill' developments on odd sites in the city centre, all helping to bring people back to live there. One of the lanes leading south, Lower Goat Lane, is typical Norwich with its simple, varied, low-keyed buildings with small shops on a slight curve. It ends by the City Hall, at a corner of the Market Place.

St Giles Street leads uphill past the City Hall, at first gently, then more steeply. It is unlike most other streets in Norwich in that it is dominantly Georgian, with a succession of sizeable brick houses. They are enlivened half-way along by two Edwardian buildings, especially no. 43 with a really vigorous baroque front in stone, designed by the brilliant local architect George Skipper. Probably by Skipper too is a more staid but strongly detailed classical building (no. 49), also in stone, with columns on the upper floor. The climax is St Giles' church, set on a brow in a green churchyard, round which the street turns – towards where one of the city gates used to stand. Gate and city wall (on this stretch) have long since disappeared, and now a ring road sweeps round outside the line of the wall (of which fragments remain to the north and south-east) – so severing the centre of the city from the suburbs as surely as the wall, in the past, separated the entire city from the fields around. But the ring road was a good idea; otherwise most of the traffic on it would try to get through the central city streets. A footbridge crosses the road from St Giles Street to the Roman Catholic cathedral.

Norwich is unusual among English cities in having two cathedrals both of which are of accepted cathedral scale. The Catholic one was built in 1884–1910 at the expense of the Duke of Norfolk – because of his family's historic and titular connection with the county. The architect was George Gilbert Scott the second, son of the first Sir Gilbert, and it is a splendid piece of Gothic Revivalism, especially inside. It became a cathedral only in 1961.

This itinerary ends with a few individual buildings. The Assembly Rooms in Theatre Street, built in 1754, were saved in 1950 by a benefactor who gave them to the city; they consist of two splendid rooms separated by a large hall, the work of the local architect Thomas Ivory. Probably only Bath and York have finer Assembly Rooms, although Bury St Edmunds has its Athenaeum. The main part of Norwich's shopping centre, south of the Market Place, is visually a jumble. It was fairly badly damaged by bombing, and the 1950s and 60s rebuilding was characteristically insipid. Survivals from the Edwardian era or earlier stand out; the most striking were designed by George Skipper, in Orford Place and White Lion Street. Skipper's *tour de force* is the original building for the Norwich Union insurance company in Surrey Street, dating from 1903–4, 'one of the country's most convinced Edwardian office buildings' (Pevsner), a tremendous *palazzo* with Ionic columns, sculptured pediment and wings with thickly incised stonework. It adjoins an extension of *c*. 1960.

Surrey Street still has a few fine Georgian buildings, and other fragments of old townscape survive to show that this was once an attractive part of Norwich – for instance around the two small churches of All Saints and St John at Timberhill. Past the Eastern Counties Newspapers building (1976), which is at least a decent modern building, is Rouen Road, a modern relief road named – hardly in compliment – after Norwich's twin city. Off it, downhill, one finds St Julian's church, one of the most poignant places in Norwich. A bomb dropped on the round tower in the Second World War and nearly destroyed the church – but not quite. It was successfully rebuilt on the same lines, incorporating the old north wall which remained, showing rounded Saxon windows – this is the oldest standing fabric in Norwich except for the tower of St Mary Coslany (page 52). The church is interesting for its association with Julian of Norwich, a remarkable religious woman who became an anchoress in 1373 and spent the remaining years of her long life in a cell attached to the south of the church (rebuilt as before), from which she communicated with the outside world through a window on the south side, or with the church through an opening into the chancel. While there, she wrote *The Revelations of Divine Love*, one of the most remarkable works of medieval religious literature. She took her name from the (male) saint to whom the church was dedicated.

Nearby King Street runs parallel to the river, where several medieval merchants' houses backed on to wharfs. Now it is a mixture of modern commerce and restored old buildings, the former predominating. One of the historic buildings, called Wensum Lodge, an adult education centre, is a

18 Norwich Union, Surrey Street, Norwich. The company's headquarters of 1903–4 designed with tremendous *verve* by the local architect George Skipper, who was 'every bit as . . . inventive as any in London' at the time'. (Pevsner: *N.E. Norfolk and Norwich*).

complex amalgam with 17th-century work outside; it contains part of a stone house thought to have been built about 1175 by a Jewish merchant, Jurnet. (It is sometimes called the Music House because of an 18th-century use.) The other interesting building, for long called the Old Barge and now Dragon Hall, is close to St Julian's. Recent restoration has revealed a first-floor hall of *c*. 1440–50 which may have been used for displaying woven cloth; one of the trusses has an intricate carving of a dragon in the spandrel, hence the new name. It is now open to the public.

Finally the University of East Anglia, founded in 1963, on the western outskirts – it is a great pity that a central site, which was then available, was not taken. But it takes advantage of its rural setting, with a staggered range of stepped-back buildings, in the then fashionable 'ziggurat' style, facing over lush landscape – though there is some very dreary concrete-scape behind. Nearby, and not strictly part of the university, is the Sainsbury Centre, one of the great buildings of the 1970s, designed by Foster Associates who were also the architects of the Willis Faber building in Ipswich. It is something like an aircraft hanger, but a very elegant one, with its panelled sides and lattice-arched end enclosing an expanse of reflecting glass.

Reepham

Reepham is a very small place to be considered a town, but the presence of a weekly market and the miniature-urban character of its centre justify its inclusion. The market place is a rectangle with wide streets leading off at opposite corners, a most attractive arrangement. The buildings are mostly modest Georgian, dominantly of red brick (fortunately few have been painted over), with some of greater scale facing the market place – especially Dial House, now a hotel, built soon after 1700, with columned porch, a sundial above, and elegant railings on the frontage. But what makes Reepham really memorable is its *two* churches, end to end, each once serving a separate parish. (Incredibly there was a *third* church just to the south, serving yet another parish, until it was burnt down in 1543.) Only one is used for worship; the other is the church hall – and neither can begin to compare with the churches at neighbouring Cawston and Salle, which are among the glories of Norfolk. But St Mary's (the used one) has a magnificent monument, to Sir Roger de Kerdiston who died in 1337; he lies tense, arms folded and legs crossed, on a bed of pebbles wrought in stone; this monument found its way to the *Age of Chivalry* exhibition in 1988. From behind the churchyard a pleasant lane leads past Georgian and older cottages, with an alley back to the market place.

Swaffham

Swaffham is a market town – its market today, as in the past, is the chief cause of its prosperity. In the 17th and 18th centuries it was famous for corn; today the market is a general one with stalls filling most of the available space every Saturday, drawing shoppers from miles around. The market place was a very large triangle; the usual encroachments have resulted in irregular islands of buildings at the wider northern end, but there is still a great space tapering to the south. The *clou* is the marvellous Market Cross, a circle of columns supporting a domed roof with a statue of Ceres, goddess of corn, on the top; it was donated by the Earl of Orford, in 1783. Its Victorian counterpart is the hefty Corn Exchange of 1858 with massive round arches in yellow against red brick. All around are Georgian houses interspersed with humdrum buildings; the finest is Oakley House at the far north-west corner of the market place, with a broad pediment and elaborate treatment of window heads and surrounds; another is Electric House, east of the Market Cross, in flint bound with yellow brick. The best sequence is along the southern stem, dominantly red brick with some flint, and pantiles, red and grey. The church tower rises behind; the church was rebuilt in the 15th century using the 14th-century arcades of the nave, which was lengthened to the west; the marvel is the roof with angels on the hammerbeams, angels at the tops of the king posts, and angels along the wall plates. For those who like anecdotes to heighten architectural appreciation, the church was partly paid for by John Chapman the pedlar, who dreamed he would meet a man who would help him make his fortune if he went to London; when wandering on London Bridge with his dog, a man asked him what he was doing, and he recounted his dream. The Londoner told him that he too had had a dream, about a fortune lying buried in a garden in a place to which he had never been, called Swaffham. Chapman returned, dug in his garden (with the help of his dog) and found buried treasure. Two choir stalls have carvings (from the original Chapman family pew) of the fortunate pedlar, and also one of his wife behind the counter of their shop. In fairness it should be added that the chief benefactor of the church was John Botright, royal chaplain, master of Corpus Christi, Cambridge, and absentee rector of Swaffham, who died in 1474 and whose tomb is in the chancel.

19 **Swaffham**. The enormous market place is focused on the domed Market Cross, 1783, surmounted by the goddess Ceres. Behind are a flint-fronted Georgian house, and the church with its delicate tower top and graceful spirelet.

Thetford

Thetford is an extraordinary town. Much of it is very new – the population has increased about fourfold since 1950, largely through planned development of houses and factories for people moving out of London. For the previous 900 years Thetford's history had been one of alternating stagnation and decline. Before that it was, for a time, one of the most important towns in England. The name means, roughly, 'ford of many people' – referring to an ancient crossing of the rivers Little Ouse and Thet (the latter taking its name from the town, not vice versa). The first Saxon settlement was occupied *c.* 870 by the Vikings, who developed it into an important trading centre; this was consolidated and extended by the Saxons after they reconquered it. The Viking and Saxon town was mainly south of the Little Ouse – parts of its site have been excavated by archaeologists – but since Norman times the main centre of activity has been north of the river. From 1072 to 1096 Thetford was the seat of the East Anglian bishopric, but in the latter year Bishop Losinga moved the see to Norwich. This move marked the beginning of Thetford's long decline. It was already over-shadowed by Norwich, and soon by Bury St Edmunds as well. It never developed important marketing trade, as the surroundings are sandy and infertile; it never shared in the weaving industry. A rich priory brought

some wealth in the Middle Ages, but that disappeared at the Dissolution. An engineering industry grew in the Victorian period – Burrells were famous for farm machinery, and later for fairground equipment, powered by steam; the firm's closure in 1930 was a tragedy for the town.

Thetford may not have a great deal to suggest its long past, but a walk through its complicated network of streets and footways (with the aid of a map) reveals many minor surprises and a few major ones. Assuming one starts at the station (1845 of flint, like so much of the town, with later additions in brick), the first interesting street is White Hart Street, with the birth-place, in 1737, of Thomas Paine, the radical philo-sopher, involved with the American Revolution; the house is now a hotel. Then the Ancient House, an interesting timber-framed building of just after 1500, now a museum; despite the Georgian sash windows and shop front (which add to its charm) and the low Victorian slated roof, a great deal of the original build-ing survives; the carvings on the ceiling beams of the main room suggest that an important townsman lived here. Nearby St Peter's, now partly secularized, is one of three very modest and much altered survivors of numerous medieval parish churches; it has nice flint-work. From the central crossroads by the partly Tudor

Bell Hotel one should, if one has time, go along Minstergate and under the bypass to see what is left of Thetford Priory – a monastery of the Cluniac order, like Castle Acre (page 24), founded in 1103 by Roger Bigod, the progenitor of the family which built Bungay and Framlingham castles in Suffolk. It became a place of pilgrimage because of a figure of the Virgin Mary which was said to have had miraculous powers. What survives is largely a series of stumps and foundations in flintwork, with a few telling fragments of fine stone which suggest faintly what a grand building it was. Some of the fragments rise several feet, to weird weathered shapes which at times suggest exhibits in a sculpture gallery. It is worth studying the official guide (and the plan) to make sense of the remains. Back to the Bell Hotel crossroads; Bridge Street leads to the river where there is a charming iron bridge of 1829, brightly painted; one can turn along the so-called Riverside Walk which is (and looks like) a 1960s shopping area, leading into King Street. This is the main shopping street, a mixture of 1960s and older buildings, which because of the latter, the subtle twists of the street, and, especially, some old trees carefully preserved, is on the whole attractive. The highpoint is Thomas Paine's gilded statue, given by the Thomas Paine Foundation of America, in front of the Georgian King's House which has a grand (for Thetford) facade in yellow brick with bright red brick window surrounds. The street climbs and winds eastwards to St Cuthbert's, the remaining active Anglican parish church, largely a rebuilding of 1854 but pleasant and welcoming; the dedication suggests a connection with Northumbria in Saxon times. Beyond is a confusing meeting of streets, with the market place and Guildhall of 1900. Along scrappy Guildhall Street to the much more interesting Old Market Street where two forceful buildings face each other. One is the former prison of 1796 and 1816, as grim as a dark flint building can be, with sparse arched windows in yellow brick and a grey pantiled roof. Opposite is a former Victorian brewery, as austere but livelier, with an impressive pattern of brick-bound arches on its facade. Old Market Street passes more buildings in red and yellow brick, flint and pantiles, and the chequer-fronted Dolphin Inn, to the entrance to the castle, set in a park – a massive series of earthworks, grass-grown and tree-shaded, centred on a tall motte, on which stood the Norman Bigods' timber keep. The castle was dismantled in 1174 after Roger Bigod rebelled. The earthworks had been adapted from those of an Iron Age fortress which guarded the nearby ford. From the park one can return along Castle Street, with more flint houses, to the town centre, or else go south along the trafficky Nuns' Bridges Road to cross the two rivers, in a setting still green and rural. One can follow Spring Walk westwards along the Little Ouse – laid out in 1818 to lead past a pump room hopefully built over a spring with medicinal properties in an unsuccessful attempt to establish Thetford as a spa; the walk is the spa's lasting legacy. There are then complicated walks over interconnecting watercourses, or one can go along Mill Lane and Old Bury Road, past more flinty buildings, back to Bridge Street and the Bell Hotel. On the west side of Bridge Street, south of the river, is the Grammar School, an ancient foundation with mainly Victorian buildings which occupy the site of the early Norman cathedral and, later, of a Dominican friary. Tom Paine went to the school.

Walsingham

Walsingham, strictly Little Walsingham, was the only town in England which owed its importance solely to pilgrimages. Other major shrines were in cities important in their own right, like Canterbury, St Albans or Durham, or remote rural places where towns never grew. Richelda de Fervaques, lady of the manor, dreamed that she was taken to the holy house in Nazareth, and was directed by the Virgin Mary to build a replica. She evidently remembered clearly the house she had seen in her dream, and a replica was built in Walsingham – in wood like the original. The legendary date for the building of the Walsingham house is 1061, but the middle of the twelfth century is more likely, since Geoffrey de Fervaques, who may have been Richelda's son, founded an Augustinian priory alongside the holy house in about 1153. The house, and the statue of Mary placed within it, soon became an object of pilgrimage – eventually the most popular destination for pilgrims in England after Canterbury. They came either overland, especially from London, or, presumably, from nearby ports like Cley, Wells-next-the-Sea and King's Lynn. The priory grew rich through the pilgrims' offerings and royal patronage; Henry III visited it several times. The priory church was grandly rebuilt in the 13th and 14th centuries, and the holy house was enclosed within a stone chapel in the 15th. After the Reformation the monastery was largely demolished, and eventually replaced by a Georgian country house in a landscaped park. But one part dramatically survives – the east end of the church, a towering gabled wall between complicated turrets, with a tall gaping hole, where the original window was, continued down to the ground. It cannot have become like this through natural decay; the ruin must have been 'doctored' by the Georgian landowner to look dramatic, as it still does, across a greensward and backed by trees: Parts of a vaulted undercroft and a ruined refectory survive, showing the high quality of the medieval workmanship. The ruin and its setting have a tremendous atmosphere – but are open only on certain days.

The town of Walsingham – it still looks like a market town though it now has the status of a village – is delightful; it is kept moderately prosperous by the modern pilgrims. There are a straight and narrow main street and two former market places, suggesting deliberate planning. Many of the houses have timber-framed upper storeys but flint-faced ground floors – like some of the old houses of Norwich (see colour illus. p. 51). There is a concentration of interest about half-way along the street where a red brick house with a 'Dutch' gable faces a slightly grander timber-framed one with conventional gables, at the corner of a side street that leads to the rectangular Friday Market – pleasantly informal with two houses in warm Georgian brick setting the tone. High Street continues northward past the flint gateway to the priory site and reaches Common Place, the smaller of the two old market places and the hub of the town. It is roughly rectangular, surrounded by altered timber-framed buildings (a range on the north side has had upper storeys added later), with a curious octagonal conduit house, topped by a stepped stone roof, in the centre. The homely Shire Hall, probably so called because the county quarter sessions were occasionally held there, is now a museum. As in High Street the predominant red and glossy grey pantiles help give the town a distinctive look. Down Knight Street one reaches the Anglican shrine, which comes as a surprise, since externally it is not remotely in character with medieval or present-day Walsingham.

Revival of the pilgrimages was due to the Revd Alfred Hope Patten, a dynamic Anglo-Catholic who became vicar in 1921. He placed a statue of Mary in a side chapel of the parish church, and organized pilgrimages, which grew in popularity. The new Anglican shrine was started in 1931, to the south of the medieval priory. It is centred on a second supposed reconstruction of the holy house, this time using brick, stone and plaster. The great church architect Sir Ninian Comper (page 60) designed the glittering altar but not the building as a whole, which has an atmosphere that seems part Catholic and part Eastern Orthodox, with

20 Walsingham. A corner of the town, showing houses in flint with some timber-framing, a 'Dutch' gable, and pantiles. (Colour plate, page 51)

the numerous side altars, statues, murals and mosaics. The Roman Catholics have their shrine and pilgrimage centre around the restored medieval Slipper Chapel about two miles away – where the medieval pilgrims are said to have taken their shoes off to walk the last part of their journey barefoot.

The parish church of Little Walsingham, St Mary's, is at the opposite end of the town from the Anglican shrine, reached along Church Street from the bottom of High Street. It was burnt in 1961, leaving the outside walls, tower and western porch, and rebuilt much as before. Its great treasure is the 15th-century font which, amazingly, survived the fire largely undamaged although the wooden cover on top was destroyed. It is one of the best of the Seven Sacrament fonts which are fairly common in East Anglia but rare elsewhere, and which show the seven sacraments of the Church – Extreme Unction, Confession, Holy Communion, Confirmation, Baptism, Ordination and Matrimony, together with the Crucifixion, on each side of the octagonal bowl. Possibly some will see symbolism in the survival of this font, while all else in the church was destroyed. For those who like unrestored medieval churches there is a splendid 15th-century example at Great Walsingham little more than a mile away – a small village long since outgrown by Little Walsingham. It has lost its chancel, but has an unrivalled series of late medieval pews, with carved detailed figures, animals, foliage and shields. The church was in the patronage of Walsingham Priory, and its survival partly makes up for the loss of most of the priory itself.

Wells-next-the-Sea

Wells has a strong individuality which distinguishes it from other coastal towns that are more dominantly resorts. It is firstly a port – cargo ships moor at its long quay at the head of an inlet bordered by marshes; the open sea is over two miles away. Its history is sparsely documented; it took its name no doubt from springs on its inland edge. In 1202 its overlord, the abbot of Ramsey in Huntingdonshire, obtained a grant for a market, and it may have been then that part at least of the town's dense pattern of streets and lanes was first laid out. It exported agricultural produce, first wool, later corn and malt, to London and the Continent; it had a fishing trade and imported coal from the Tyne; the huge 18th-century agricultural improvements on the nearby estate of Holkham must have stimulated its prosperity. The quay is dominated by a 19th-century granary with a gantry projecting over the road – stark in itself but giving character and scale to the whole. The prettier part of the waterfront is further east, with old houses in flint and brick, especially one which was the custom house from 1676 until a century ago. A whole series of yards opens off the waterfront, many of them public thoroughfares, leading past old storehouses and former maltings, some converted, some decaying; many have been demolished and their sites filled with new houses to varying degrees of sensitivity. The most impressive conversion is that of a warehouse into the Wells Community Hall, with theatre and other facilities. Staithe Street, narrow and containing most of the shops, leads inland by a double bend into High Street, long and low-key with well-kept houses and few shops. The buildings fronting these streets tend to be stuccoed or painted over, but alleys leading off reveal old brick and flint work at their sides and along garden walls. The great surprise is Buttlands, a space as green and expansive as most of the town is urban and tight-knit, lined on one side with fine houses almost as if it were a Georgian square. Finally, the church at the far end of the town is a rebuilding of 1879 after a fire, much as it was before.

Wymondham

Wymondham – always pronounced Windum – is a pleasant town with two landmarks, the great abbey church on the outskirts, and the little market cross in the centre. The monastery was founded in 1107 by William d'Albini, father of the builder of the castles at Buckenham and Rising (pages 39, 24). For long it was a priory subservient to the abbey at St Albans, but it became an independent abbey in 1448. As monastery and parish shared the same church, there were frequent disputes between monks and townspeople. After these were finally settled in the 15th century, there were in effect two churches end-to-end – the parish had the western church with a west tower, the monastery the eastern church, with the monastic tower in a central position between the two churches. Following the Reformation the monastic part was demolished, apart from the central tower; the parish church remained, with a tower at each end. Inside it is basically Norman, with austere arcades, and tall gallery arches above. The glorious nave roof is 15th-century, with angels flying from the hammerbeams and star-like foliage patterns radiating from the bosses. The north aisle, rebuilt in 1440–5, is wider than the nave – and has another hammerbeam roof with intricate tracery patterns in the supporting brackets and on the panels. The culmination of the interior is the richly detailed, gilded, reredos, with a crucifix high in the roof space in front – typical works of Sir Ninian Comper, the great Anglican high church architect of the inter-war years. Outside, the two towers counterpoise each other marvellously when seen from different angles. The older is the eastern tower, built from about 1390 and now a shell, with its tall outer arch open to the air, and above that two octagonal upper storeys ending in a flat top. The west tower, started in 1445, is square, solid and slightly taller; its design is attributed by John Harvey in his *English Medieval Architecture* to James Woderofe, who worked in Norwich Cathedral and was responsible for the Erpingham Gate there.

Wymondham obtained a market charter in 1203, and it may have been then that the triangular market place developed, on the brow of a slight eminence – an effect wonderfully enhanced by the placing of the Market Cross near one apex. This is an octagonal building,

21 Market Cross, Wymondham, one of the most delightful of its kind, built 1617 after a fire had devastated the town – in the last years of the timber-framed tradition.

with timber-framed upper storey, conical roof and open-sided ground floor, built in 1618 – three years after its predecessor, along with much of the town, was destroyed by fire. At this time timber-framing was still the normal method of building, and the destroyed parts of the town were so rebuilt after the fire; several timber houses probably dating from then, though much altered, survive around the market place and along the narrow streets leading off. But many were refronted or rebuilt in brick in the 18th century, a time when the town was a centre of worsted weaving, and the making of wooden spoons was a cottage industry – an adjoining hamlet is called Spooner Row.

Damgate Street, leading east, is a pleasant small-scale street of timber and brick houses, with a memorable view across fields to the church. Church Street must have escaped the fire. At its entrance is a 15th-century flint-built former chapel, once used by a guild and later a grammar school; now it is a library; the nearby Green Dragon, timber-framed, is of similar date. Middleton Street has the town's best Georgian building, Caius House, of deep red brick with wide pilasters, classical pediment and columned doorcase – the last surviving between two inserted shops. Finally, Bridewell Street, on the opposite side of the town, ends in front of the former Bridewell or prison, a handsome classical building of 1787, which, according to the excellent leaflet *A Walk around Old Wymondham*, was built along lines suggested by Howard the prison reformer. It served a large part of Norfolk, not just Wymondham.

Yarmouth

The site of Yarmouth did not exist in Roman times. There was a wide estuary into which the waters of the Yare, Waveney and Bure flowed, with a small Roman port by its northern shore at what is now Caister, and a fort on the south side, part of which survives as Burgh Castle. A few hundred years later an island of sand and shingle emerged in the estuary, which was occupied, at first seasonally, by fishermen. Permanent settlement followed, and by Norman times Yarmouth was a town; over a hundred households were recorded there in Domesday Book. From then until the present century it was a major fishing port, especially for herring, which were smoked and salted. Fishermen from many other ports landed and sold their catches in Yarmouth – the Cinque Ports of Kent and Sussex had special privileges in this respect which led to frequent clashes with the local fishermen, culminating in a battle between Yarmouth and Cinque Ports ships off the Flemish coast in 1297. From then the Cinque Ports were in decline, but fishermen from Rye and Hastings, as well as Brighthelmstone (now Brighton), sailed every autumn to fish off Yarmouth until the 18th century.

In the 14th century Yarmouth began to suffer through silting. First the northern end of the estuary was blocked, making the site of the town a peninsula, not an island. The peninsula is nearly a mile wide in its main part, narrowing to the south; the original town was on its western side, facing the riverside quays. Tidal action in the later Middle Ages caused the peninsula to lengthen steadily southwards, until it reached almost to Lowestoft, preventing the river from reaching the sea for many miles – much, as in Suffolk, Orford Ness blocks the River Alde from the sea today. The town authorities tried six times to cut a new outlet, but each time the sea defeated them, until in 1560 Dutch engineers succeeded in forming a new river mouth where it is now. The town steadily regained prosperity, developing general trade as well as fishing. Merchants' houses surviving in part near the quay, especially the Elizabethan House, testify to the town's late 16th-century recovery.

Yarmouth had a peculiar street plan. The town was hemmed in by a strong wall, built between 1285 and 1346 (much of it survives), except on the western side where it faced the riverside quays. In the north-eastern corner of the walled town was, much as today, a very long market place, with the monastic church of St Nicholas at its northern end; King Street, as now, led from the market place southwards. Between the market place and King Street on the one side, and the quaysides on the other, there developed a dense network of parallel alleys called Rows, mostly only a few feet wide, which were lined with small houses, cottages and storehouses. It is often asked why Yarmouth in particular should have developed in this way. Most fishing towns and villages were densely built, since fishermen did not need, and could not have made much use of, garden plots; Yarmouth was the biggest medieval English town dependent primarily on fishing, and so it is not surprising that it was probably also the most densely built town. There were well over a hundred Rows, not all opening directly on to the quayside; some ran between parallel streets behind. Most survived until the present century, but slum clearance, bombing and redevelopment have left only a few, mostly only in part; none is now lived in. What survives of the Rows can give only an inkling of what the heartland of Yarmouth was like up to less than a century ago.

Outside the walls were the Denes, extending for the length of the shingly peninsula, where nets were dried, and where no substantial buildings, except windmills, were built for several centuries. In 1759 a bath house was built by the beach, marking the beginning of the resort, but extensive development beyond the walls and along the sea shore did not start until the 1830s. A very ambitious scheme was promoted by a building company in 1841 including a huge crescent, squares and terraces which would have made Yarmouth an eastern Brighton or a seaside Bath, but very little of this was built as intended. The town prospered in the railway age as a popular rather than a fashionable resort, and by the beginning of this century there were promenades, piers, popular theatres and all the trappings of a big pleasure resort. Meanwhile the port flourished, the herring trade reaching its peak just before the First World War. Hundreds of Scottish fishermen sailed south every autumn and landed their catches at Yarmouth, bringing their wives and daughters who cleaned and dressed the fish on shore. The fishing trade declined sharply after the first war and is now locally extinct (though it continues at Lowestoft), but Yarmouth developed as a general port, and the quays much extended, are busy. Modern Yarmouth has two sides, the boisterous side facing the beach, the serious side focused on the river, with the town centre in between, though nearer to the latter.

Partly because of bombing and redevelopment the historical fabric of Yarmouth is patchy, but some of the patches are of great interest. The following parts are described: (1) Around St Nicholas' Church: (2) The Quays: (3) King Street and the Walls: (4) The Victorian Seaside: (5) Nelson's Column.

(1) Around St Nicholas' Church

The great church of St Nicholas was founded around 1100 by Bishop Losinga, the builder of Norwich Cathedral. Like the church he also founded in another rising port, King's Lynn (page 29), it was associated with a small priory as well as being parochial, so that its claim, often made, to have been the largest medieval parish church in England is invalid, since such a distinction must go to a church which was never monastic. Repeated enlargements turned Losinga's cruciform church into a rectangular one, which was outwardly much restored in Victorian times, and inwardly completely gutted through fire bombs in the Second World War, though the central tower, the lower part of which is still Norman, stayed upright. The interior was reconstructed, not entirely as before, by the inspired architect Stephen Dykes Bower, designer of the extensions to the cathedral at Bury St Edmunds, and has a splendid spatial effect. Next to the church is the brick-built vicarage of 1718, with a shell-hood over the door, and behind this the 14th-century priory refectory survives, adapted as part of Priory School.

The church stands at the northern end of the long rectangular space which further south forms the Market Place; at this end it is intersected by roads but part has been made into a pleasant green. Facing the green is Yarmouth's most endearing building, the Fishermen's Hospital, founded in 1702 by the borough council for retired fishermen and their wives. It has cottage-like houses facing a formal courtyard with Dutch-style gables and an archway topped by a cupola.

The shopping centre extends south from the Market Place. Regent Street leads to the Quays, past Fastolff House, an Art-Nouveau fantasy designed by 1908 by a local architect, J. W. Cockrill; its terracotta facade is like an echo of the work of Charles Mackintosh in Glasgow.

(2) The Quays

The area beside the old Quays is the true historic centre of Yarmouth. It extends along the river front, with successive roads called North, Hall and South Quays, bordered on the other side by buildings of different dates. Hall Quay is the traffic hub, as it adjoins the bridge over the river, last rebuilt in 1930, which brings vehicles in from the south. The dominant building is the Town Hall of 1880–2 in dark brick with a tall cupola. To the north are solid Victorian banks mixed with earlier buildings, including the Bull's Head which, characteristically, looks Georgian outside but is older within. The finest range of buildings faces South Quay. Nos. 1–3, just south of the Town Hall, have Georgian fronts but are partly older behind. No. 4 is the Elizabethan House, owned by the National Trust but used as a museum by the county council. Its yellow brick facade of 1809, placidly classical, gives no inkling of the Elizabethan splendour within; the inside is largely as fitted in 1596 by Benjamin Cooper, a merchant, with spectacular ceilings and overmantels. A visit here should be a 'must' for all historically minded people coming to Yarmouth (but they should note that Yarmouth museums close on Saturdays as well as Sundays). The series of grand Georgian-fronted houses continues; no. 5 has a red brick front with fine doorcase; nos. 7–8 have flat-fronted bay windows, nos. 11–12 iron balconies; no. 16, beyond a busy turning, has a classical loggia, and no. 17 a big bowed front rising through three storeys. The climax of the series is the Custom House, no. 20, built in 1720 by John Andrews who was called 'the greatest herring merchant in Europe'; it has a red brick front with round-topped windows (an early 18th century fashion), and a classical porch added about a hundred years later.

The surviving fragments of the Rows lead off from the Quays, or from parallel streets behind. Along one Row is part of a 17th-century house, now another museum; along a parallel Row is a fragment of the medieval Franciscan friary. The Tolhouse, fronting a street parallel with South Quay, has a very interesting exterior of flint and stone, largely 13th-century; it was built as a house but was converted early into a civic hall and court; it was damaged internally by bombing and has been restored as yet another museum.

(3) King Street and the Town Wall

One of the very few classical churches in East Anglia, St George's dates from 1714–6, designed by John Price, an architect of Richmond, Surrey, to a baroque design derived from Wren, in brick with stone dressings, doubly curved corners and a white painted cupola, standing by a busy road junction. It is no longer used as a church. The part of King Street leading south from the church has fine Georgian fronts over modern shops, some with bow windows.

To find the best remaining section of Yarmouth's town wall one should turn down Alma Road off the southern end of King Street. The wall originally enclosed the town on its northern, eastern and southern sides, with rounded towers at intervals, and two major gateways to north and south, both long since demolished. Much of the wall and some of the towers survive, the most impressive of the latter being the South-Eastern Tower facing the oddly named Malakoff Road. The lower part is of flint and rough stone like most of the wall, but it was heightened, perhaps in the 16th century, to a curious and impressive chequer pattern in brick and flint, with a gabled roof. It was used for a long time as a herring smoking house.

(4) The Victorian Seaside

The most impressive part of Victorian Yarmouth is in and around the street called Camperdown, leading at right angles off the sea front. The development of the area was started in the 1840s as a modified version of the grand scheme originally proposed. Camperdown has Victorian bay-windowed houses, impressive in their regularity, but its chief feature is the Wellington Arch of 1847, an *arc de triomphe* spanning a minor street leading off, flanked by smaller pedestrian arches which help to give it scale. A lesser arch spans a street off the other side of Camperdown. Kimberley Terrace, facing the sea across a formal green and now containing the Carlton Hotel, was built in 1841–2 and shows how fine the sea front might have been if the rest had been built like that; alas it was not. Shadingfield, now a restaurant, was built about 1865 by a Norfolk landowner as his seaside villa; later it was owned by the Sutton family with whom the Prince of Wales (later Edward VII) stayed no less then eight times from 1872 to 1899. But even this did not give Victorian Yarmouth fashionable cachet.

(5) Nelson's Column

Nelson's Column is, with the Elizabethan House, the Fishermen's Hospital, the South-East Tower and the Wellington Arch, one of the several surprising features of Yarmouth. It was built from public subscription to commemorate Lord Nelson who was born in Norfolk (though at the opposite end of the county, near Burnham Market). The site was then the open South Denes; only in recent years has it been surrounded by industrial buildings, over which it towers incongruously. It was finished in 1819, twenty-four years before its counterpart in London; it is interesting that the architect was the Norfolk-born William Wilkins, who was later to design the National Gallery beside the London column – as well as buildings in Cambridge including the Gothic screen at King's. The figure at the top is not Nelson, but Britannia herself, in artificial Coade stone, facing towards Nelson's birthplace.

Suffolk

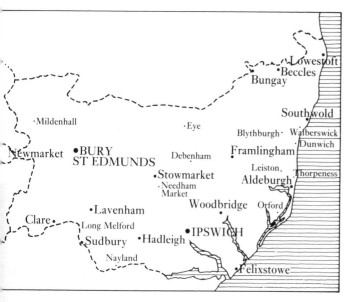

Aldeburgh and Leiston

Aldeburgh – fashionable and famous for its festival – was formerly a port. Like so many places on the eastern coast it has suffered from both erosion and silting. Once it was on a peninsula – the old *burh* or defensive place – with a wide inlet to the north, long since drained. To the south is the Alde estuary (the river name is derived from that of the town, not vice versa), which over several centuries has been deflected southwards by an astonishing shingle spit, now extending well to the south of Orford. Despite the disadvantages of the long approach, the estuary provides good shelter for small vessels, and in Tudor times Aldeburgh throve on coastal trade, as well as fishing and shipbuilding. There was decline in the 17th century, accentuated in 1650 when the Johnson family, shipbuilders on the Alde, moved to Blackwall on the Thames where prospects were better – they helped to stimulate the growth of the maritime East End. In Georgian times Aldeburgh was small and poor – as depicted by George Crabbe, a native and sometime local curate, in his poem *The Borough*, which gave inspiration for Sir Benjamin Britten's *Peter Grimes*.

In the 19th century the leading local family was the Garretts. Richard Garrett came to Leiston, then a small village, as a blacksmith in 1788. His son expanded into making agricultural implements, and of his two grandsons Richard developed the Leiston firm further, while Newson Garrett moved to Aldeburgh. He promoted the town as a resort, and built large maltings at Snape, up the estuary. He was prominent in local affairs, and so was his daughter, Elizabeth Garrett Anderson who, as mayor of Aldeburgh in 1908, was the first woman to hold that office anywhere in England. She was better known as a pioneer woman doctor, while her sister, Dame Millicent Fawcett, was a radical feminist who campaigned for women's votes.

Sir Benjamin Britten, a native of Lowestoft, settled in Aldeburgh and with Sir Peter Pears inaugurated the festival in 1948, with much help from local people and the newly-formed Arts Council. In 1967 part of the Snape maltings was converted as the festival concert hall reopened triumphantly, after a fire, in 1969.

Aldeburgh has a prevailing Victorian character with Georgian elements, based on a pattern of parallel or converging streets which derives from the town's Tudor heyday. It was much more extensive then; erosion in the 17th and 18th centuries resulted in the loss of at least one street and dozens of houses. The Moot Hall, the town's *clou*, was some way inland; now it is right by the shore. It is timber-framed with a pantiled roof, probably built at about the time when the town received its first charter, in 1529, but it was thoroughly restored in 1857 when the tall chimneys were added. It had a public room and council chamber (still used as such) on the first floor, while the ground floor was originally partly open. Now it is an interesting museum (see colour illus. p. 69). The High Street is wide and urbane in its main part; it narrows southward past smaller houses, partly Georgian or older, with roofs in rich red pantiles. But the prevailing image of Aldeburgh is that of its shingle beach, separated by a low sea wall from the narrow promenade which is overlooked by big-bay-windowed Victorian – or occasionally faintly Georgian – houses and hotels, the whole pleasantly informal yet sophisticated. To the south is Slaughden, the one-time maritime quarter. Originally the shingle spit between the sea and the estuary here was much wider; Slaughden was a cluster of houses with warehouses and boatyards facing the estuary. The spit was narrowed through erosion and the village disappeared; a sea wall built after the Second World War prevented the sea linking again with the estuary. Now there are moorings for pleasure craft, and broad inland views over the estuary bordered by marshes, gently rising fields and patches of woodland.

The church, on high ground west of the town proper, was rebuilt from 1525 and not finished till after the

Reformation, though the tower is a little older. It is broad and spacious but lacks the clerestory and high roof characteristic of nearby larger churches. There is a sumptuous pulpit of 1652 and a vivid window by John Piper in memory of Benjamin Britten.

Leiston, four miles from Aldeburgh, is a small industrial town, strange in Suffolk, which grew round Garrett's engineering works. Under Richard, Newson Garrett's brother, the firm pioneered the use of steam engines in farm machinery, and later in other fields. By the end of the century it had a big export trade. After changes in ownership, it closed in 1980. A local trust bought the oldest parts of the factory buildings and has restored the Long Shop of 1852 as part of a remarkable museum, housing Garrett products, including early steamrollers and traction engines. The Long Shop itself was a pioneer in line production – the machines or vehicles were moved slowly along the floor as component parts were added, some from balconies on either side. The other notable building in Leiston is the church, rebuilt except the tower in 1853 by the eccentric architect E. B. Lamb (who also designed Eye town hall, page 82). It has a fantastic interior, broad and low with a very complicated roof. For more conventional Gothic architecture one should go to the remains of Leiston Priory, to the north-west.

Beccles

Beccles lies on a bluff above the River Waveney, which has been navigable through most of the town's history. It was a borough in Domesday Book, and many of its street names end in -*gate*, the Danish or Viking term for street, indicating their influence. Except for the church, the best buildings are Georgian, but the town's main industry – printing and book production – developed in the 19th century. The hub of the town is the New Market. This, clearly, was once a big open market place, but the usual process of infilling by permanent buildings where there were once market stalls has turned it into an irregular circuit of spaces, dominated by the town's two key buildings. One, the King's Head, has a fine early Georgian front; the other, the church, has the rare (for England) feature of a detached tower or campanile, finished in 1547 – the abrupt roofline suggests that a taller, more elaborate, top was contemplated. The big church is an amalgam of 14th- and 15th-century work; its finest feature is an exquisitely detailed porch of two different stones. The church's west front is close to the edge of the bluff, now embanked with flint and brick walls, which explains why the tower could not have been built in a normal western position. Steps descend to Puddingmoor, a road which runs parallel with the river and connects further south with Ballygate, one of the town's two most attractive streets. (The element *Bally* seems to be related to the word bailey, and to the beginning of many Irish names, signifying a fortified place; presumably there were early defensive works, otherwise unrecorded, on this site.) At the far end of the street

22 New Market, Beccles. The brick quoins on the right belong to the Georgian King's Head; the church tower was completed in 1547; the irregular block of buildings on the left are encroachments on what was originally a large market place.

is, surprisingly, a grand neo-Norman Catholic church, St Benet's, built in 1889 and intended to be part of a monastery, which was never established. Going back towards the town centre, Ballygate gradually unfolds, each slight bend revealing more delights. First there is a strange flint-faced building, a Victorian restoration of a school founded in 1631; then, opposite, the former rectory with pilasters and pediment, in deep red brick like most of the Georgian houses of Beccles. The classical theme is continued with more modest houses overlooking the river, and then, in a narrower winding part of the street, in buildings of cottage scale ending with a magnificent vista of the church tower, with an Art-Deco cinema, the Regal, providing an interlude.

North-east of the church is the Old Market, a rectangular space with prominent Georgian houses counterpoising each other at opposite ends. Northgate, a long and interesting street, leads from a corner of the square, but before walking along it it is worth turning into The Score, which ends in a grassy strip leading to the river bank. A score, as in Lowestoft (page 102) was simply a way from higher ground to the waterside. Presumably goods were unloaded from boats and carried up to the market places, and vice versa, but the grassy surface suggests that this ceased long ago. Northgate, like Ballygate, is lined intermittently with grander houses among many pleasant smaller ones. First there is Northgate House, with heavy brick detailing and classical doorcase, then Staithe House, more complex and with 17th-century features, then the smaller Oswald House with a Dutch-style end gable, seen on other buildings along the street. Montagu House is comparable to the rectory in Ballygate, with pediment and brick quoins. At the far end of the street, past converted maltings, are the riverside quays, alive with pleasure boats.

Bungay

Bungay is a remarkable little town, its main part built tightly at the neck of a head-shaped peninsula round which the River Waveney flows. There was probably a Saxon fortification; a castle was built c. 1165–70 by Hugh Bigod, earl of Norfolk, son of Roger Bigod, a Norman baron to whom the manor was granted, together with others including Framlingham (page 83), soon after 1100. Later, Bungay thrived as a river port, but was devastated by fire in 1688. It quickly recovered, and prospered through the 18th century as a place of trade and a centre for the local gentry. Today, like Beccles, its main source of livelihood is printing and book production; the industry began in 1795 and developed in the 19th century, printing, among much else, the first edition of *Alice in Wonderland*. Today the products include paperbacks and bibles, in many languages.

The town was rebuilt after the fire to the medieval plan, and the market place is extremely irregular, thanks to encroachments on its original area. Its western side was defined by the outer ditch of the castle, long since filled and built over. The townscapes vary intriguingly as one walks round the intricate spaces. Two Georgian former coaching inns are prominent landmarks, but the best view in the market place is southward, with St Mary's church tower rising beyond the open-sided octagonal Market Cross. This was built in 1689, immediately after the town fire, and has a domed roof surmounted by a symbolic statue of Justice in painted lead, put there in 1754. St Mary's Street curves round to the church, passing first a house with a Venetian window, then a range of timber-framed buildings with the original carved sills of their first-floor windows – these would be fairly unremarkable in some other Suffolk towns but are notable in Bungay because they are among the few buildings that escaped the fire.

St Mary's has a very fine tower with octagonal corner buttresses and tall pinnacles, built in the 1440s and attributed, by the writer of the church guide, to Reginald Ely, the first master mason of King's chapel, Cambridge. The church was made redundant when Anglican worship was concentrated in the other church, Holy Trinity. Luckily it has not been converted to secular use, but remains open and consecrated, still used occasionally for services. It had been part of a small nunnery; after the Reformation the eastern end of the church fell into ruin, and picturesque parts survive in the churchyard.

Beyond the churchyard is Trinity Street, a delightful street of Georgian houses, leading to Holy Trinity, the still active church. The round tower, possibly pre-Norman, is one of many in this part of East Anglia, though they are usually found in smaller villages rather than towns. Beyond the church, past a house called Trinity Hall with fine carved brickwork of c. 1690–1700, and down Staithe Road, it is possible – especially

Opposite **The Moot Hall, Aldeburgh** was surrounded by other buildings when built c.1530 – a typical 'town house' with public rooms upstairs and originally open-sided ground floor; the chimneys date from 1857.

with the aid of the useful leaflet *A Walk round Bungay* published by the Bungay Society – to find a path which crosses the Waveney over a weir, and then runs beside the river into Bridge Street, which climbs back to the market place. From the rural riverside one looks across to the backs of the red-tiled houses on Trinity Street with St Mary's tower behind.

Bungay Castle is reached from an alleyway off the market place. It is memorable for the remains of two rounded towers which guarded the entrance, added in 1294 by Roger Bigod, a descendant of Hugh the original builder. Of Hugh's keep only the base remains, but this contains a cavity which is interesting in military history. He rebelled against Henry II, and in 1174 was forced to hand over his castles and territory. Work was started, on the king's orders, on dismantling the castle through undermining – which meant cutting a cavity or 'mine' at a crucial structural point in the base of the building, and substituting the excavated stonework by temporary wooden props, which were then set on fire, causing the masonry above to collapse. Before the undermining was completed, Hugh was pardoned and his castles – Framlingham as well as Bungay – were returned to him. The unfinished cavity remains, overgrown, as a reminder of the origin of a word, *undermine*, used so often today in a figurative sense.

Another way from the castle leads through a yard and a passageway into Earsham Street, which curves sharply back, round the line of the castle ditch, into

23 **Bungay** is a largely Georgian market town to a medieval plan; the domed Market Cross dates from 1689 with a later figure of Justice on top; the church tower was built *c*.1470–80.

the market place; it has Georgian houses well placed on its curve, and one of the excellent neo-Georgian post offices built in East Anglia between the wars (as in Woodbridge, page 113). In Broad Street is a small museum, which helps one understand better this tiny but exceptional town.

Bury St Edmunds

Bury is one of the pleasantest towns in England – it is surprising how many people concur with such a judgment. Until the Reformation it was a major religious centre. Sigbert, first Christian king of East Anglia, founded the original church at the place then known as Bedricsworth (this spelling, like Sigbert, is a modern approximation to the various Saxon spellings). In 903 the remains of Edmund, last king of East Anglia, killed by the Vikings in 870, were enshrined here. His tomb became one of the foremost places of pilgrimage in England.

In 1020 the church was refounded as a Benedictine monastery. Its great abbot, Baldwin, who came from St Denis near Paris in 1065, started the rebuilding of the church, completed after his death in 1097 on a scale matching that of the great cathedrals. Baldwin laid out a new and bigger town beside the abbey – which had displaced much of the older town.

Baldwin's street pattern is still that of the present town centre. It forms a grid, not quite rigid but with sufficient irregularities, in alignments and spacing, to make the townscapes much more interesting than they would be with a completely regular pattern. There was originally a very large market place, but this was soon encroached on through market stalls becoming permanent, leaving the present L-shaped space in Cornhill and Buttermarket as today's marketing area. One street, Churchgate Street, was aligned directly

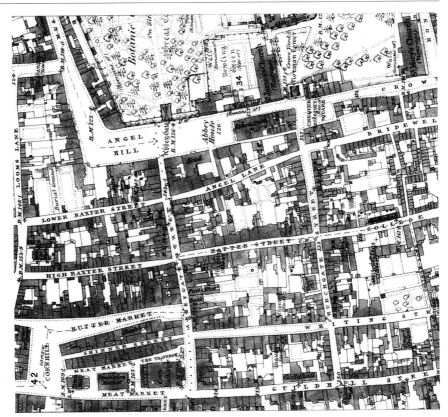

Map V, Bury St Edmunds. This map of 1887 shows the rough grid of the town laid out by Abbot Baldwin *c.*1080, to the west of the huge abbey precinct, with the later churches of St. James (now the cathedral) and St. Mary on the edge of the precinct. The original market place was bounded by Cornhill, Butter Market and Meat Market; the buildings bordering Skinner Street are encroachments.

on the west door of the abbey church. If this orientation were deliberate, it provides a rare, perhaps unique, example of axial planning in a medieval town – there is no other obvious example in England and few if any in Europe of a street being laid out directly on the axis of a major building in post-Roman or pre-Renaissance times. Parallel with Churchgate Street is Abbeygate Street; this leads into another large medieval square, Angel Hill, where the fairs were held, outside the gate to the abbey.

The medieval town was very much controlled by the abbey, and lacked the civic independence of Norwich, Ipswich or King's Lynn. Relations between town and cassock boiled over in 1327 when townspeople burnt much of the abbey and slew some of the monks. There was more unrest in 1345–50, and again at the time of the peasants' uprisings of 1381. Nevertheless Bury throve as a marketing centre for a huge area, and by the 15th century as a weaving centre as well. The prosperity was so great that the town survived the closure of the abbey in 1539 and continued to flourish.

Bury's second heyday was in the 18th century. This was partly due to continuing trade, stimulated especially by improvements to the tiny River Lark, a tributary of the Ouse, made navigable up to the town in 1698. But what gave Bury its special Georgian distinction was its status as a fashionable centre for the aristocracy and landed gentry of East Anglia. There were assemblies, theatrical performances and other gatherings, especially at the time of the Bury Fair which was held annually over several days in September

– a period which seems to have provided the high-point of social life for all classes.

Bury became largely a brick- and stucco-fronted town. Older timber-framed houses survived in plenty, especially in the secondary streets, but as elsewhere they were plastered over, or wholly refronted in classical taste. Numerous substantial town houses were built, those occupied by prosperous tradesmen or professional people not being easily distinguishable from those where 'county' families or their relatives lived. At first the local brick was red, but buff bricks became fashionable well before 1800, and during the 19th century were made in large quantities, especially in Woolpit nearby.

Bury did not stagnate in Victorian times. Rather it continued at much the same tempo as in the Georgian period, the railway providing good local communications but not main-line services. Classical architectural traditions continued, culminating in the Corn Exchange of 1862, symbol of the final burst of prosperity (before modern times) of East Anglian farming. Only with the agricultural slump at the end of the century did Bury become something of a backwater, which it remained till the Second World War. Renewed agricultural prosperity made the area important again. Industries developed – and were positively encouraged in the late 1950s and 1960s when planned London 'overspill' housing was built around the town. The population grew markedly, but Bury seems so far to have taken these changes in its stride, and its increasingly busy centre remains, on the whole, astonishingly attractive, with only a few bad or nondescript patches. The most striking modern developments have been on the outskirts – especially the big sugar-beet factory which provides the remembered landmark for traffic skirting Bury on its way to the coast.

A good place to start a walk round Bury is the Corn Exchange with its temple-like front, successfully subdivided about twenty years ago when shops were inserted. Beside it a narrow street, The Traverse, leads to Cupola House, built for an apothecary in 1693 and now a restaurant. It was one of the first classical houses in the town, and its octagonal cupola formed a sort of summer-house on the roof. Beyond is a greater gem – what was till recently the Town Hall, of 1774, designed by Robert Adam, now confusingly called the Market Cross (a reversion to an old name). It is cross-shaped, with ground-storey arched in stone and tall upper storey, mainly in buff brick, where columns and pediments enclose Venetian windows. The upper floor was fitted from the start as a theatre, which it remained until the Theatre Royal, described later, was built in 1819. The ground floor, at first open-sided, was used for marketing.

All this area was part of the original market place laid out by Abbot Baldwin about 1090, later encroached on by the predecessors of the buildings in The Traverse and the parallel Skinner Street. The present, much smaller, market place extending from Cornhill at a right angle into Butter Market is packed with stalls on Wednesdays and Saturdays. The dominating feature is Moyses Hall, one of a small number of stone-built houses of the late 12th century surviving in some measure in English towns; others are in Lincoln, Southampton, Norwich and King's Lynn, but Moyses Hall is the most nearly intact. It has two rooms on each floor; those on the ground floor were

Opposite top
Clare. These timber-framed buildings, variously altered, back on to the castle site.

Opposite bottom
Nethergate House, Clare. The central part, with its very fine chimney of carved brick, was probably built in the mid 17th century by a cloth merchant, incorporating older timber wings.

24 *Above right*
Old Town Hall, Bury St Edmunds, officially the 'Market Cross', by Robert Adam, 1774, in exquisite brick and stone. The ground floor arches were originally open.

25 *Above*
Cupola House, Bury St Edmunds dates in its present form from 1693 and is a prototype 'Georgian' building, but the jetty at first-floor level suggests that it is basically timber-framed. The cupola was, so to speak, a summer house on the roof.

used for merchandise, with access direct to the market place, while the merchant and his family lived on the upper floor. Moyses Hall has been used for various purposes, including an inn, workhouse and police station, but it has been a museum since 1899. Sir Gilbert Scott gave it needed restoration in 1858 and added the turret.

Butter Market funnels attractively southward, with the facade of the Suffolk Hotel on the left. It leads to Abbeygate Street, a busy shopping street, with an interesting variety of upper floors, and a few striking old shop fronts. The chemist's on the corner of Watling Street looks plainly Georgian outside, but inside the timber structure of a medieval house is revealed. Took's has a three-gabled roofline and Georgian Gothic shop windows. On the corner of High Baxter Street is a tell-tale building. The modest facade to Abbeygate Street is stuccoed above the shop front. Round the corner is exposed timber framing on the upper floor, showing that the building, behind its main frontage, is Tudor. Further down Abbeygate Street is Ridley's, which has a long, many-paned Georgian shop front with an iron balcony above, set in an earlier 18th-century house. Finally, on the corner with Angel Hill is another chemist's with Ionic columns between the windows.

Angel Hill is a very big rectangular space, once a fairground and now used for car parking but, because of its satisfactory scale, and the dignity of its dominant buildings, it remains one of the most impressive spaces in East Anglia. Strangely, it seems to have an affinity with Trinity Great Court in Cambridge, because of the varied styles and disposition of the buildings, and the dominant gateway. This is the Abbey Gate, which led into the service yard of the abbey and to the abbot's own house beyond. The gate was built after the terrible riots of 1327; it is 'strong and yet as exquisitely decorated as only that moment in medieval English architecture could do' (Pevsner: *Suffolk*). The niches have lost their statues, but the restored portcullis indicates how serious were the precautions against disorder. It now leads into a municipal park. The pathetic remains of the eastern part of the once great abbey church are approached through the park – a few jagged masses or shafts of rubble, and exposed foundations. The visitor with little time to spare might give them a miss.

Across the square from the Abbey Gate is the Angel Hotel, built as a country-house-like inn in 1779 (but including a medieval vault). At right angles, containing Angel Hill marvellously on its southern side, is the Athenaeum. An existing building, already used for assemblies, was remodelled in 1789 by the owner of the Angel, and further improved in 1804; it has a ballroom with a curved ceiling in the Adam style, though unlikely to be by Adam himself. A delightful alley, Athenaeum Lane, punctuated by a porch, leads into Chequer Square, another of the surprises of Bury. It is a rectangle, smaller than Angel Hill, with Georgian houses on three sides, mostly in red or buff brick, one of them with an iron balcony. On one corner is the magnificently Norman Abbey Tower, built by Abbot Anselm *c.* 1130–40 at the ceremonial entrance to the abbey. It was exactly on the axis of the west door of the abbey church, on which Churchgate Street was already aligned (page 70). The gate was thoroughly restored in the 1840s, but most of the details are authentic, even if much renewed. It was a bell tower as well as a gateway, and has for long served the neighbouring church of St James, now the cathedral, in the former role.

The first church at Bury had served the townspeople for worship. When it became part of the abbey, and grandly rebuilt, the town had to be provided with separate buildings. So the predecessors of the present churches of St James and St Mary were built, sited in front of the abbey – which their successors have outlasted. The original church of St James was rebuilt from about 1502, almost certainly under John Wastell, master mason for King's chapel at Cambridge and Saffron Walden church; he is known to have lived in Bury. The medieval chancel was lost, and replaced in Victorian times. In 1914 the church became the cathedral of a new diocese covering Suffolk. It was enlarged eastwards – roughly doubled in size – in 1960–7; this was certainly one of the most remarkable building achievements of that contentious decade. For it is Gothic, not copyist but individualistic; a masterpiece, at least internally, of the underrated architect Stephen Dykes Bower. The lengthwise vistas are superb, especially that from the modern choir back to the medieval nave, which has a hammerbeam roof designed by Scott in 1865–9 (Wastell's roof had long since disappeared) This creative enlargement of an already fine building goes some way towards compensating for the catastrophic ruination of the abbey church four hundred years before.

One substantial part of the abbey church *does* survive, the core of the lower part of the west front, behind the present cathedral. This was once something like the western end of Lincoln or Ely, but broader. All the upper parts have gone; the fine stone facings have been stripped leaving massive rubble walls within which, astonishingly, houses were later formed. Their windows, Georgian or Victorian, are set in the rubble as if it were natural rock. There was a dispute several years ago between official and romantic preservationists. The former wanted to strip off everything post-medieval, leaving what remains of the original; the latter wanted to repair and use the houses as they are. The romanticists won, but there could have been limited compromise. The house set within the remains of the arch of the great west door has neo-Norman windows which are not remarkable; this house (alone) might have been dismantled, opening out the old arch as a way to the ruins beyond, and giving an inkling, much more than is possible now, of the huge scale of the original building. Perhaps this could still be done, with the remaining houses repaired and reoccupied.

The romanticists have also won in the treatment of the huge churchyard which extends south of the abbey ruins. This is a traditional churchyard with all the tombstones standing, long grass and half-wild plants around them; there is no more than minimal tidying. Long may it remain so. At the top of the churchyard, reached up Crown Street from Chequer Street, is St Mary's church. This is the other of the two churches built in front of the abbey site, the counterpart of the present cathedral. The nave with its magnificent roof, where hammerbeams with angels alternate with arched braces, was started in 1424; there are few finer churches even in Suffolk.

The first-time visitor to Bury might well end his exploration here, exhausted. But there is a great deal more to see. St Mary's Square, round the corner, is a green space surrounded by Georgian houses with, on one side, Greene King's brewery – an amalgam of Victorian and modern buildings which, despite their scale, manage to fit in with the surrounding streets. They extend along Westgate Street, facing the Theatre Royal which was rescued and restored in 1975. It was first opened in 1819 to succeed the theatre in Adam's former Town Hall, already described. The architect was William Wilkins, later to design buildings in Cambridge as well as the National Gallery.

A succession of parallel streets, part of the Norman grid, leads north off Westgate Street – first College, then Whiting and finally Guildhall Streets, each more interesting than the one before. In Whiting Street, close to an intersecting lane which links the three streets, is a striking timber-framed building, now divided, with two gabled wings and a recessed central part, originally a hall. One wing is plastered, with Georgian windows, the other has had the plaster stripped, the timbers exposed and mullioned windows restored to the original pattern – providing an interesting contrast in ways to treat timber buildings. Guildhall Street is continuously interesting. There are old paned shop fronts under first-floor jetties towards the southern end and, among the many grander Georgian houses, no. 81–3 has pedimented wings which were designed by Sir John Soane (the central part is earlier). Churchgate Street leads off to the east, with the view down to the Abbey Tower, already described. On the way down is the former Unitarian chapel of 1712, which has a superb front in brilliant red brick, with carved classical details in the brickwork of the doorway and cornice.

And there are many more fine streets in Bury. Northgate Street has Georgian houses, Well Street pleasant early Victorian ones, and St John's Street has a typical Bury mixture of altered timber-framed and later build-

26 Angel Hill, Bury St Edmunds. The Abbey Gate was built after serious rioting by townsmen in 1327 had caused damage to the abbey; the portcullis was a necessary protection. The Regency columns on the chemist's shop and the Art-Deco signpost of the 1930s provide fascinating contrasts.

ings. It leads to St John's, the town's third Anglican church, built in 1843 with a fantastic, and very effective, three-tiered spire, all in buff brick. Some way further north is the station, a splendid building of 1847, probably designed, like Stowmarket and Needham Market (pages 106, 104) by Frederick Barnes of Ipswich, though it is also attributed to Sancton Wood. It has baroque turrets, big recessed arches over the outside canopy, and a former station master's house in Jacobean style. Nearby is a contemporary railway arch over the road, broad and elliptical, with solid piers and cornice, not the least elegant of the monuments of Bury.

Clare

Clare is historically one of the most important towns in East Anglia. The name is probably of Celtic origin, and may mean warm or bright – referring no doubt to the waters of a stream flowing into the Stour. There was an important Saxon village, which came into the hands of Richard FitzGilbert, a close associate of William the Conqueror, who took the name Richard de Clare. He obtained numerous other estates including Tonbridge in Kent where, as at Clare, he built a castle. The estates passed through a succession of Gilberts and Richards (with one Roger), who were earls of Hertford after 1140 and, through marriage, earls of Gloucester from 1218. The latter inheritance brought them land in Wales, especially round Cardiff, while a branch of the family held Pembroke Castle and adventured into Ireland, leaving the family name there. The de Clares were great builders of castles, culminating in that of Caerphilly, which Gilbert the Red, son-in-law of Edward I, built around 1270. Gilbert's son, also Gilbert, was killed by the Scots at Bannockburn, so ending the male line (as some Celtic patriots would

say, justly). His inheritance was split between his sisters; Clare itself came to Elizabeth de Burgh (she kept the name of the first of her three husbands, the last of whom she long outlived). She lived at Clare Castle in tremendous style until her death in 1360, employing, it is said, about 250 people in her household. She founded what became Clare College, Cambridge. Clare Castle came into royal hands and was abandoned. The town grew wealthy with weaving, sending broadcloths to London for export in the 15th and 16th centuries, and the lighter 'New Draperies' later. This trade declined, and Clare is now little more than a large village, though a handsome and urbane one (see colour illus. p. 72).

The approach to Clare is impressive from the west along Nethergate Street, wide and grass-bordered. The first old house on the left, The Cliftons, has a plain exterior and slate roof, from which rises a cluster of richly decorated Tudor brick chimneys. Nethergate House on the south side has Tudor timber-framed wings and a more classical centrepiece, the latter prob-

27 The Ancient House, Clare, a medieval house pargetted over in the 17th century with contorted decorative patterns (35, 64).

ably dating from about 1644 when the house was altered by its owner, Francis Crosse, a clothier. It too has a tall brick chimney. The street narrows and twists eastward, and used to end at the castle gate (hence Nethergate). Almost all that is left now of the once mighty castle is a series of romantically overgrown earthworks, including the tall motte with a fragment of masonry on top. The site, extending to the River Stour (which is the boundary between Suffolk and Essex) is now the Clare Castle Country Park. The branch railway from Cambridge to Sudbury used to run through the castle site; the track is grassed and the pleasant little station of 1866 is converted into warden's office and shelter. Nearby are the remains of Clare Priory – in fact it was an Augustinian friary – now occupied again by Catholics who have converted one of the monastic buildings into a church. The original friars' church has almost gone, but the prior's house remains, altered after the Reformation.

The market place laid out by the de Clares north of the castle was at first very large. It was encroached on at an early date, leaving a still spacious 'Market Hill'

and a parallel High Street connected by alleys, with the parish church to the north. High Street has attractive buildings on its western side, mostly medieval or Tudor in origin. The most intriguing is on the corner with Nethergate Street, where a gracefully rounded late Georgian shop front takes the corner under a jutting upper storey. Facing the church is the Ancient House, a 15th-century building plastered over in the 17th with pargetting in relief – one of the most striking examples of this traditional treatment after the Ancient House in Ipswich (35) and the Sun Inn in Saffron Walden. The church was reconstructed in the late 15th century but, as often, much of the older fabric was incorporated. The low 13th-century tower suggests the original scale. The 14th-century arcades were taken down and re-erected at a greater height, on new tall bases, with additional carved detail. The chancel was again rebuilt in 1617–19 in 'Gothic Survival', with simplified tracery, and red brick mixed with the rough stone. North of the church is the wide Callis Street with more old houses, especially The Grove, set back on the right, with four gables; it was a medieval house altered in the 17th century, the outer gables being original and the middle ones added then.

Debenham

Debenham is a former market town where a great deal of the medieval and Tudor fabric survives, modified

and updated. Unusually, there is not much of Georgian date (it must then have been in decline), but there is a

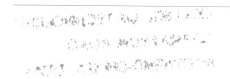

little Victorian. The village – that is its present status – has a most attractive plan. It begins at its southern end with an irregular green, then the narrowing High Street climbs and slightly curves to a brow, beyond which a tapering green, the former market place, descends. House after house is two-storeyed, timber-framed, often jettied, usually plastered (rightly) and colour-washed, and roofed in dark grey or red pantiles. One or two have passageways into yards, taller than the ground storeys to enable waggons to pass through. A rather grander house than most, jettied and brick-nogged, stands on the brow where the old market place (now green) begins. Next to it, on the green, is a small restored early 17th-century market house, for some time a school. On the left, facing the green, is a row of flint and buff brick houses, early Victorian, lending variety, while more timber-framed houses line the street continuing northward – one, much altered, was the 15th-century Guildhall, illustrated in its original form in Dymond and Northeast's *History of Suffolk*. The church is on the hump of the hill, behind the houses on the east side of High Street. Unusually for Suffolk it has a low tower, either Saxon or very early Norman, with a later western porch; to come through these into the airy, spacious 15th-century nave is a memor-

28 Debenham, an unspoiled former market town, with plastered timber-framed houses, roofed in pantiles, one with a tall passageway to admit waggons; the temple-like Victorian chapel adds to the character of the scene.

able experience. Outside, the church has a nice texture of flint, rough and fine stone, and patches of brick.

Dunwich and Blythburgh

Dunwich is the 'lost city' of East Anglia. Almost all the site of the former town is now sea. In Roman and Saxon times the coast was generally about a mile further out than it is now, but there was a wide-mouthed harbour into which flowed the waters of the winding River Blyth and several smaller streams. The town grew to the south of the harbour entrance. In 630 Felix, a Burgundian bishop, was invited by Sigbert, the already Christian king of East Anglia, to evangelize his pagan kingdom. Felix founded his first church – the original cathedral of East Anglia – at *Domnoc* which is usually thought to have been an early form of the name Dunwich – although Felixstowe has been suggested as an alternative location. Dunwich throve as a port, probably reaching its peak in the early 13th century when, although no longer a cathedral see, it had at least eight parish churches and several monastic foundations. But decline was beginning. The great storm of 1287, which wrought havoc on the Cinque Ports further south, also caused erosion, and damage to the harbour, at Dunwich. There was a worse storm in 1328 which blocked the harbour mouth, and caused a new one to be formed a mile to the north; later action of the sea shifted the harbour mouth even further away – to the great benefit of the hitherto small villages

29 Blythburgh. This house, with its thatch and weatherboarding, indicates the present rural character of what in the Middle Ages was a busy port.

30 **Blythburgh Church,** rebuilt in the 15th century in flint with frilly stonework when Blythburgh was a flourishing port at the head of an estuary.

of Walberswick and Southwold. Dunwich tried to curtail the growth of those rival communities, but was weakened by further attacks from the sea. Erosion has continued steadily ever since – the last remaining church was abandoned in 1755, though its final fragment disappeared down the cliff only in 1919. The present line of crumbling cliffs runs roughly along the line of the landward defences of the medieval town.

Blythburgh, at the head of what was a tortuous estuary, was probably as old a place as Dunwich. The East Anglian kings evidently had a palace there; King Anna, son of Sigbert and father of St Etheldreda, foundress of Ely, was slain nearby in 654 and buried in a church he himself may have founded – possibly on the site of the present church. A market was recorded in Domesday Book, and a small priory was established in about 1130. Blythburgh prospered in the 15th century when Dunwich was declining, and the parish church (which was not the priory church; this has disappeared) testifies to this. Except for the rather modest tower, the exterior is superb, with a lantern clerestory and long unbroken rooflines lined with lacy stonework along the parapets of south aisle and porch. The interior is splendidly spacious; the most humanly interesting features are the carved pew-ends depicting symbolically Avarice, Hypocrisy, Pride, Greed, Drunkenness, Sloth and Slander, as well as the four seasons. Blythburgh's prosperity did not long survive the completion of the church, no doubt because the harbour silted and ships became bigger. Now it is a small village.

Walberswick was on a peninsula between the Blyth estuary and an arm of Dunwich harbour to the south (the latter is now marshland), and prospered when the entrance to the harbour shifted conveniently near. It was an important port, for general merchandise and fishing, from the 15th to the 17th centuries. The orig-

inal village, of which there is now no indication, was near the mouth of the southern creek, but the later port developed on the south side of the Blyth opposite Southwold – the present mouth of the river was formed artificially in 1590. During the 17th century there was steady decline from a prosperous town into a fairly small village – a process hastened by a series of fires. Now there are Georgian and later houses round a small green; was it the market place? Artists have painted round here for a hundred years or more. Architectural drama is concentrated on the church, which lies well away from the main part of the village, beside the only road in or out. It was comparable in scale to the churches of Blythburgh and Southwold when it was completed in 1493, incorporating a grand tower which had been added to a previous church about sixty years before. In 1695 the impoverished parish obtained permission from the bishop to pull down most of the building, keeping part of the south aisle and, fortunately, the tower. The demolition of the rest was not complete; there are creeper-covered ruins behind the surviving aisle, which make the tower look all the more dramatic. It is strong and simple, of flint with sparse stonework, except for the crown which has a richly carved frieze and a flushwork parapet with thin corner pinnacles. It has some resemblance to the more elaborate tower at Eye, where there is a similar concentration of decoration at the top. A contract survives, dated 1426, for building the tower; the master masons were Richard Russell of Dunwich and Adam Fowle of Blythburgh. The first was Member of Parliament for Dunwich. This evidence is doubly interesting, showing not only that there was a master mason (essentially an architect) practising in Dunwich at that time, but also that his profession was prestigious enough for him to become one of the town's two M.P.s

Dunwich returned two Members to Parliament right up to the Reform Act of 1832 – an anomaly as great as that of the equally depopulated Old Sarum in Wiltshire doing the same. The voting – such as it was – was under the control of the Barne family, who owned much of the adjoining land. As squires they built most of the small village we see today, straggling along what had been the road approaching the town, with a church dating from 1830. In the churchyard are the impressively detailed remains of a Norman leper hospital – standing at a suitable distance away from the town when it was built. Not far away are the scant ruins of a Franciscan friary, which stood on the landward side of one of the town gates. Beyond is the crumbling coastline, as unstable now as it has been over the last seven hundred years.

Northgate Street, Ipswich.
On the left, the brick gateway,
c.1480, built as the entrance to
his local house by the same
cleric who built the Deanery
Tower at Hadleigh (**34**); in the
background Bethesda Baptist
Church, a splendidly
conservative building of 1913.
The trees of Christchurch Park
rise behind. (*see p. 92.*)

For the final, evocative, view of Dunwich one should go southward for about a mile to Dunwich Common, a piece of heathland bordering the cliffs, which the National Trust bought in 1968. From it one looks northward along the coast and tries to imagine – it is difficult – the town spreading down what was probably a gentle slope from the level of the present clifftop well out to where is now sea. The town would have been punctuated by church towers, and masts might have been visible in the background, rising from the harbour to the north of the town. Then one turns southward and receives a jolt. For, beyond what is now the wilderness of the Minsmere bird reserve, we see the bulk of Sizewell 'A' nuclear power station, with 'B' being built beside it, and 'C' threatened for the future. Will they eventually be eroded as Dunwich was?

Eye

Eye was a feudal town. It was taken over by William Malet, an associate of William the Conqueror, together with many other manors in Suffolk. He built a castle at Eye – which was encircled by streams and marshes, hence the name, meaning 'island' – and founded a market. As William died in 1071 the castle and market must have been established between 1066 and then. William's son Robert was disgraced for plotting against the king in 1110. Later the lordship came into the hands of the de la Pole family, earls of Suffolk, who lived in nearby Wingfield; Eye castle decayed. Although it has never been more than a small market town, Eye received municipal charters and was a borough right up to the local government reform of 1974.

The Malets' castle had a keep on a tall motte, and a large outer bailey whose outline – represented by Church and Castle Streets – determines the form of the town. The market place was outside the bailey to the west – originally a rough rectangle, it became encroached on early by islanded buildings, so that its site is now a confusion of streets and alleys, including Broad and Cross Streets. Curiously, the dominant notes in Eye are largely Victorian, although it was not particularly prosperous in that period. The Town Hall is a rumbustious building of 1857 in red and brown brick which would look striking if it were cleaned – the work of the highly individualist architect E. B. Lamb (page 67). The best house is Linden House in Lambseth Street, the broad street leading north, with a lovely early Georgian front in blue-grey brick with rich red detailing. What survives of the castle is the tree-planted motte seen across gardens, topped by Victorian walling, which looks at first sight like part of a keep – which it is not. Beyond is the church with a magnificent tower of c. 1450–80, decorated with flushwork in thin vertical strips of stone interspersed with dark flint. The porch, of similar date, was attractively refaced on its sides in brick in the 18th century, making a vivid contrast of colours. The interior was remodelled as a high church shrine under Canon Donald Rea, vicar from 1934 to 1966, with Sir Ninian Comper as architect. The great screen, however, is mostly medieval, including the coved woodwork supporting the rood loft – a rare survivor from the rigours of the Reformation. Comper added the rood, or crucifix, with attendant figures, as he imagined they would have been in the Middle Ages. The paintings of saints in the lower panels are restored medieval, but folk-art rather than great art. But the archway within the screen is a lovely piece of medieval wood carving. Next to the church is the restored 16th-century Guildhall; one should remember that guilds in small towns such as this were religious clubs associated with churches, not trade organizations as some were in the big cities.

Felixstowe

Felixstowe is entirely new as a town; little but the name and a church are older than Victorian. St Felix brought Christianity to East Anglia in 630, and it has been suggested that his first church, usually thought to have been at Dunwich (page 79) was here, even though the name Felixstowe is not recorded till the late Middle Ages; before that it was called Burgh, and what is now the suburb of Walton was once more important. Nevertheless there was a church of St Felix somewhere in the vicinity in early times, refounded as a priory in 1105. It probably stood in or near what came to be called Walton Castle – a Roman coastal fort which was converted into a castle, and suffered from erosion; the last remains disappeared in the 18th century. The priory was relocated, on a smaller scale than before, near Walton village in the 14th century.

History started again in the 1870s when a local landowner, Colonel Tomline, promoted a railway, opened in 1877, and a new dock which he hoped would compete with Harwich across the Orwell estuary. The dock did not succeed till long after his lifetime, but the railway stimulated seaside development, so that by 1900 a quiet, informal, fairly exclusive resort was developing beside the low, picturesque cliffs. Its heyday was the Edwardian decade, and its *clou* was the Felix Hotel, built in 1901–3 to look like a grand Jacobean mansion at the top of a tumbled cliffside; it is now Harvest House, the offices of a major company. The architect was T. W. Cotman of Ipswich (page 90), who was skilled at creating a romantic skyline, as he did here with many gables and a dominant cupola. Even more dramatic is the house he built on a headland further north, Cobbold's Point, for Felix Cobbold, the Ipswich banker and brewer, now part of Felixstowe College. It is a romantic composition with tall chimneys rising above steep roofs. The seafront between Cobbold's Point and Harvest House, and from there to the town centre, still has informal Edwardian charm, with semi-wild planting carefully maintained on the low but broken cliff slopes. This is seemingly far from the huge modern docks, which face not the open sea but the Orwell estuary. The moribund Victorian dock began to be transformed in the 1950s; now it is Britain's biggest container port. The growth of the modern port out of almost nothing is comparable to that of Victorian Cardiff or Middlesbrough, but, for various reasons (including the far smaller number of people employed there compared with Victorian ports) this did not result

in Felixstowe becoming a big city. It still looks, and feels, like an Edwardian seaside town.

Felixstowe has two notable churches; the medieval St Peter & St Paul (now in a suburb but once the focus of a scattered rural community), delightfully rustic, with the stump of a tower capped by a pyramid, and an eastern part of 1871 built of brick set to an irregular pattern; and the truly remarkable St Andrew's, near the station, built in 1930–1. The architect of the latter was Hilda Mason. She had been assistant to Munro Cautley, of Ipswich (page 90) before training as an architect; this was her *tour de force*. She tried to adapt the medieval Suffolk style to reinforced concrete construction, and created a remarkable building, with big rectilinear mullioned windows, octagonal turrets and a superb interior where the horizontal and vertical elements are very much like those of a late Perpendicular church – a resemblance accentuated by the flat Tudor forms of the arcades. Hilda Mason worked on the church in association with Raymond Erith, later known for his new Georgian creations and hardly for buildings like this. Both architects resigned following a dispute with the vicar over the brilliantly coloured stained glass which Miss Mason had designed, and Mr Erith's intended choir fittings. These were never inserted. Although the present east window, by another artist, is effective, we have been denied the brilliant pattern of colours which had been intended within the concrete framework of the other windows.

Framlingham

Framlingham Castle is unlike all the others in East Anglia of which there are substantial remains. At Orford (colour plate, page 88), Castle Rising, Castle Hedingham, Colchester and Norwich there are great keeps. Framlingham never had a stone keep. What we see was mainly built after 1190 by Roger Bigod, earl of Norfolk, to replace a smaller fortress built by his grandfather, lord also of Bungay (page 68), but destroyed by order of Henry II after his father, Hugh, had unsuccessfully rebelled. Roger regained the king's favour, and the castle he built was on a grand scale. It was one of the first in England to dispense with a keep, relying for its strength on massive encircling walls with projecting towers at intervals, originally with moat and earthworks outside. We can now walk along the top of those walls and appreciate how well they commanded the gently undulating country round. The last Bigod died in the 14th century; the castle passed through a complicated succession to John Howard who was

created Duke of Norfolk in 1483, dying at Bosworth Field two years later. Three generations of Howard dukes lived at Framlingham; they adapted the castle as a residence rather than a fortress, and added the curiously incongruous chimneys of elaborately carved brickwork to the tops of the towers – these were built almost entirely for ornament, since only three ever connected with fireplaces. The third Howard duke was disgraced under Henry VIII and forfeited the castle. It was in royal possession when Mary Tudor came there after the death of her brother in 1553; she was proclaimed queen of England in Framlingham, her standard flying above the castle gate. Afterwards the Howards regained the castle but did not live there again; in time, through marriage, their main seat

Overleaf **The Tide Mill, Woodbridge,** on the Deben estuary, splendidly restored *c.*1970. Behind the trees across the estuary is the site of the Sutton Hoo ship burial.

31 *Top* **Church Street, Framlingham.** The slight twist in the street helps to make a perfect picture, with the church tower and churchyard trees in the background.

32 *Above* **Double Street, Framlingham.** The sharp bend shows the modest 'vernacular' classical houses to best advantage (Map VI).

Map VI, Framlingham. The town appears as an adjunct to the castle (**33**), and may originally have had outer defences following roughly the line of Fore Street to the south of the map. The sharp curve of Double Street (**32**) and the triangular shape of Market Hill may have originated from the need to fit them into the defended area. The map is of 1891.

became Arundel Castle in Sussex.

In 1635 the castle was sold to Sir Robert Hitcham, a lawyer, who died a year later and left it, with other lands, to Pembroke College, Cambridge, with the strange condition that the castle be dismantled, the materials sold and a poor house, school and almshouse founded in Framlingham. Fortunately the whole castle was not demolished; the outer walls were left, but most of the domestic buildings within the walls were pulled down. Only the great hall remained for a time, converted into a poor house. This was rebuilt in 1729 in brick, and contains the museum. Next to it is a gabled warden's house built soon after Hitcham's bequest.

It is a good idea to walk from the castle into the town along Double Street, a delightful thoroughfare on a sharp curve, lined with frontages of varied bricks and renders. Double Street ends directly opposite the churchyard entrance, which has graceful iron gateposts. Overlooking the churchyard is Regency House, an

older building refronted in 1815 with slate hanging (exotic in East Anglia), its upper bay window enveloped in a curved iron balcony and verandah. The church is complex; the tower, built from 1483, is tall, simple and elegant with flushwork on the buttresses

33 **Framlingham Castle.** The turreted curtain wall, *c.*1180, was an advanced piece of defensive work for its date. The ruin is that of a projecting tower; the Tudor chimneys were added by a Duke of Norfolk when the castle was a ducal residence.

and heraldic lions acting as pinnacles on the corners at the top. The nave has a hammerbeam roof, its framework partly hidden with wooden panelling almost like the springing of a fan vault. At the Reformation the third Duke of Norfolk of the Howard dynasty started to rebuild the chancel as a mausoleum for his family, who had previously been buried in Thetford Priory, then doomed to destruction. The chancel was incomplete at the time of Howard's disgrace, but was finished by order of Edward VI. The Duke's own tomb (he died in 1554, soon after his rehabilitation) is magnificent – a work of French Renaissance inspiration. There are other tombs to members of the family, including the poet Earl of Surrey; to Sir Robert Hitcham who bought the castle; and, very interestingly, to the Duke of Rich-

mond, illegitimate son of Henry VIII, who married a Howard and died in 1536 – he was buried in Thetford Priory but his tomb was soon moved to Framlingham when the priory was dissolved.

A path leads into the roughly triangular market place, with a slope and a small encroachment in one corner. The tone is set by the range of brick-fronted houses on the eastern side, Georgian or partly earlier, shaded by a row of lime trees. There are other interesting buildings in the streets west of the market place, including the starkly elegant Unitarian chapel of 1717, and the Hitcham and Mills almshouses of 1654 and 1703, but the best of the town is concentrated in the Market Place, Church Street and Double Street.

Hadleigh

Hadleigh is one of the group of towns on the Suffolk–Essex border that throve in the heyday of the weaving industry, but its origins go back much further. Guthrum, the leader of the Vikings who killed King Edmund of East Anglia, and who was himself defeated by King Alfred, died in 890 at *Haedleage* (the name means heathery clearing). About a hundred years later part of Hadleigh was granted to the Archbishop of Canterbury; like Bocking in Essex it became a 'peculiar' under his direct jurisdiction, not the local bishops'. The rectory of Hadleigh was well endowed; from 1472 it was held by Walter Pykenham, Archdeacon of

Suffolk, who built himself a house in Ipswich (colour plate, page 81) as well as what is called the Deanery Tower in Hadleigh. (The rectors, like those of Bocking, came to be known as deans – hence Deanery).

Hadleigh became a market town in 1252, and by about 1300 there were weavers, fullers and dyers on the archbishop's manor. In the early 16th century it was second only to Lavenham among Suffolk woollen towns. Later the weaving trade declined; Hadleigh, unlike Colchester and Braintree, did not adapt to the 'New Draperies' and became dependent mainly on corn marketing. It stagnated after the mid 19th century; only recently has it grown significantly.

The town at first sight seems little more than one very long, fairly wide street with a slight curve at its northern end. It has a low profile; few buildings are more than two storeys high; shops are small though prosperous, and the scale is pleasantly domestic. Very many of the houses are timber-framed, though almost always plastered over – the stripping of plaster to reveal beams has luckily not happened as much here as in some other towns. Many are recognizable hall houses in origin, with their halls long since subdivided, and gabled wings on either side. A good example is no. 47–9 (Hicks), probably 15th-century with later plastering and windows; a 16th-century northward extension has a carved Tudor door. Another, called Sun Court, is on the outside of the curve, while no. 99 has painted pargetting showing coats of arms and Tudor roses – this work is dated 1618 but the building itself is older. A 17th-century building next to the White Lion, at the other end of the street, has more pargetted devices. Also remarkable is the so-called Coffee Tavern nearly opposite the entrance to Church Street; the upper storey has triple windows, the centre parts arched like

34 Deanery Tower, Hadleigh was erected *c.*1500 by a cleric as a gateway to a great house never built; it is a magnificent piece of Tudor brickwork, though the central chimney dates from 1830.

simpler versions of the Ancient House at Ipswich; the date 1676 is inscribed on one of the windows.

But the really memorable architectural group in Hadleigh is centred on the church, reached from High Street either by Church Street or, preferably, Queen Street – the latter is a formal classical street of 1838, ending with rounded corners to the churchyard. The church is big, though without the obvious grandeur of Lavenham or Long Melford; it has a low tower crowned, quite unusually for Suffolk, with a tall leaded spire. Inside it is light and graceful, with slender 15th-century arcades. West of the church is the spectacular Deanery Tower, built by Archdeacon Pykenham from 1495; it was intended only as a gatehouse to the palatial house which he proposed to build behind but never did; it is entirely of brick with carved details and fretted skyline – but the tall chimneys were added in the 19th century. The group is completed by the Guildhall, on the southern side of the churchyard. This is a tall three-storeyed jettied building of the 1430s, with lower wings added a little later, and a rear wing of about 1460 where the town's guilds met – they were, as in other small towns and villages, social and religious organizations, not directly connected with trade. Parts were converted later into a school and almshouses, and the whole has recently been well restored. The timbering is exposed, and the plaster between the timber studs has been very effectively limewashed to a traditional deep ochre. These three buildings are individually splendid, but what makes them so memorable as a group is their contrasting building materials – stone and flint on the church (with lead on the steeple), brick on the Deanery Tower, timber-framing on the Guildhall. Yet all three were built within a short span of years – their respective materials were appropriate for different types of buildings. A painting by Gainsborough depicting the church and Deanery Tower – one of his few topographical works – hangs in his birthplace in Sudbury.

Ipswich

Ipswich is a confusing town. It is an ancient port, a busy commercial centre and, in parts, an attractive and visibly historic town. It has dreadful buildings of the 1960s and 70s facing dreary traffic roads that might be anywhere, as well as others of similar date which are far more acceptable. But the historic parts of the town are surprisingly extensive and worth exploring. In many ways Ipswich is like Norwich without a cathedral, castle or working market place. It has networks of narrow streets on medieval alignments, numerous timber-framed houses variedly altered, and many flinty churches. There are few notable buildings from the 18th century but many good ones of Victorian date – the earlier examples carrying on Georgian traditions, the later ones often in fanciful forms with colourful facades that fit in well with the historic townscapes.

Ipswich was *Gippeswic*, the trading centre (*wic*) at a corner – where the Orwell estuary opened out and made a right-angled bend; an excellent place for a port. It was founded in the 7th century, almost certainly by one of the remarkable dynasty of East Anglian kings who had their seat near Wood-bridge and were associated with the Sutton Hoo burial. Its prosperity as a port continued right through the Middle Ages and into the 17th century – it was an outlet for East Anglian cloth and agricultural produce, and a base for merchants with wider interests. It declined relatively in the 18th century but recovered in the 19th. The construction within the estuary of the Wet Dock in 1840–2 – the largest enclosed dock in the world when built – initiated the modern development of the port.

The interesting parts of Ipswich are covered in three itineraries: (1) Cornhill to St Margaret's and Christchurch Mansion: (2) Cornhill to the Orwell: (3) The Quays and Fore Street.

Opposite
Orford Castle. The keep was built from 1165 of septaria (rough stone quarried near the coast) with fine stone dressings, overlooking what was then a busy port.

(1) Cornhill to St Margaret's and Christchurch Mansion

Cornhill is the hub of Ipswich – for centuries it was the market place. Now it has something of the character of an Italian *piazza*, since nearly all traffic has been removed and the space paved. The former Town Hall, very English Italianate of 1868 by the Lincoln architect Bellamy, has come into its own since cleaning has revealed the varied buffs and whites of its stone. The Post Office of 1880, heavily classical in white stone, is a good neighbour. In complete contrast is Lloyds Bank opposite, designed in 1888 for a then independent bank by the local architect T. W. Cotman, said to have been a nephew of the watercolourist. It looks highly picturesque with its fretted sky-line and deep red brick enlivened by white stone dressings, but the ground floor was drastically altered in *c*. 1930 when a traffic way was driven through it. Cotman designed other lively buildings in Ipswich and Felixstowe (page 83); one is the Crown and Anchor hotel in nearby Westgate Street.

An alley called Thoroughfare leads off beside the Post Office, then turns into an enclave of half-timbered neo-Tudor buildings designed in 1934 by Munro Cautley – author of the book *Suffolk Churches*, by far the fullest source of information on the subject. Cautley's make-believe is thoroughly successful. Thoroughfare leads into Buttermarket, which, with the parallel Tavern Street, forms the heart of Ipswich's shopping centre. Both are pleasant, slightly winding streets of moderate scale. The climax of the townscape is the Ancient House (or Sparrowe's House), which cannot fail to astonish even people familiar with it through photographs. It is older than it looks outside, being a partly 15th-century house with a small courtyard. In about 1670 Robert Sparrowe, a grocer and spice merchant who must have traded widely round the world, remodelled the two street frontages with big bay windows and pargetting in relief. The windows have rounded central arches – of the type which late Victorian architects like Norman Shaw loved to imitate, sometimes called the 'Ipswich window'. The plasterwork shows scenes representing the four known continents – Europe with a Gothic church, Asia with a domed mosque, Africa with a figure under a sunshade (or umbrella) and a crocodile, and America with (presumably) an Indian smoking a pipe, together with what must be a buffalo. In addition there are a pelican, a vase, a shepherd and shepherdess, a Charles II coat of arms, and much else. This is by far the finest piece of pargetting in England; the next best is on the Sun Inn at Saffron Walden.

The Ancient House forms the foreground of a colourful view up Dial Lane, dominated by the tall slender tower of St. Lawrence – one of Ipswich's numerous old churches, now closed and, like some of the others, awaiting a new purpose. The tower was rebuilt in 1882, with greater elaboration than before, by the local architect Frederick Barnes, known also for his railway stations at Stowmarket and Needham (pages 106, 104). Next to the church is a charming Art-Nouveau shop front – the work of another Ipswich architect, J. S. Corder. Dial Lane leads to Tavern Street; northward is Tower Street, with an assortment of predominantly Georgian buildings facing St Mary-le-Tower, traditionally the chief church of Ipswich but largely rebuilt in the 1850s and 60s. Its churchyard is marvellous. Except for a small formally treated area on the approach to the south door, it is mostly

35 *Opposite*
The Ancient House (or Sparrowe's House), Ipswich is one of the most extraordinary houses in England (now a bookshop), with upper floor windows and pargetting of about 1670. The scene in the centre of the photograph, right of the corner, is of a shepherd and shepherdess under a tree. The core of the building is 15th century.

maintained in a half-wild state, with the tombstones remaining *in situ*, and many trees growing amid the carefully controlled undergrowth. Vicars and churchwardens who think churchyards should be turned into suburban-type gardens with excessively mown lawns should be brought here. A path leads to Oak Lane, a typical Ipswich alley with a striking timber-framed building at its far end, on the corner of Northgate Street. This is basically late medieval, but was elaborately restored twice, the first time in 1882 by the architect T. W. Cotman who bought it to save it, the second in 1913. The corner post, with a carving of a smith and anvil, is original.

Northgate Street has a great variety of buildings, some altered medieval with jettied fronts, some straightforward Georgian. On the west side is a brick gateway with stepped gable, the entrance to the former house of Walter Pykenham, who was archdeacon of Suffolk from 1471 and also, as rector of Hadleigh, builder of the great tower there (34). Nearby was, until 1794, the town's North Gate – Ipswich never had stone walls, only earthen ramparts (long since flattened). Now the view along the street is closed by the classical portico of Bethesda Baptist Church, built as late as 1913 (see colour illus. p. 81).

A roaring road now follows the line of the ramparts. Off it leads Soane Street, passing the entrance to Christchurch Park and Mansion, and St Margaret's, the finest old church in Ipswich. Its tower is of a specific local type, with large double belfry windows and two-tiered flushwork parapet, but its crowning glories are the clerestory, richly carved outside, and double hammerbeam roof. Christchurch took its name from an Augustinian priory founded in the twelfth century. Its site was bought by a City of London merchant, Paul Withipool, who in 1548 built the mansion in its original form for his son Edmund, enabling him to set up as a landed gentleman while also remaining a City magnate. It was altered in the 17th century when the 'Dutch' gables were added. It was bought in 1894 by Felix Cobbold, a local banker (of the bank now Lloyds in Cornhill) and presented by him to the town council. Now it is a well-stocked museum with many period rooms, and a collection of paintings including some by Gainsborough – who lived in Ipswich for several years after moving from Sudbury in 1752 (page 108) – and by Constable. The hilly park is informally landscaped and almost rural.

(2) Cornhill to the Orwell

South of Cornhill the streets are twisty and confusing; some are of medieval origin, others were formed in Victorian times. King Street ends in front of a classical arch, built in 1850. This opens into a distinctive Victorian enclave, centred on Museum Street – which, with its double twist, looks as if it had been a medieval lane, but was laid out in the 1840s. Its best buildings are in Suffolk buff brick, whose pale creamy colour has been brought out by cleaning. With their doorcases and pediments they suggest – like buildings of comparable date in Bury St Edmunds – that the Georgian tradition survived long in Suffolk. Elm Street, an ancient street, leads to St Mary-at-Elms, one of the few old churches in central Ipswich still in use (it is Anglican High Church), with a brick Tudor tower and a Norman doorway containing what may be the original door and hinges. The illusion that this

36 Silent Street, Ipswich.
Sixteenth- or seventeenth-
century houses, with a carved
post and bracket on the jettied
corner. Till recently these
houses were plastered over.

is a country church is heightened if one looks into the informally maintained churchyard behind the church; overlooking it is a plastered 15th-century house that might be in a Suffolk village.

Nearby is one of Ipswich's most astonishing buildings, the offices of Willis Faber and Dumas, opened in 1975. Designed by Foster Associates – architects also of the Sainsbury Centre in Norwich – it seemed startling when built and still does, with its irregular rounded shape, fitting into the streets around, and its shiny walls of opaque black material. The walls reflect the buildings round, which appear in fascinatingly distorted forms; this, in a strange way, helps the new building to accommodate with its surroundings.

One of the buildings reflected by Willis Faber is the Unitarian meeting house, built in 1699 – only about ten years after it became legally possible for such a dissenting chapel to exist. It is timber-framed and plastered, with two tiers of domestic-looking windows, indicating the internal arrangement with galleries on three sides, the fourth having an elaborate pulpit. It is one of the best-preserved early nonconformist churches in the country. Round the corner, Willis Faber reflects another, more conventional church, the medieval St Nicholas in flint and stone, awaiting a new use. Also reflected – just – is an attractive line of old houses, many restored after long neglect, on St Nicholas Street, which, with its continuation St Peter's Street, forms the ancient route from the town centre to the river. Silent Street comes in from the east, and at its junction is one of the town's set-pieces of picturesque old houses, most of them now with exposed timber-framing though old photographs show them to have been plastered. More old houses, retaining their plaster, front St Peter's Street, which ends at the tall tower of St Peter's church. This may have been the site of the first church in Ipswich; it was well endowed in Saxon times. In the twelfth century an Augustinian priory was founded, incorporating the church. Yet it was never rebuilt on a grand scale; now it is empty, though recently repaired, and awaits a new use. Could not this or another Ipswich church be turned into a museum, as has been done successfully in Colchester and elsewhere? Something is needed to illustrate the history of Christianity in Suffolk – and where better than in an old Ipswich church? The priory was suppressed in 1528 by Cardinal Wolsey to provide the site and some of the revenue for a new school which was intended to rival Eton. But Wolsey fell, and his college lasted only two years. The new buildings were never finished; all that remains is a small brick gateway.

(3) The Quays and Fore Street

The ancient quays of Ipswich were at the head of the Orwell estuary. In the 1840s the setting was transformed; a narrow channel was constructed to take the flow of the river, some land was reclaimed, and part of the estuary, in front of the old quays and wharfs, became the Wet Dock. The beginning of the dock can be seen from Stoke Bridge, where a Victorian warehouse faces the river. A few hundred yards down is the entrance to the New Cut, taking the river flow off to the south-east, while the quays and wharfs continue along the side of the Wet Dock. The quayside road provides a fascinating walk. Great warehouses and grain mills face the water, projecting over the road on iron columns, their façades clad in corrugated sheeting. Under a succession of these projecting buildings, the road emerges on the open Common Quay, in front of the remarkable Custom House of 1844, designed by a local architect, J. M. Clarke, who sadly died young a few years later. It has a portico above an Italianate staircase which contains a massive semi-circular recess, brought out in incised stone against the bright red brick of the building above. Beyond the Custom House the quayside – now called Neptune Quay – is becoming smartened. Old restored wherries and barges are moored; waterside buildings have been converted into bars and restaurants. But the most striking landmark is a former Victorian warehouse with a projecting front, just beyond the Custom House; it has been restored as offices and the projection re-clad with glazing and rounded rooflines.

A lane – Wherry Lane – leads into Salthouse Street which, roaringly trafficked, joins Fore Street. This used to be one of the most fascinating streets in Ipswich, beginning on the eastern edge of the shopping area, and curving with a broad bend to run parallel with the quayside. It is still a very interesting street, but has suffered through commercial decline, demolitions in key places, and heavy traffic in its eastern part. This part, east of Salthouse Street, still has a fascinating series of buildings on its southern side, originally backing on to the quay. The best-known among them form the recently restored premises of Isaac Lord, which include a gabled timber-framed house fronting the street with a passageway through to a yard, ending with a brick and timber warehouse which backs on to the quay. The great historian W. G. Hoskins described them in a broadcast thirty years ago, and what he said is quoted in Pevsner's *Buildings of England: Suffolk*: 'This type of house has no direct entrance from the street – or had none originally. It has a long side-passage off which the doorways open to give access to the shop and to the kitchen behind. The passage then emerges into the open at the back into a long courtyard with long ranges of warehouses or lofts stretching back along the site until we emerge directly on to the Quay. On the main street the merchant had his tiny shop and behind that came the kitchen and the buttery. The other living rooms were piled up above. At the back door, so to speak, the merchant's ships unloaded straight into his warehouses. At the front door, he was selling pennyworths of goods to retail customers. In between, he carried on the wholesale business that was the mainstay of his livelihood; he covered the range of trading, from importer to retail shop-keeper.' Both the description and the reality provide a vivid example of an old trader's premises, where living and trading, loading, storing and selling were integrated on the same site. Perhaps the nearest parallels are at King's Lynn. East of Isaac Lord's are other interesting buildings, notably the restored former Neptune Inn, partly medieval, partly 17th-century and later.

One can return to the town centre along the curving course of Fore Street. Conspicuous on the curve, but empty at the time of writing, is a three-gabled building with rounded 17th-century windows which are simpler versions of those on the Ancient House. In Foundation Street, further west, is a picturesque group of almshouses dating from 1846, the rebuilding of a foundation (hence the name of the street) by Henry Tooley, a 16th-century merchant. The parallel Lower Brook Street is one of the nicest streets in Ipswich, with a high proportion of the town's good Georgian houses, and also an early Victorian terrace carrying on the Georgian tradition.

Lavenham

In the heyday of the weaving trade Lavenham was one of the richest towns in England. It was not large, but exceptionally wealthy because of the prosperity of its leading merchants, or master clothiers, especially the Springs. There were three generations of Thomas Springs in the weaving trade; the first died in 1440 and the third, the richest, in 1523. The latter's son did not remain in the trade, but set up as a landed gentleman. The prosperity of Lavenham quickly diminished after the departure of the Springs, but this was part of a trend which affected all the local cloth-weaving towns in the mid 16th century. Spinning continued in the town through the 17th and 18th centuries – but this was mainly to supply the worsted weavers of Norwich. Horsehair weaving, in small factories, developed in the 19th century. Lavenham had become a small obscure town before the recent boom in tourism. It is often called one of the most authentic late medieval towns in England. This is true with reservations. There are many timber-framed houses from the town's heyday – variedly altered in later times but often partly restored back to what was considered to have been their medieval appearance. But Lavenham in the past never looked as spick and span as it does today; in Tudor times there would have been much visible squalor amid prosperity – while the filth underfoot would have been far more objectionable than the modern tourists' litter. And the town was probably more colourful. Although most timber-framed houses had their timbering exposed before about 1600, the plastering in between the timbers

37 *Above*
Lady Street and Water Street, Lavenham. The three arches formed a Tudor shop front, with shutters instead of glazing. The timbers have, correctly, not been blackened and the plastering is finished to a deep colour, possibly as it was in Tudor times. The jettied house to the right has not had its plasterwork stripped.

Opposite
Southwold Church, built 1430–60, is the *beau ideal* of an East Anglian church, with its lantern clerestory, elaborate porch and strong tower with not over-elaborate flushwork. The shafts rising above the belfry lights suggest that a pinnacled crown was intended, but the flat top is very effective. (*see p. 106*)

was usually washed over in a strong colour, such as red-brown or rich ochre. Some are still so treated, but there is a tendency, as elsewhere, to paint the plaster surfaces white and the timbers black – following a tradition which developed in the Welsh border country but which is alien to Suffolk. Weavers and spinners – usually in the employ of master clothiers – normally worked in or near their homes, so that the former wealth of Lavenham is evident in the houses – those of both the master clothiers and the more substantial artisans – and, above all, in the church.

The church is on the western edge of the town. It was rebuilt *c.* 1485–1525, largely at the combined expense of the Springs and of the de Veres, earls of Oxford – whose main base was at Castle Hedingham, Essex, but who had a local manor house; this was an unusual partnership between members of the aristocracy and *bourgeoisie*. The tower is huge, built of flint and stone dressings, with square corner buttresses like turrets in themselves, supplemented by smaller stepped buttresses. One wonders if a decorative top to the tower was ever intended, but the strong flat parapet is tremendously effective. One enters the church through a sumptuous porch, embellished with shields and insignia of the de Vere family. The interior is of a typically East Anglian late medieval type, with almost flat roof supported by slightly curved tie-beams, and panel patterns above the arcades. It is very similar to the naves of Saffron Walden, Great St Mary's, Cambridge, and Burwell, Cambridgeshire, and as the first was certainly built under John Wastell, master mason of King's chapel, Cambridge, one wonders whether the others were Wastell's work too. The chancel, and the main screen, date from the 14th century – retained when the rest was rebuilt. The south chapel was built to commemorate the third Thomas Spring and Alice his wife, as a Latin inscription in stone proclaims outside, yet the great clothier is actually buried in the opposite, north, chapel behind a glorious wooden screen with naturalistic carving.

38 Water Street, Lavenham
is not quite as it looked in Tudor
times, although nearly all the
structures date from then or
before. There would have been
cobbles and dust instead of
asphalt and white lines, and less
of a black and white effect.

The main thoroughfare of Lavenham, first called Church Street then High Street, curves splendidly downhill below the church, then veers uphill. Blaize House on the outside of the curve (nos. 11–12), is a typical pair of restored late medieval houses (now combined), with timber-framing re-exposed after having been plastered, partly original mullioned windows on the upper floors, and doorways with fine carving. Fir Tree House, on the opposite side, back towards the church, is a charming Georgian intruder, in rich red brick with flat bay windows; there is a similar facade further down the street. In between, no. 88 is an altered house of 'Wealden' type, with central part recessed under the eaves. The focal feature in the view is the Swan Hotel, a gabled timber-framed composition. Water Street, one of the town's most interesting streets, leads off to the right, but it is a good idea to go first along High Street and turn down the narrow Market Lane into the Market Place, which was the heart of the Tudor town. Its dominant building is the Guildhall, built in 1528–9 for the Corpus Christi Guild, the chief social organization of the town – which, however, lasted for less than twenty years more, going the way of most guilds, as religious organizations, at the time of the Reformation. In the 18th century it was a prison, condemned by John Howard the prison reformer in 1784 for its bad conditions and closed; it became a workhouse, then a store, till bought by a Suffolk grandee, Sir Cuthbert Quilter, in 1887; he restored it and his son gave it to the National Trust; now it is a community building, open to the public, with a museum of the weaving industry. Although some of the structure, particularly inside, is restoration work – not surprisingly in view of the building's history – much of the external carved detailing is original, especially round the main doorway, on the bressumer beams supporting the overhangs, and at the corner. East of the Guildhall is a slightly older range, with a recently revealed Tudor shop front (it had been hidden behind accretions). But the finest gem of the market place is Little Hall, on the eastern side, a 15th-century hall house. The central hall was subdivided with a new floor in the 16th century, when a chimney was inserted. The north wing, with its gable and distinctive diagonal timber braces, is the original solar; the south wing is a 16th-century addition. The house has been sensitively restored, with warm orange-ochre colourwash between the timbers, thoroughly traditional and much more attractive than the off-white used on the plasterwork of the Guildhall. Little Hall is the headquarters of the Suffolk Preservation Society, whose folder, *A Walk round Lavenham*, is an admirable guide for an exploration of the town. It directs the walker into Barn Street, with the 16th-century Molet House, then into the parallel Shilling Street, which it says is 'perhaps the most interesting street in Lavenham, not generally explored by visitors'. It is lined mainly with smaller houses or cottages, of the sort which would probably have been occupied by the actual spinners and weavers; some are visibly timber-framed, others have been much altered or rebuilt in later times. But there are also more substantial houses, notably Shilling Grange, 17th-century and restored in the 1920s. Shilling Street comes into Water Street, which leads back to the centre of the town. Among its many interesting buildings is De Vere House, dismantled and re-erected in the 1920s – convincingly. Some of the detailing, like that over the door, is certainly original. Further on is The Priory – a misleading name, since it was merely owned by an Essex priory and was never monastic itself. Recent repair has revealed its complete history. Its core is 13th-century; repeated enlargements and alterations have resulted in the present attractive frontage with three gables, two of them set back behind the garden wall, with elaborately carved medieval bargeboards. On the corner of Lady Street is another exceptional building, with a triple Tudor shop front, one of its wood-framed windows now glazed. Early shop fronts are rare, though there is another, already mentioned, in the market place; there are others in Saffron Walden. Facing this building across Lady Street is the Wool Hall, built for St. Mary's Guild, and a counterpart to the Guildhall in the market place. It was used as a wool store as late as the 17th century – the wool would then have been used by spinners for Norwich weavers. In 1911 it was actually dismantled with the intention of rebuilding it elsewhere; after protest a benefactor paid for it to be re-erected on its proper site. Now it is part of the Swan Hotel.

Long Melford

Long Melford is well named. The town or village – either term is used – extends on both sides of an ancient crossing of a small stream; the 'mill ford', represented by a bridge. On one side is a huge green, on the other a very long street; from the top of the green to the far end of the street is nearly two miles. Along that length are a magnificent church, a very large number of timber-framed houses, and a major country house – and there is another country house a short distance away. All these were built in the 15th and 16th centuries when the town was a prosperous centre of the weaving industry.

The green is wedge-shaped, with the point near the bridge. It is sadly more open than it was before some fine elms were killed by disease, but this has its compensations. A pleasant line of houses borders the green on the west; the grounds of Melford Hall are on the east; the church forms the climax on the highest ground, at

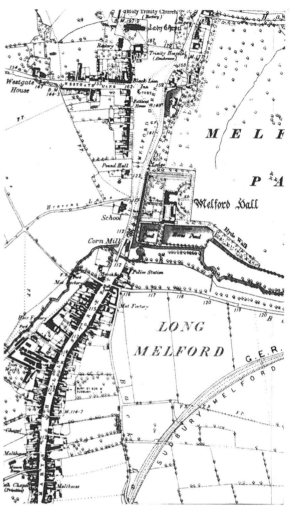

39 Long Melford Church. Elaborate flushwork in flint and stone; the Gothic lettering on the frieze spells the names of benefactors towards the rebuilding of the church in the 1480s. The gables to the right are those of the nearly separate Lady Chapel.

Map VII, Long Melford. This map of 1885 shows the incredibly long street, crossing a stream and then opening into a huge wedge-shaped green with the church at the far end, and Melford Hall to the east.

the north-west corner of the green. The only structure actually on the green is a little brick conduit house, which covered the source of the Tudor water supply. Melford Hall, a National Trust property, is a brick-built mansion set back a little from the green. Mr. Barry Wall, whose *Long Melford through the Ages* is the best introduction to the town, shows that it was originally a mansion built about 1520 by the abbot of Bury St Edmunds as a country retreat. It was altered by Sir William Cordell, an Elizabethan lawyer, and by various later owners. The gateway from the green dates from about 1815, with later lodges. Looking north, the church rises behind the long Trinity Hospital, an almshouse founded in 1573 by Sir William Cordell and

rebuilt, very effectively, in 1847. It forms a perfect foil to the church.

North of the church there is a view towards Kentwell Hall in its park (the house is open on certain days). Like Melford Hall it is mostly Tudor with later alterations. The Clopton family owned the estate from about 1400 – John Clopton, patron of the church, succeeded to it in 1446.

The church has the scale of a small cathedral, although unmistakably a parish church with its great long unbroken space, lantern-lit with a tall clerestory. The main part was largely rebuilt between 1480 and 1484, as indicated by flushwork friezes inscribed in Gothic lettering along the clerestory and south aisle.

These list the donors towards the rebuilding, including John Clopton of Kentwell Hall, and many townsmen and their wives. The five western bays of the nave arcades come from the previous church; the remaining arches are similar in dimensions but different in detail. The general impression is of great length, emphasized by the rhythm of fairly narrow arches of modest height, and the long lantern of the clerestory. At the north-east corner, approached through a small door and a flat-vaulted vestibule, is the tiny Clopton chantry chapel, which Mr Barry Wall suggests in his book was built as an isolated chapel before the church was extended and linked with it. John Clopton's tomb is set under a recess between the chapel and the high altar, with the Renaissance monument to Sir William Cordell, who died nearly a hundred years later, on the opposite side of the altar. The most unusual feature of the church is the Lady Chapel, virtually a separate building, though abutting on to the east end of the main church. As another elaborate flushwork inscription explains, it was started by Clopton and completed after his death in 1497. Mr Wall suggests that the present rather awkward three-gabled roof of the Lady Chapel is not original, but dates from the 17th century when this chapel was converted into a school. The chapel has an unusual plan with central space and ambulatory round, suggesting a shrine. The church's original tower has long since gone; the present one is a refacing (c. 1900) of a Georgian one.

The main part of the town is the almost endless street beginning at the bridge at the south end of the green. It was part of an important medieval highway from London through Braintree and Sudbury into the heartland of East Anglia; this succeeded a Romano-British route which followed nearly the same alignment at Long Melford, though diverging to the north and south. The street bends gently, and varies subtly in width, with intermittent patches of grass and occasional trees beside the all-too-busy carriageway. Building after building is basically medieval or early Tudor. Many were originally hall houses with gabled wings, and, although in every case the open central hall has been subdivided by an intermediate floor (with or without a heightening of the roof) the basic forms of the original houses can frequently be seen. As elsewhere, facades originally with exposed timber have been plastered and windows altered to sashes. Many of these three-part houses have been split into separate ownerships and, of course, shops have been opened in the ground floors of several. Here and there are Georgian fronts, some in brilliant red brick made locally, others, of later date, in the characteristic Suffolk buff brick – but, more often than not, these facades conceal older timber-framed structures behind. A few solid Victorian rebuildings continue the architectural sequence. Long Melford does not display its charms as openly as Laven-ham, where more of the old houses have had their plastering stripped to reveal their original beams; this makes Melford seem in a way more 'genuine'.

Lowestoft

Lowestoft began as an inland village where St Margaret's church now is. In the 14th and 15th centuries a maritime town developed along the coastal ridge on the line of the present High Street, with narrow lanes (called scores) descending on the broad shingly beach where fishermen's stores and curing houses were built. Its herring trade flourished when that of Yarmouth was in difficulty because of the blocking of the harbour entrance there. True, Lowestoft had no harbour at all, but it was relatively easy for fishing boats to be hauled on to the beach, or anchored offshore. After Yarmouth recovered, with the reopening of its harbour in 1560, Lowestoft again became less important than its neighbour, though it must have been fairly prosperous in the Georgian period. Its growth as a modern town began in the 1830s when the shingle beach south of the old town was breached by an artificial cut, linking with the land-locked Lake Lothing and Oulton Broad beyond. With the construction of a canal further inland, joining the rivers Waveney and Yare, it became possible for small ships to sail through Lowestoft and up to Norwich. The company which promoted these works soon went into difficulties, but was bought in 1844 by Samuel Morton (later Sir Morton) Peto, who was involved with the building of Nelson's Column, several London theatres, the Houses of Parliament and, later, railways all over the world. He developed the harbour facilities; for a time Lowestoft had a connection with Denmark, importing cattle which were dispatched by train to the London markets. (The town's Victorian history is recounted in Robert Malster's *Lowestoft east coast port*, to which the writer acknowledges his debt.) The Danish trade ceased, but the railway company took the port facilities over and developed the fishing trade. Herring continued to be caught and cured but, unlike Yarmouth, Lowestoft also developed trawling, for cod and other white fish. In the 1850s and 60s fishermen moved to the town from Barking – which had hitherto been a fishing port but was then becoming swamped by London – and also from Brixham in

Devon, whose trawlers were famous in the age of sail. Most trawlers were still sailing vessels up to 1914, although the herring boats were steam-driven before then. The crowded harbour and boisterous fish market became major attractions for visitors to Lowestoft as a resort. This role was largely the creation of Sir Morton Peto, who laid out the hitherto open land south of the harbour with a broad esplanade, staid seaside houses and hotels. The southern breakwater at the entrance to the harbour was adapted as a seaside pier – providing visitors with a nice contrast between the fishing port on one side and the beach on the other. It was supplemented by Claremont Pier, further south, in 1903.

Victorian Lowestoft is now very disappointing, partly because many of its main buildings have been lost through bombing and subsequent reconstruction. Georgian Lowestoft survives in some measure along High Street, but of medieval Lowestoft there is splendid evidence – the parish church of St Margaret. It stands where the original village church was, grandly rebuilt in the mid-to-late 15th century to serve the prospering port, although over half a mile away. The surroundings have been built up during the last hundred years, but the church is as far from the modern town centre as it was from the old town. The western tower is comparatively modest; it belonged to the earlier smaller church; the copper-sheathed spire is a replacement of the medieval one. The interior with its long unbroken space is of great beauty. The pillars of the arches are broader across than they are lengthways, giving a delicate but lofty screen-like effect to the arcades. The roof is unusual; it has hammerbeams, on which rest arched braces supporting tie-beams; its quality was brought out by sensitive painting and gilding of the details by the architect G. F. Bodley in 1899. Fittings are not (apart from the medieval lectern) particularly distinguished; it is the overall effect which makes this one of the most memorable church interiors in East Anglia.

The old town, north of the modern town centre, is still a distinct entity. It is mainly High Street, running along the seaward side of the ridge, with the buildings on its eastern frontage standing on the brow – though this is evident only through occasional gaps, or from below. It has a slightly faded, slightly self-conscious charm, with varied small shops in buildings of differing dates. Some are fairly pretentious Victorian, attractive in their busy skylines, but many are more modest and earlier. Some have roofs in traditional red and grey pantiles. There are a few Georgian gems, notably no. 55, in bright red brick with Venetian windows. Flint House, no. 80, has a Georgian front in knapped flint with brick-framed sash windows; the date 1586 indicates that it is older than its front suggests. At one end of this house is a passageway into Wilde's Score. This is one of the many scores which were characteristic of old Lowestoft; the name means a path down to a waterside, used in nearby villages as well as Beccles (page 68). Several remain off High Street, with names like Spurgeon's Score, Maltster's Score, Martin's Score and Mariner's Score. Most are stepped in their steepest parts, and descend between old garden walls into what is now an industrial area at the bottom. Originally most of the population, including the fishermen, lived on the high ground along or off High Street, while the buildings and apparatus connected with fishing were on the coastal strip, the scores providing links. But by about 1800 many poor houses had been built amid the fishing huts, stores and curing houses of the shoreside area, while the more prosperous people lived on High Street – especially in the houses on the eastern side with their gardens plunging down the hillside between the scores; early Victorian guidebooks wrote of the 'hanging gardens of Lowestoft'. Now the shoreside area has been largely redeveloped for commerce and industry, shutting off the beach from this part of the town – including the Ness, England's eastern extremity. Nevertheless some of the old curing houses survive, converted to other uses, near the bottom of the scores.

Finally, although it is not part of the town, one should mention Somerleyton Hall. This, a few miles inland, was built from 1844 by Morton Peto – at the time when, already a very successful building contractor, he was beginning to invest in Lowestoft. It is in a fanciful Victorian amalgam of styles with a fine garden, now a popular showplace. He also transformed Somerleyton village for his estate workers, with deliberately picturesque cottages, many of them thatched, round a large green. Nearby was a brickworks whence came much of the material for building Lowestoft – and parts of London as well. Alas, Peto went bankrupt in 1866 – his companies were overstretched, particularly in their foreign enterprises – and the estate was sold to another industrialist, Sir Francis Crossley from Halifax.

Mildenhall

Mildenhall was a very small town where the Breckland gives way to the Fens – it drew its sustenance from the latter; in the Middle Ages there was a fish market, supplied from the Fenland waters. The quietude of the area was shattered between the wars when one of the first important airfields was formed nearby; some of the famous air races, such as those to Australia, started from Mildenhall. The airfield, and the adjoining one at Lakenheath, are now Anglo-American bases. The old parts of the town are pleasant and low-key, with predominant Georgian plastered facades under mottled tiles of Cambridgeshire type. The generally small scale of the town helps to emphasize the grandeur of the church, a building of many parts, less impressive as a whole than Lavenham or Long Melford, Blythburgh or Southwold but equalling them in total interest. The tall tower is disappointingly plain, but the same cannot be said of the rest of the church. The oldest features are a small vaulted north chapel and the finely detailed chancel arch, both mid 13th-century. The east window is slightly later, with its decorative geometrical tracery pattern, almost like embroidery in stone. The nave

must be late 15th-century, with arcades deeper than their piers are broad (as at Lowestoft, page 102), giving the combined effect of slenderness and depth. But the greatest glory is the series of roofs; that of the nave has alternate tie-beams, with traceried arched supports, and hammerbeams, embellished with a multitude of angels. The aisle roofs are if anything more remarkable, and more easily seen. They are single-pitched with hammerbeams on the lower sides; the northern one has a wonderful series of scenes carved on the sides of the hammerbeams. Munro Cautley in *Suffolk Churches* (where they are illustrated) lists as subjects: St George and the dragon, with a king and queen looking from a castle and the rescued maiden with her dog; the baptism of Christ; the sacrifice of Isaac; a hunting scene; the Annunciation: – a fascinating mixture of the sacred and the ordinary. And even more angels are carved into the wall posts which support the roof.

Nayland

Nayland was one of the old clothmaking towns of the Stour valley, although it was not as important as Lavenham or Hadleigh in their heyday. Unlike them it stands right on the Stour – Constable's river – which forms the boundary between Suffolk and Essex. After the decline of the heavy cloth industry in the mid 16th century, Nayland produced lighter cloths or 'New Draperies' for a time, but its commercial importance has long since ceased and it is now a large village of exceptional charm. A high proportion of the houses are timber-framed, generally plastered over and colourwashed in the East Anglian tradition, though a few prominent ones have their timbers exposed. The market place has a pleasing, and wholly irregular, shape, best seen coming from the north. The buildings curve gracefully round to the right, but they jut out from the left in three successive stages, with the top of the church tower rising above the roofs. The church is modestly grand, with finely moulded arches; its most remarkable feature is an altarpiece by Constable, one of only two paintings of this type he did – according to the local guidebook it was given to the church by a relative as a thank-offering for his success as an artist. The church is hemmed in by buildings, especially on the south side, where an alley passes Alston Court – a

complicated house of *c.* 1480 onwards; what one sees from outside are two gables and the large window of a hall in between, with a curved door hood dating from about 1700. There are also long wings embracing a courtyard. Northwards the market place narrows into Church Street, and off to the right is Fen Street, where there is a delightful row of houses set back in gardens behind a stream, an offshoot of the Stour, whose primary purpose must have been to drive a nearby mill. Did clothworkers live here and make use of the water for processing? Church Street leads into another long street at right angles, with more timber-framed houses.

Although it is smaller and was never a town, mention must be made of Stoke-by-Nayland, better known than Nayland because of the prominence of its church, whose tower is a feature in some of Constable's paintings, like that of Dedham across the valley. Stoke was the mother church of which Nayland was a chapelry; its tower, with heavy diminishing buttresses and tall pinnacles, is of a Home Counties rather than East Anglian type. It has an affinity with the tower of Prittlewell church, now in Southend, not surprisingly since the priory of Prittlewell held the patronage of Stoke church.

Needham Market

Descriptions of Needham have sometimes been unflattering: 'a featureless little town' is a comment by an otherwise perceptive writer. This was written before

a bypass took away through traffic, making it possible to enjoy the long street with its succession of buildings of the usual East Anglian variety – a great deal of

Georgian overlay, in red or buff, with classical porches; much surviving timber-framing, usually under plaster; spicy Victorian buildings here and there. It is a typical street town which developed along an important highway after the bishop of Ely, lord of the manor, started a market in 1226. It recalls Long Melford, without the pronounced curve that the street at Melford has; at Needham there are infinite subtle deviations on the frontages, which increase the enjoyment which the buildings themselves bring. There is a concentration of interest in the centre, where a former inn on the corner of Bridge Street has a carved angel on the angle bracket. Opposite is the Limes hotel, of Georgian brick with steps to the door, and a little further on is the church, scarcely remarkable outside. Inside there is fantasy – a very complex roof, with slender horizontal and vertical members, rich with carving, all rising from a hammerbeam, and containing a clerestory within its structure; Colin Platt in his *Travellers' Guide to Medieval England* calls it a 'church all over again in the air'. The rest of the building is simple and much restored – it was a chapelry of the village church at Barking two miles away. Who sponsored and designed this unique roof we do not know; the arms of Bishop Grey of Ely (1458–78) are carved above a door, but there is nothing obvious in or near Ely from that date to suggest that the carpenters came from there, apart from the splendid roof at March, which was also an Ely possession.

Needham is not quite all one street. Along Hawksmill Street, which has old houses on a raised pavement, is a fine Victorian mill on the River Gipping, recently converted into houses. And if one returns by train, the station building (1849 by Frederick Barnes of Ipswich) is like a scaled-down Jacobean mansion with flanking towers – more ambitious, though perhaps less pleasing, than Barnes' station at Stowmarket.

Newmarket

Just as Cambridge was a trading centre before the university developed, so Newmarket was a market town before it became famous for racing. It is first recorded, as *novum mercatum*, in 1219. The market originally took place along the important road from London into East Anglia, forming the basis of the present High Street; later it was relocated to the north. The High Street became a thoroughfare of inns, shops, and, from the 17th century, fashionable houses. James I was the first king who came to Newmarket for sport – but for hare coursing, hunting and hawking, as Mr Peter May makes clear in *The Changing Face of Newmarket*. Charles I followed these pursuits too, but it was he who caused horse racing to be established as a serious sport on Newmarket Heath – which, with its chalky turf, is ideal for the purpose. James I built palaces in the town; the first, finished in 1610, collapsed three years later; Inigo Jones was commissioned to draw plans, which still survive, for its successor. Unfortunately this was demolished during the Commonwealth. Charles II was a great promoter of racing – he rode his own horse Rowley – and built a new palace, fairly modest by royal standards, on the south side of High Street. Most of this disappeared in the early 19th century, but parts survive within an externally Victorian building facing Palace Street (a back street to High Street).

Newmarket looks impressive when approached from the west, past the racecourses and then the prominent baroque Cooper Memorial of 1910. The ancient High Street veers downhill, with a bit of raised pavement on the right, surmounted by Georgian and Victorian classical buildings, and turns out of sight at the bottom of the slope; a rounded hillside capped by a patch of woodland makes a perfect backcloth in the distance above the roofs. Just at the turn is the town's best building, the Jockey Club as rebuilt in 1933 by Sir Albert Richardson, the early 20th-century Georgian, in admirable classical style, discreet yet forceful, with two broad bowed bays in brick and an elaborate inset stone-framed entrance. The nearby Post Office, dated 1951, could have been by Richardson too. After that there is visual disillusionment; the main part of what should have been a fine street is undistinguished – owing partly to inadequate recent buildings, some of which replaced vigorous Victorian ones. At the far end the street gains character again, especially from the Rutland Arms, a gentlemanly late Georgian inn set, unexpectedly, round a courtyard that is partly older. The climax is the rumbustious Victorian clock tower of the sort that it used to be fashionable to decry; it now seems splendid after the insipidity of much of the present High Street architecture. Several roads meet here; one of the lesser ones, leading to Moulton, climbs past the galloping turflands to the hilltop wood which provided the backcloth as we approached from the west.

Further west, traversing the racecourse, is the Devil's Dyke, an earthwork dated to the sixth or seventh century which descends to the Fens, almost certainly thrown up by the emergent East Anglian kingdom against invaders from the Midlands.

Orford

Orford has a splendid castle keep, very different from the rectangular ones at Castle Hedingham and Colchester. It is polygonal (circular inside), with three projecting towers that rise taller than the main part, and a sloping base of fine stone which contrasts well with the rough local 'septaria' of the rest. Only the keep survives (it was kept as a sea-mark); all the rest of the castle has disappeared (see colour illus. p. 88). It was built from 1165 by Henry II, to offset the seemingly menacing power of neighbouring barons, particularly the Bigods at Framlingham (33). Orford was a small port when the castle was built, but the regular plan of the present townlet suggests that most of it was laid out in conjunction with the castle. Like so many East Anglian ports it was prosperous up to the 16th century, then declined. Until that time it faced open sea, but in the following centuries the shingle spit of Orford Ness was built up to its astonishing present length, separating the River Alde from open waters for many miles (page 66). The town declined to a village and 'pocket borough' with two M.P.s (until 1832) whose 'election' was controlled by a neighbouring landowner.

There is a long former market place with the castle rising over trees beyond one end and the church at the other. The church has a spacious 14th-century nave and aisles, and a remarkable ruined chancel probably of the same date as the castle. The surviving arcade of narrow rounded arches on tall, weathered circular piers is very impressive. The nicest part of Orford starts south of the church. Church Street runs between Georgian and later houses to a crossroads; Broad Street going west, now grass-bordered and loosely developed, was probably once a more urban street. Quay Street, leading south, is also grassy, but this is deceptive. An old bird's-eye view, shown at the castle, indicates an artificial inlet where the grass strip along the street now is; it came roughly as far as the crossroads. Small vessels could thus have got near to the heart of the town – this would have been specially useful for bringing supplies and building materials to the castle. It is not clear when this inlet was filled in. Quay Street continues to the now lively little quay with its pleasure boats and oyster fishing, shut off from the open sea by the Ness.

Southwold

Southwold is the most attractive town on the East Anglian coast. It is now a quiet resort; in its 15th-century heyday it was an important port. Until the 13th century it was a small village, but in 1259 it came into the hands of the de Clare family (page 77). They promoted its trade, profiting from the erosion of Dunwich nearby, and the move northwards of the mouth of Dunwich haven and the Blyth estuary (page 80). With the demise of the Clares it became a royal holding, and obtained a borough charter in 1490. A hundred years later the mouth of the River Blyth was stabilized where it is now, but a period of misfortunes followed. There was a serious town fire in 1596, and a worse one in 1659. The harbour silted, and hostile ships hindered trade during the Dutch wars – the indecisive battle of Sole Bay was fought offshore in 1672. In 1745 the harbour was improved, and Southwold became for a time the base for a fishing fleet; there were also salt-works. Then trade declined again because of further silting. Growth as a resort began soon after 1800 when the first villas were built overlooking the sea and the many green spaces. The growth has been gradual, and Southwold never ceased to appeal to the discerning.

Except for the church, Southwold's buildings are modest; it is their collective effects, in relation to the sea, streets and spacious greens, that make the town so marvellous. The itinerary starts in High Street – which looks like that of an inland market town, slightly wavering, and widening into the triangular Market Place, from which two narrower streets continue. There are fine Georgian facades; the so-called Manor House, built by the salt-works owner about 1753, has decorative brickwork and keystones. Bank House of 1716 (Lloyds Bank) also has keystones and a fine round-topped porch. (These and other facts are taken from the excellent folder *Southwold* published by the Suffolk Preservation Society – the basis of a more detailed walk round the town.) The Swan Hotel is a nice amalgam, a Georgian inn with Edwardian bays and a discreet 1930s extension; it has delightful ironwork over its projecting sign, as has the Crown further north. Some of the older houses are roofed in pantiles, both red and dark-glazed.

Queen Street leads from the market place to South Green, a splendid sprawling space with two salients to the sea front. Buildings front it with total informality; some are Regency but most are Victorian, and many would not look remarkable on a suburban road; it is the ensemble and setting that matter. Among those that stand out are Regency House of 1828, later lengthened and heightened, with a bowed and shuttered façade; South Green Lodge on one of the salients, built about 1820 and altered, with an iron balcony (a feature on several of the houses); and no. 18, conspicuous on a corner site, red-blooded Victorian with a broad turret, endearingly incongruous in its genteel setting. The green narrows at its far end where it is called Constitution Hill; it is continued by Ferry Road, which curves round the edge of the marshes, commanding a view to the boats on the river half a mile away and to Walberswick beyond. If one does not have time to go further, one should turn north along the coast, first to Gun Hill, a green space where ancient guns point out to sea. Stone House, south of the guns, is built, unusually for Southwold, of flint with buff brick dressings. One of the salients of South Green opens up to the left, but a narrow promenade curves round on the clifftop to emerge at the end of the second salient. Here is a group of houses called Centre Cliff, originally a terrace of 1829, with later additions.

40 Southwold. One of the many informal corners of this delightful town, with the lighthouse of 1887, and the sea in the background.

Further along the front are two more coastal greens, with East Street leading inland back to the market place. Behind St James' Green is the lighthouse, the *clou* of Southwold, built as late as 1887 – over forty years after the stuccoed pub in front. St James' Green narrows inland, and then East Green opens up – the numerous greens are a remarkable feature of Southwold, but the legend that they were left after the 1659 fire as fire-breaks is unconvincing. Adjoining East Green is Adnam's brewery – which is what many people know of Southwold for. Then suddenly there is the splendid view of the parish church, the *beau ideal* of East Anglian churches, built between 1430 and 1460, all of a piece. It is of the usual flint with stone dressings, strongly composed but not exuberant outside except for the slightly later porch. The tower has gradually diminishing buttresses, ending below the parapet,

leaving the top few feet clear and vertical. The shafts over the belfry lights suggest that pinnacles were intended (or once existed), but the present flat termination is extremely effective. Inside there is splendid unity, although Victorian restoration was – necessarily – more thorough than in some churches; the roofs are reconstructions. The screen is original, with the matchless series of medieval paintings in the lower panels – the apostles on the middle; angels on the northern part, 'some depicted in the feathered costumes of the guild actors, others in the silks and furs of rich merchants', as Norman Scarfe writes *Suffolk in the Middle Ages*. If the church does not sate the appetite, there is a museum nearby (closed in winter) in a small building with a Dutch-style gable. (See colour illus. p. 97)

Stowmarket

Stowmarket has grown steadily since the River Gipping was made navigable from Ipswich in 1793. The main-line railway followed in 1849; now the station is an important stop on the electric line to Norwich. It looks uninteresting from the train, but the main frontage is extraordinary, with a broad 'Dutch' gable over the entrance, flanked by heavy classical pavilions, and with wings which look as if they belonged to a Jacobean mansion; the architect was Frederick Barnes (pages 90, 104). Narrow streets twist and converge on the Market Place, which cannot be appreciated because of traffic. There is a nice view eastward, including a shop

front with Doric columns, and a small but conspicuous corner building with upper-floor windows in rounded recesses, flanking the entrance to an alley which ends with the church tower – this used to be crowned by a graceful Georgian spirelet, now an ugly stump. For the rest there is the Museum of East Anglian Life, potentially outstanding but still in the making; there are exhibits illustrating farming, domestic life and crafts, as well as re-erected buildings – notably the 14th-century Edgar's Farmhouse which was moved from a site that had become unsuitable, only a few hundred yards away.

Sudbury

Sudbury was the south *burh* or stronghold of East Anglia, set on a bluff above a bend of the River Stour. There was an early church, the forerunner of the present St Gregory's, and a mint existed in 980 – indicating that it was by then a place of trade. In the Middle Ages the de Clare family were overlords, and in the 14th century the town was already a centre for the weaving trade. Archbishop Simon of Sudbury, beheaded in 1381, was the son of a local cloth merchant who supplied the fabulous Elizabeth de Burgh, last of the de Clares (page 77) with her wardrobe requirements. Sudbury's weaving wealth never equalled that of Lavenham at its peak, but the town developed broader interests. Its status as a market and distribution centre was strengthened by the canalization of the river down to Manningtree under an Act of 1705. Meanwhile weaving declined – Thomas Gainsborough's father was a Sudbury clothier who went bankrupt a few years after the artist's birth. But by the end of the 18th century Sudbury began to prosper again from textiles. Silk merchants, hitherto based in Spitalfields, London, where wages were relatively high and there was little room for expansion, set up in Sudbury and in places such as Halstead, Essex, where they employed people with traditional textile skills both to throw (spin) and to weave silk – at first using hand machinery, later working in small factories. To this day there are wide-windowed former silk-weavers' houses in the town, and two silk factories still flourish. Sudbury prospered as a market town until the late Victorian agricultural slump. Its population then remained static, or slightly declined, until the 1950s and 60s, when there was planned rehousing of Londoners (mainly in the adjoining parish of Great Cornard), and corresponding development of industries. The present population of about 15,000, including Cornard, is about twice that of forty years ago. But Sudbury has been stimulated rather than swamped by those developments. Most of the new building has been east and north-east of the market place; the town's growth west and south has been constrained by ancient meadows bordering the Stour. There are two itineraries: (1) Market Hill and Friars Street to the Meadows: (2) Cross Street to Stour Street, Gainsborough's house and St Gregory's.

(1) Market Hill and Friars Street to the Meadows

Market Hill – the market place – is specially attractive, whether one sees it full of stalls (on Thursdays and Saturdays) or (as on Sundays) nearly empty. It has a distinctive shape, something like a rectangle broadening out at both ends into branching streets, with a slight pinch on the southern side. Moreover there is a slope, small but perceptible, up from west to east and south to north. The dominant building, St. Peter's church, is almost at the highest point to the east. It was originally a chapelry of the town's principal church, St Gregory's, but was rebuilt grandly from about 1480. The tower is well proportioned, with stepped buttresses and thinly pinnacled parapet, but it has recently lost a Georgian spirelet which gave it added distinction. It became redundant in 1972, and has been converted into a much-used meeting place, while the chancel, screened off, remains consecrated.

Thomas Gainsborough has pride of place at the focus of the square; his

41 Former Corn Exchange, Sudbury, now converted to a public library behind the baroque facade of 1841. Corn Exchanges were built in the mid 19th century heyday of agriculture, before the slump which followed cheap imports of corn from 1870.

statue dates, belatedly, from 1913. The buildings on the south side form a lively group. Lloyds Bank occupies a deep-red brick house of about 1760 with two storeys of flat-fronted bay windows over an Ionic porch. Nearby is the vigorous baroque front of the former Corn Exchange of 1841, converted in 1968 into a public library. Before it was built, corn had been sold around the Tudor Moot Hall which stood near the centre of the market place. This was demolished, together with several other buildings which had encroached on to the square, around 1830–40, so restoring the market place to what had been its original extent. The loss of the old Moot Hall was sad, but there was gain in obtaining the present visual effects.

The market place was outside the early medieval town, and may have first developed in the 14th century. Friars Street, which has a distinctive curve, probably reflects the line of the south-eastern defences of the Saxon *burh*, while what are now Gainsborough and Stour Streets were the main streets of the original town.

Friars Street runs out of the south-west corner of Market Hill almost as a river flows from a lake. It curves at first gently, then more sharply. At the beginning there are busy shops, which thin out gradually so that most of the rest of the street is residential. The Friars Restaurant is a restored 16th-century timber building which was originally the hall of one of the town's guilds. There follows an informal sequence; nos. 27–9 have a mansard roof – a feature fairly common in eastern England; no. 31 has a pedimented doorway. Next to the latter is a humble house with entrance on narrow Bullocks Lane. Thomas Gainsborough, returned from his youthful years in London where he had recently married, lived here from 1748 until 1752, when he moved to Ipswich. While here he painted his famous picture of Mr and Mrs Andrews against a recognizable local background, and finished the woodland scene which is usually called Cornard Wood. Bullocks Lane is worth going down; it leads past the Georgian Red House which has a crinkle-crankle garden wall, seen round the corner in Meadow Lane. Back to Friars Street; no. 33 has a stuccoed Regency front added to an older building, very similar to no. 26 nearly opposite. The varied sequence continues; there are plaster-fronted timber-framed houses, and a stark buff brick terrace of about 1830 which helps to frame a fine view back along the curving street.

Further on is the Priory Gate, a two-storeyed timber house with a blocked archway. This is nearly all that survives of a Dominican friary founded in 1272 – it was the gateway to the prior's house. Opposite the street line is set back attractively, with a row of colourful houses. Friars Street joins Church Street, which turns to All Saints, one of Sudbury's three old churches, serving what was in essence a medieval suburb on the south-western side of the town. It was rebuilt in stages *c*.1450–1500 and achieves moderate grandeur, especially inside, with its tall, narrow, strongly detailed arches. The roofs are mainly original, with the richest details over the north aisle. There is a lovely screen at the end of the aisle, now in front of the organ, which was paid for by Joan Dennys, a widow, through her will of 1460.

Church Street reaches Ballingdon Bridge, crossing the Stour into the old suburb of Ballingdon with its long and interesting main street. Lanes and paths lead off to the Meadows – a succession of traditional grazing fields bordering the river and its side streams; they carry communal rights held by certain inhabitants of the town, which date back to the Middle Ages. From the paths across the Meadows there are views back to the town which cannot have changed in essence for centuries. All Saints, tower rises over old roofs to the east, while further north the land rises to the bluff on which the town originally grew, with the tower of St Gregory's seen in the distance.

(2) Cross Street to Stour Street, Gainsborough's house and St Gregory's

Cross Street leads north from the Stour at Ballingdon Bridge. The buildings on its western side back on to the Meadows. The street looks scrappy at first sight but it has interesting buildings. The Old Moot Hall is a restored early Tudor house which may originally have been the meeting place of the town council before the slightly later Moot Hall (already mentioned, and long since demolished) was built in Market Hill. Nearly opposite is a terrace of 19th-century houses which originally had wide windows on their first floors, lighting rooms where latter-day silk weavers would have worked. Cross Street continues as Mill Hill, curving past the entrance to a big, mainly Victorian former mill (on an ancient site) recently converted to a hotel. Mill Hill climbs into Stour Street, the town's most interesting street, with a series of timber-framed houses, variedly altered, which were probably the homes of merchants or master clothiers. The first, on the right, is Salter's Hall, showing a flint end elevation which was built in the early 19th century when the adjoining house was demolished. The main facade with its gable and jettied upper storey is largely 16th-century work, including an oriel window with a carved sill showing a packhorse loaded with wool, a tame-looking lion

42 *Above*
Gainsborough Street, Sudbury was once called Sepulchre Street. John Gainsborough, a cloth merchant, added the handsome brick front to the house on the left (older behind) which he bought in 1722, and where his famous son Thomas was born in 1727. It is now a gallery and museum.

43 *Above right*
Stour Street, Sudbury has a succession of merchants' houses; the nearest, Salters' Hall, has a carved sill under the oriel window; others beyond have former halls, long since subdivided into two storeys, between gabled wings.

and a man standing between the two. Salter's Hill is now linked, through an intervening smaller house, to another timber building called The Chantry – the whole group is used as a private school. The Chantry (the name, like Salter's Hall, has no antiquity) has a central hall – long since subdivided with an internal floor – between two gabled and jettied wings. Its great feature is the carving on the shaft and bracket at the corner, showing angels and the Yorkist rose (suggesting a date before 1485). Another former hall house further east must have looked like The Chantry, but there is now a Georgian façade where the hall was, between the surviving gabled wings. Finally, at the end of Stour Street, facing down Gregory Street, is yet another altered hall house. The first modifications were by Thomas Carter, a cloth merchant, in the late 17th century; the building was changed again after his death in 1706 when the sash windows were probably put in, and the western wing separated as another house. It should be added that this information, and a great deal else about Sudbury, is taken from Barry L. Wall's *Sudbury through the ages* – an invaluable and informative book, tracing the town's history and describing many of the streets in detail.

Stour Street is continued by Gainsborough Street (originally it was Sepulchre Street), which goes on to Market Hill. Thomas Gainsborough's birthplace, now a gallery and showpiece, was bought by his father, John Gainsborough, a cloth merchant, in 1722, five years before the artist's birth. It was probably a medieval timber house which had been altered in the 17th century; John added a classical front in dark brick with brighter red bricks round the heads of the windows, which gives no indication from the street of the older structure behind. The business failed in 1733, but fortunately John Gainsborough's nephew, also John, bought the house and, presumably, revived the business, enabling the family to go on living there. Thomas went to the grammar school, where his uncle was master, and was allowed to roam the countryside during much of the school time, coming back with sketches of landscapes, trees and other subjects. Thomas left for London in his 'teens, to return in 1748 to the house already described in Friars Street – but his birthplace remained with the family until sold in 1792 to a silk manufacturer. Clearly, weaving took place in back rooms on the upper floor where there are large 'weavers' windows' overlooking the garden; were these put in after 1792? Apart from its associations, the house is fascinating on its own account – the medieval original, the 17th-century remodelling, the sumptuous front added by a cloth merchant whose business declined, the weavers' rooms, the later use for silk making. Now it is well maintained, with a garden beautifully re-created at the back.

St Gregory's is a little to the north. The dedication – to the sixth-century pope who evangelized England – suggests a very early foundation, but the building is mainly 14th- to 16th-century. It is famous for its connection with Simon of Sudbury, son of a clothier, who was successively chaplain to the Pope, bishop of London and, from 1375, archbishop of Canterbury; he became Lord Chancellor (a post then usually held by a bishop) in 1380. It was in the last capacity that he instituted the poll tax that helped to fuel the Peasants' Revolt of 1381; he was beheaded by the rebels outside the Tower of London. His body was buried in Canterbury Cathedral (it was he who initiated the building of the glorious nave there), but his skull is said to have found its way to Sudbury – at least a skull is preserved in the vestry of St Gregory's which, without certainty, is claimed to be his. Simon founded a college of priests on the site of his father's house next to the church; this was closed at the Reformation and a hospital now stands there.

Thorpeness

Thorpeness is an extraordinary place. It is a planned seaside village, started in 1911 by Stuart Ogilvie, who had inherited the land on which it is built. The centrepiece is not the beach but The Meare, a shallow artificial lake, intended to be a play place for children – numerous little islands and other features were given names from Peter Pan; Ogilvie was a friend of J. M. Barrie. Around are half-timbered or weatherboarded houses, set along contrivedly winding roads, looking like cottages in a model industrial village or an early garden city. But this low-key suburban effect is start-

44(B) *Below* **Thorpeness** was a seaside village and miniature fantasy world started by Stuart Ogilvie in 1911. The view is through an arch under a water tower concealed as a tall gateway, including living accommodation as in the House in the Clouds.

44(A) *Left* **The House in the Clouds, Thorpeness** was built as a plain water tower in 1923. It was later converted into a fantastic house by the insertion of five storeys below the tank, which was concealed under weatherboarding, with false windows and a pitched roof.

lingly jolted in a few places by fantastic buildings. One, The House in the Clouds, down a quiet side road, was built in 1923 as a plain water tower, but converted into a house by filling in five storeys below the tank, which is camouflaged by a pitched roof, weatherboarding and false windows, making it look like the overhanging upper floor of a house in a children's story. A windmill from a site two miles away was re-erected nearby to provide wind power for the pumps feeding the tank. Nearly as astonishing is the Westbar, seen along a half-timbered street called Westgate – another water tower, its tank concealed by Gothic window shapes and corner turrets, with residential floors below and an archway at ground level. A Gothic almshouse, originally for retired workers from Ogilvie's estate, is another enlivening feature. Development facing the sea is looser, apart from a crescent of gabled houses of the 1930s on a low headland – the last to be built as part of the original scheme. Recent infilling on the remaining spaces is more ordinary, but Thorpeness keeps its feeling of comfortable fantasy. And no one would guess by looking that the Sizewell nuclear power station is over the brow to the north.

Woodbridge

Woodbridge is a repeatedly rewarding town. It is a very complex place which reveals surprise after surprise as one walks through its streets and spaces. There are three centres of activity; the riverside, the shopping centre (mainly along the street called Thoroughfare), and the market place; there is a tendency for visitors to one or two of these not to be aware of the other(s). For exploring the town the booklet *Woodbridge, a short history and guide*, by C. & M. Weaver, is invaluable.

The riverside is best seen first from River Wall just behind the station. One looks across the Deben estuary, with boats in the foreground, the Tide Mill in the middle distance and woody shores in the background. A short distance behind the other side of the estuary is the site of the Sutton Hoo burial, where in 1939 the outline of a ship was found, containing the buried possessions (now in the British Museum) of a Saxon ruler, almost certainly Redwald, a king of East Anglia who died about 625 – he was the father of Sigbert who brought Christianity to East Anglia (page 79). His palace was at Rendlesham about six miles away. The origin of Woodbridge is uncertain; it is possible that the ending *-bridge*, which hardly makes sense as there is no obvious site for an early bridge, is in fact a corruption of *-burh*, meaning a fortified place. It became an important port, especially in the 15th to 17th centuries, when local produce was sent to London and abroad. It also developed a ship and boat building industry. Unlike other old ports of East Anglia, it did not suffer from silting or erosion, and retained a significant coastal trade right into the present century. Today the Deben (pronounced Dee-b'n, unlike Debenham, where the e is short) is full of pleasure craft.

The Tide Mill is late 18th-century with a striking mansard roof. The corn ground there was not all local; some was brought in by barge from elsewhere, and much of the flour was shipped to London. It continued working until the 1960s, though latterly with mechanical power, and was bought for preservation in 1968. Now, well restored, it is a showpiece; the walls are once again clad in weatherboarding (latterly corrugated iron had replaced the boarding). The old basin where tidal water was impounded, to drive the wheel on the ebb tide, is now a marina (see colour illus. pp. 84–5).

45 Approach to the Church, Woodbridge. The alley leads from Market Hill to the church porch with its flushwork decoration with thin stone mullions and Gothic tracery contrasting with the dark flint. The top of the tall tower has similar treatment.

The shortest way from the riverside to the rest of the town is along Quay Street, but a nice alternative is Doric Place, a winding path leading north off the street called Quayside. It passes secluded Victorian houses, none of them in the least Doric, and emerges on Thoroughfare, the busy shopping street (pedestrianized on Saturdays) – long, narrow and writhing, with interesting upper storeys; some of the most prominent are Victorian, especially Lloyds Bank by T. W. Cotman (page 90). Thoroughfare's western continuation is Cumberland Street, entirely residential past the Post Office and delightful for all its considerable length. The Post Office is one of several in East Anglia built in the 1930s in a solid neo-Georgian style, effective in their settings, as at Bungay (page 70). Opposite are real Georgian houses in rich red; one has a carved brick frieze. Further on are Georgian fronts to older buildings, plastered jettied houses, and much else in a typical East Anglian succession, culminating in another house with carved brickwork.

Back along Cumberland Street – it needs to be enjoyed in both directions – to the main crossroads, and up Church Street, almost as alluring but very different – narrow, curving, climbing and lined with small shops; one has a fine pair of early Victorian small-paned windows. It bends round the churchyard and enters Market Hill, but it is a good idea to see the church first, revealing another theme in Woodbridge's history. The original church became part of a priory established c. 1193; priory and town used the same building until the present church was built in the 15th century. Its tall tower, with gracefully stepped buttresses, changing shape as they rise, and leaving the top of the tower clear, was built c. 1450. It has flush-work patterns round its base and on the parapet; even more elaborate is the flushwork on the porch, including tracery, heraldry, wheel patterns and fancy lettering. The priory was pulled down after the Dissolution; Abbey House, standing on its site south of the church, now a school, was an Elizabethan merchant's house.

A passage leads from the church into Market Hill, a townscape of subtle delight. Originally it was an approximate rectangle, on a spur of high ground – perhaps laid out in Saxon times, or else in the 12th century when the priory obtained the right to hold a market. In the middle is the Shire Hall, originally built about 1575 and altered since, with 'Dutch' gables at the ends; the ground floor was at first open-sided. It is called the Shire Hall because it was the judicial centre of the Liberty of St Etheldreda (or St Audrey), a kind of sub-county within Suffolk which survived into the 19th century. The area was originally controlled by the monastery at Ely – possibly granted by Etheldreda herself when she founded Ely; she was the great-grand-daughter of Redwald of the Sutton Hoo burial. Market Hill now consists of two small *piazzas* linked by the short narrow streets that flank the Shire Hall. The street to the north has an appealing succession of gables; the space to the west has been paved and tree-planted, around an engaging little Gothic pump-house of 1876.

All the streets leading from the corners of the market place are full of interest. Church Street disappears downhill from the south-east corner, curving between Georgian houses and the churchyard to the point where we left it earlier. Seckford Street leads from the south-west corner to Seckford Hospital, another of Woodbridge's surprises. It was founded in 1587 as an alms-house by Thomas Seckford, a lawyer who held offices of state, and a merchant with interests in London as well as locally; he lived in Abbey House beside the church. He endowed it with land in Clerkenwell, London, the income from which increased hugely – hence the scale of the present building of 1835–42, in a Gothic-Classical overlap style, rising behind impressive railings. The Seckford foundation also benefits Woodbridge School and other local organizations.

A lane leads from Seckford Street into Theatre Street, the parallel street leading back into the market place, with two interesting timber-framed buildings. One has the tops of former windows now spanning the entrance into a yard, with the carved figure of an angel on one side. Opposite is the inn called the Angel, with carvings on a bressumer beam. Angel Lane descends alluringly beside the inn, past recently restored cottages. Back to Market Hill, and New Street leading down from the north-east corner. Projecting from an inn called the Bell and Steelyard is a gantry which contained a mechanism for hoisting and weighing waggons, loaded and unloaded, on their way to and from the market, as a prelude to charging tolls. Further down, New Street twists between closely spaced rows of cottages – those on the right were threatened by a road-widening scheme, and restored in 1975–8 after the scheme was rescinded.

New Street ends in a distinctive area developed in the 1840s, when Woodbridge was especially flourishing as a market town and port. The building in the fork between St John's Street and Hill has an impressively rounded corner. At the top of the latter is St John's church of 1844–5, Gothic in brown brick with a strange tower, gable-topped on each side. Alas, the crowning spire was taken down in 1975 and not replaced. The architect was J. M. Clarke, who later designed the Custom House at Ipswich (page 94).

Essex

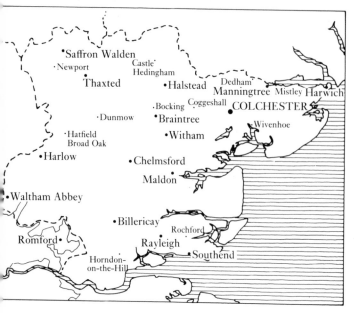

one long street, aligned generally north–south, with subtle curves and twists – part of an ancient route from East Anglia to Tilbury ferry and Kent. It was prosperous in late medieval times, as surviving timber-framed houses show – especially a many-gabled group east of the church, variedly plastered or weather-boarded or, in one case, with timbers recently exposed. The church was a chapel-of-ease to Great Burstead parish church about a mile and a half away, and has a small brick tower of *c.*1500; otherwise it was plainly rebuilt around 1780. A much altered timber house, now a restaurant, opposite the church is said to have been the home of Christopher Martin who helped to organize the Mayflower voyage in 1620; two other Billericay people accompanied him and his wife among the hundred or so aboard. There is, indeed, a Billerica in New England. The town prospered in Georgian times too; there are several individualistic houses of the period, such as no. 43 High Street, now an estate agent's, with red brick quoins and a recessed central part, and no. 51, reached down a passage, also with quoins but with its middle part brought forward. Burghstead House at the south end of the street, set back behind iron gates, is later and plainer. The High Street still holds out as a historic thoroughfare, but it cannot afford to lose many more of its indigenous buildings, still less to suffer another hurt like that caused by an ungainly office block built about twenty years ago at a crucial point on the outside of the street's curve.

Billericay

Billericay developed in the 13th century; it had a market charter in 1253. Till recently it had little more than

Braintree and Bocking

Braintree and Bocking together form a very complicated town. They grew at the junction of two ancient routes which are still important – the old Stane Street, latterly A120, from Colchester westward, and the present A131 from Chelmsford northward, which for centuries has been part of a major route from London into East Anglia. There was a Roman town – part of its site has recently been excavated – which was deserted by Saxon times, when there was scattered rural settlement. The part of the area, north of Stane Street, became the parish and manor of Bocking, of which the Archbishops of Canterbury were overlords, while the southern part – Braintree proper – was held by the Bishops of London. In 1199 the Bishop established a market, and this was the beginning of the present town of Braintree.

From the 13th century almost to the present day Braintree, and, more particularly, Bocking, were important textile centres. At first their product was the heavy East Anglian broadcloth, but from the late 16th century the lighter 'New Draperies' prevailed under the influence of Flemish refugees who came to Colchester and elsewhere (page 125); 'Bockings' became the name of a type of light cloth. This trade declined in the late 18th century, fortunately to be replaced by silk manufacture. At that time Spitalfields in London was the main centre of silk weaving, which had been introduced

Braintree area by 1800, where he set up in partnership as a silk spinner. George Courtauld was not always successful in his many enterprises, but the same could not be said of Samuel – a thrusting and inventive entrepreneur, who converted the Bocking mill for silk spinning, bought another mill in Halstead (55), and expanded into silk weaving. The firm came to specialize in crape, especially the black variety associated with mourning, for which there was a great Victorian demand. Until the end of the 19th century Courtaulds was mainly an Essex firm, but in the present century it has developed in the Midlands and the North. The Bocking factory closed in the 1980s. For the rest, Bocking Churchstreet is a fairly typical Essex village, with a straggle of old houses, together with solid Victorian cottages built by the firm for their employees, and a windmill to the north.

(2) Bradford Street, Bocking

For many centuries, the main centre of population in Bocking parish was Bradford Street, which begins about a mile from Bocking Churchstreet and extends towards Braintree town. It developed along the important medieval road from London into East Anglia, which was used by pilgrims to Bury St Edmunds and possibly also to Walsingham, as well as traffic to and from the Suffolk wool towns. Many of the master clothiers lived in houses fronting the street, where there were also storehouses or wool halls where wool might be brought and sorted before spinning, the spun yarn collected for distribution to weavers, and woven cloth stored before or after fulling and finishing. In addition there were many inns. The buildings along Bradford Street are a diverse collection dating from any time from the 13th century onwards, often altered, adapted or partly reconstructed several times over. As in so many places they are frequently far older than their facades suggest.

Coming from the north, Bradford Street starts at a bridge over the small River Pant (or Blackwater), adjoining a late Victorian Catholic chapel designed by J. F. Bentley, architect of Westminster Cathedral. Opposite is Bradford Mill, picturesque and weatherboarded, standing on the site of older mills used for fulling. The real street begins with Tudor House opposite Church Lane – a jettied building of about 1520, restored in 1974. The excellent booklet *Discovering Bradford Street,* to which the author is indebted, says that the ground-floor windows were glazed when the house was first built, but that the first floor was then only shuttered – interesting evidence from the time when glass was just becoming cheap enough for middle-sized houses. Opposite, a splendid series begins with Maysent House, no. 89, whose Georgian front conceals a partly 15th-century structure behind. Adjoining is Wentworth House, no. 87, a three-gabled house of complex history. The southernmost section, with the lowest gable, is 14th-century; the rest was reconstructed in the 16th and early 17th centuries. The fine shell-hood over the door is late 17th-century, and the windows are Georgian. The whole is plastered over, in the East Anglian tradition, to an attractive buff colour at the time of writing. This is an admirable example of a house adapted and modified in several stages over a long period. Further on is the Woolpack, formerly an inn, also three-gabled. The two end wings were built *c.*1590 and the central section reconstructed *c.*1660 (*Discovering*

46 *Above*
Bradford Street, Bocking is a
marvellous street with buildings
of all dates associated with the
weaving trade. The nearest
range on the left (Nos. 67–9),
with a Georgianized front, is
converted from a 13th century
timber-framed building which
had an upper hall. The nearer
three-gabled building (The
Woolpack) is 16–17th century,
the further one (Wentworth
House) is 14–16th century.

47 *Right*
**Tudor House, Bradford
Street, Bocking**, an early 16th
century range with carved
bressumer beam, Georgian
windows and some
weatherboarding.

Bradford Street). Although, again, most of the windows are Georgian, the bay window under the jetty of the southern wing is original Elizabethan. Beyond the Woolpack are two of the oldest buildings in the street, though their exteriors give few clues to this. No. 75 has a gable end with exposed timbering at the top. Mr M. C. Wadhams of Essex County Council has identified this as an early 14th century structure which had a first-floor hall. He has also found that nos. 67–9 nearby, with a long Georgianized front to the street, is basically of 13th century date – one of the small but increasing number of timber-framed houses in Essex which experts have recently identified as dating from as early as this. It too had a first-floor hall, long since subdivided. As there is no evidence that there was ever any provision for internal heating in nos. 67–9 or 75, Mr Wadhams has suggested that they were probably both wool halls rather than houses. Open-hearth fires would have been difficult in first-floor halls, and there were no chimneys; in any case a fire of any sort would have been very risky in a wool hall. If they were indeed wool halls, they would show how early the weaving industry developed in Bocking. Another possibility is that they were pilgrims hostels.

From the opposite side of the street there is a splendid view back, past the gables of the Woolpack to those of Wentworth House, ending with the white classical frontage of Maysent House, the whole range following the gentle curve of the street. Turning southwards again, Bradford Street continues, climbing gradually, first with a curve then straightening, past house after house which either shows its basic medieval or Tudor timber-framed form, or else has a wholly classical frontage, till it approaches Braintree proper. There are few more fascinating streets in East Anglia.

(3) Braintree town centre

Many people are put off Braintree by the impression it gives along the circuit of roads that take through traffic out of the town centre. In parts it looks like a Midland industrial town. (A bypass will soon be opened.) Once inside the traffic girdle, the town centre is surprisingly attractive – a tangle of narrow streets widening into small spaces, interconnected by labyrinthine lanes. This pattern seems to have happened through infilling. On an accurate map one can discern the outlines of what was probably a large, roughly square space which may have been the market place laid out by the bishop in 1199. This became built over by irregular blocks of buildings, sometimes separated by arms-length alleys. A few vignettes should be mentioned. One is the view from Bank Street, past the prominently timber-framed Swan inn to a tall octagonal water tower with round-headed arches – a country cousin of Colchester's 'Jumbo'. Another is the view eastward along the widening street engagingly called Great Square, closed by a broad and architecturally busy Georgian-fronted building now the Constitutional Club, with the turret of a 'post-modern' supermarket visible through a gap beside it; the Club has a three-gabled 17th-century back elevation, revealed from near the supermarket. South-east from Great Square the buildings close in, and then open up again round the present market place – dominated by the heavily neo-Georgian town hall of 1928 by Vincent Harris. It contains a Heritage Centre which helps to make clear the town's complicated history.

Castle Hedingham

Hedingham is now an attractive village; in the Middle
Ages it was a small town subservient to its castle. The
de Veres were one of the longest-lasting dynasties in
the history of feudalism. The first Aubrey de Vere was
a follower of the Conqueror; his grandson became earl
of Oxford under Henry II; there were eighteen de
Veres until the last one died in 1625. All except the
last two lived in Hedingham Castle, which was built
by the second Aubrey, father of the first earl, in c.1135.
The keep is externally almost intact; its most serious
loss is that of the low forebuilding, which contained
the entrance staircase. A. C. Edwards in his *History of
Essex* calls it 'the best-preserved Norman keep in
western Europe' (a term that begs a question, since
only in England are buildings of the period called
'Norman'; he should have said 'Romanesque'). It has
outer walls of smooth Barnack stone, with wide shallow
buttresses which give the keep architectural elegance
as well as military impressiveness. All the other buildings in the three baileys, where the family lived in later
times, have gone.

The village is densely built. In the middle is the
parish church, of two periods. The brick tower, clerestory and battlements are Tudor, probably built by
the thirteenth earl, a close associate of Henry VII. But
inside it is a superb late Norman building, veering to
Gothic, built by the first earl. It has rounded arches,
pointed chancel arch and remarkable east window in
the form of a circle with spokes – original in design
even if the stonework is restored. Colin Platt, in *The
Traveller's Guide to Medieval England*, refers to the
southern European influence in the 'typically "classical" flavour of its beautifully proportioned arcades',
brought in, he suggests, through de Vere's international
contacts.

The townscape is delightfully tight near the church.
There may have been originally a fairly large triangular
market place, most of which disappeared early through
infilling, leaving only the minute but very colourful
Falcon Square, where timber-framed houses jostle with
a big sombre Victorian building, while an impeccable
Georgian house stands by the entrance to the churchyard. Lanes hem in the churchyard, with cottages
facing the church. The wider main street has buildings
of bigger scale; it turns sharply south-west into Queen
Street where the dominant feature is the mansion-like
former vicarage, with a central Venetian window and
a semicircular one above – a combination found in
other houses in the area; there is a similar façade in the
main street at Halstead (page 133).

Chelmsford

Chelmsford is a thoroughly disappointing town. It
became the county town of Essex simply because of
its central position, but remained quite small until the
early 19th century. There was an important Roman
town, Caesaromagus, on the southern side of the
present town centre, but this was abandoned, and in
Saxon and Norman times there was sparse rural settlement. The land belonged to the Bishops of London,
one of whom in 1199 obtained a grant for a market and
laid out a new town, mainly of one long curving street
leading from the bridge over the small River Can, near
its confluence with the Chelmer. This is the present
High Street, long since narrowed at its northern end
where originally it opened into a market place. Almost
the only older buildings of distinction are the former
Shire Hall and the present cathedral. The first has a
splendid classical front of 1789–91 in Portland stone,
closing the view along High Street. Behind is the parish
church, which became a cathedral in 1913 when Essex
was formed into a new diocese. The most suitable
churches, architecturally speaking, for this new status
were either on the fringes of the county, like Waltham
Abbey, Saffron Walden or Prittlewell (Southend), or
in remote rural places like Thaxted. So the medium-
sized church in the county town was chosen. It looks
good outside, with a flushwork porch and a very pleasant 15th-century tower, rising to a delicate parapet and
crowned by an 18th-century steeple, its top sheathed in
copper. The nave and south aisle collapsed in 1800 and
were well rebuilt under John Johnson, architect also of
the Shire Hall. Here he reproduced the original Gothic,
and created a charming coved ceiling to the nave,
brought out effectively in colour. But there is nothing
suggestive of a cathedral.

Coggeshall

Coggeshall was once a busy town. There was a market
in the 13th century, but real prosperity came with
the cloth trade from the 15th century. At first heavy
broadcloth was woven, but Coggeshall became a centre
for the lighter 'New Draperies' under the influence of
the Flemish refugees who came to Colchester and elsewhere in Essex in the 1560s and 1570s. 'Coxall Whites'
were the special local product ('Coxall' represents the
old pronunciation of the name, now usually rendered
in three syllables as spelt). As elsewhere, the industry

timber and plaster, brick or stucco, with gables or eaves, the effects enhanced by the subtle variations in street alignments, even on the former Roman road. The three major 'sights' – the church, Paycockes and the barn – are at opposite extremities of the town.

The best street is the pleasantly long Church Street, which narrows, twists past a prominent tree, widens, and goes on to its climax where the 15th-century Woolpack inn adjoins the church. A bomb wrecked the tower and half the nave in 1940. Rebuilding under Stephen Dykes Bower – architect to Bury St Edmunds cathedral and Yarmouth parish church – has brought the building back to what it was (though he designed the tower differently); it has a superb spacious interior, with tall slender nave arcades, original on the south, renewed on the north.

Paycockes, owned by the National Trust, is on the

50 *Bottom* **Market Hill, Coggeshall**, looking north to Stoneham Street. On the left, Georgian fronts added to older houses. The weatherboarded clock tower dates from 1887.

51 *Below* **Albert Place, Coggeshall**, off Church Street. The near house, with its unexceptional stuccoed exterior, reveals in its exposed carved bressumer that it was originally a jettied timber-framed house. Beyond is typical Essex weatherboarding.

48 *Previous page* **The Woolpack, Church Street, Coggeshall**, next to the church, a 15th century or earlier house with central hall long since subdivided, and gabled wings.

49 *Top* **Church Street, Coggeshall** is a typical, infinitely varied East Anglian townscape with basically timber-framed houses altered and modified from the 17th century to the present day, the effect enhanced by the subtle twists in the street.

declined in the later 18th century, but for a time was partly replaced by silk manufacture and even the making of velvet; after about 1850 these trades too declined. The population dropped from *c*.3600 to *c*.2600 between 1850 and 1900. Now the town is much appreciated for its charm. It has a subtle street pattern, based on the west–east Roman road, which only very recently has ceased to carry through traffic. From this a space, called Market Hill, branching into Stoneham Street northwards and Church Street north-eastwards. All these streets are lined with low-key buildings, in western outskirts. It was built *c.*1500 by John Paycocke, a cloth merchant, for his son Thomas on his marriage. In the 17th century it was occupied by the Buxtons, then leading local merchants. The house later declined and was subdivided, but in 1904 was bought by a descendant of the Buxtons and thoroughly restored, under the architect P. M. Beaumont and the locally based craftsman Ernest Beckwith (who was also responsible for the restoration of Thaxted Guildhall, page 154). Much of what we see is theirs, but the basic structure is original, including the finely detailed carving along the bressumer of the facade, with the initials TP. It still gives a good idea of the sort of house in which a leading merchant in a Tudor boom town lived, and it has a delightful garden, which reveals gabled rear wings, older than the main part of the house.

The Abbey Barn is reached along Bridge Street which leads south, crossing first a mill stream then the River Pant (or Blackwater). For long in a state of collapse, it has been splendidly restored and is open to the public. Some of the structural timber dates from the 12th century, though the barn was reconstructed as we see it today in the 14th. It belonged to a Cistercian abbey, founded in 1140, which stood to the east, along Abbey Lane – where the most poignant survival is St Nicholas' chapel, built about 1225 outside the monastery gate and restored in Victorian times. It is remarkable because it is partly built of brick, with rough stone – almost the earliest known example of the use of brick in England since Roman times (apart from the re-use of Roman bricks, which did not happen here). Of the abbey itself there are a few fragments in farm buildings, past which there is a public footpath, with a charming view southwards to the partly weatherboarded Abbey Mill, now a house.

Colchester

Colchester's claim to be the oldest town in England is probably justified. There was an extensive Iron Age settlement in the vicinity, which was one of the Romans' first objectives in their invasion of AD 43. They established a military base in the area of the modern town centre. With the conquest of the rest of England, the military importance of the base disappeared, and in AD 50 it was enlarged to form a *colonia*, or colony of retired soldiers and their families. A temple of the emperor Claudius, deified in his lifetime, was built – probably the greatest religious building in Britain at the time. In AD 60 Boadicea destroyed town and temple. The town was quickly rebuilt, but never quite regained its first importance.

Colchester, like most towns in Britain, decayed after the Romans left. Perhaps the main Saxon settlement was for a time outside the walls to the south-east – the St Botolph's area, where there were two early churches. But by the end of the tenth century the walled town was substantially occupied again, and has ever since been an important place of trade. After the Norman conquest the largest castle keep ever erected in England was built on the site of the long-destroyed temple of Claudius, of which the floor and foundations remained to provide a solid base for the new keep – explaining its very large ground area.

Medieval Colchester was one of the chief centres of the East Anglian weaving industry. Much of its output was sent by water from the Hythe, the port area on the Colne estuary to the east of the town; a high proportion went to London, to be handled by the merchants there. The weaving trade started to decline after about 1520 but, as at Norwich, was reinvigorated in the 1560s and 1570s through the arrival of refugees from the Spanish persecutions in Flanders. They introduced the manufacture of 'New Draperies', including light products called bays – or baize – which found ready foreign markets. Ironically a high proportion went to Spain and Portugal, where they were used for clerics' and nuns' clothing.

Colchester suffered traumatically in the Civil War. Its sympathies had been largely Cromwellian, but in 1648 Royalists made a last-ditch rally, occupied the town, and held it against a Roundhead siege for two and a half months. Many buildings were wrecked, including the formerly monastic St Botolph's church. The weaving industry recovered for a time, then suffered a slow decline. But it was reasonably prosperous through most of the 18th century and enriched several merchants who, with other traders, professional men and local gentry, lived in the many houses with handsome Georgian fronts which still embellish the town.

Colchester became a military centre during the Napoleonic wars and again in the Crimean War, after which barracks became permanent features of the southern side of the town. Industries developed in the Victorian period, especially engineering, and the town continued to thrive as the marketing, shopping and servicing centre for a wide area, as it does today. The University of Essex, founded in 1964, is set in Le Corbusier style buildings within a Georgian park outside the town to the east. Although there has recently been a great deal of intensive building in the town centre, which is booming commercially, Colchester has managed to retain its integrity surprisingly well. This is partly because much of the new shopping development has taken place on backland, where there were few notable buildings, and partly because a great deal of effort has been put into conserving and improving some of the older areas.

Many people approach the town on its northern side, either from the distant station or from the ring road. Inchoate development suddenly changes to historic townscape at the place where the north gate to the walled town stood. North Hill climbs, with a slight double twist and a succession of Georgian and earlier fronts, immensely varied yet harmonious. At the top, just assertive enough, is the Georgian brick tower of St. Peter's church, which is partly medieval – one of the few of the town's numerous old churches still used for services. Beyond is the heart of the town; High Street leads to the east. But it is worth diverting to the west first, along narrow Balkerne Passage, to see one of the town's three major landmarks, a huge water tower, invariably called 'Jumbo'. (The other two are the Castle and the Town Hall.) The tower was built in 1882 by the borough engineer Charles Clegg, who must have thought he was designing a latter-day Roman monument. It has four huge brick arches, a central shaft containing steps and pipes, and a tank with a distinctive low-pitched roof crowned by a cupola. The tower is now redundant and its future is decidedly uncertain; any conversion would be tricky, to say the least. Next to 'Jumbo' is the Mercury Theatre opened in 1972, and beyond is what is left of the Roman Balkerne Gate, the three making a telling multi-period group. The remains of the gate are highly confusing and need the help of drawings or models (in the Castle museum) to be understood. It had two main and two subsidiary arches, and stood forward of the wall which was built round the *colonia* in the second century. Later in the Roman period the whole gateway was blocked – henceforth the main approach to the town was from the south. The gateway crumbled; in the 17th century a public house was built on top of the remains, and this survives, much altered, with a concrete balcony recently placed in front of it. On either side much of the Roman town wall

52 **Water Tower, Colchester**, built 1882, always called 'Jumbo', with the remains of the Roman Balkerne Gate in front, and the Roman town wall to the right.

can still be seen – built, like the remains of the gate itself, of alternating layers of rough stone and tile-like bricks. It is much weathered, but it still reaches, as on other surviving parts of the Roman circuit, something like its full height. Essentially it is a retaining wall, since the ground level within is higher than that outside – a characteristic of many ancient cities. In front is a roaring road, Balkerne Way, formed in the 1970s – it runs, logically, outside the wall to free the town centre of traffic. It is crossed by a footbridge, from which there is a view of the Roman wall backed by trees, the public house over the crumbled gateway and, rearing behind, the water tower.

High Street, still handsome for the most part, follows the line of the main Roman thoroughfare, with some distortion at its eastern end. The *clou* at its western end is the so-called Fire Office, built as the Corn Exchange in 1820 and for long used as insurance offices. Its loggia projects over the pavement, allowing views between Doric columns to an interesting series of buildings opposite. One has Georgian bows on its two top storeys; next to it is a solid classical inter-war building of stone and brick, built as a bank and now a bookshop. The climax of the street is the Town Hall, built in 1899–1902 on the site of a smaller building which replaced, in 1843, a medieval Moot Hall. A drawing by an antiquarian of the time, A. J. Sprague, records an extraordinary twelfth-century window arch, discovered during the latter's demolition, with rich decorative and figure carvings; this and another drawing of a more fragmentary Norman door shows what a tragic loss the demolition of this ancient municipal building was. But its present successor is a superb piece of *fin-de-siècle* architecture, by John Belcher, in deep red brick and stone. It is effectively placed where the street widens, its slender tower rising to an elaborate two-tier crown, topped by a statue of the town's patron saint, St Helen(a), who was the mother of the emperor Constantine and who, by long but improbable tradition, was supposed to be a native of Colchester. She lived in the Middle East and gained fame as the discoverer of what was claimed to be Christ's true Cross. Her statue stands on the tower top, holding a cross, looking to the east.

High Street widens east of the Town Hall, then narrow, and twists out of sight. The widest part was occupied by an islanded row of buildings and a small medieval church, St Runwald's – until they were sadly demolished in Victorian times. Even more regrettable was the demolition, in 1955, of St Nicholas' church which stood on the south side of High Street just where it twists – a site conspicuous from either direction. It had a spire added in 1876 by Sir Gilbert Scott, which photographs show was tall and slender, a striking landmark counterpoising the Town Hall tower in views along the street and from outside. It is hard to forgive the church authorities for letting the spire go. There is still a dramatic view from near where the church was, with the Town Hall tower in the middle distance and 'Jumbo' rearing up beyond the buildings in the background. Till recently most of the town's main shops fronted High Street; now the centre of activity is the Lion Walk shopping area to the south. This derived its name ultimately from the Red Lion hotel, a basically medieval building with original Gothic wooden-framed windows facing High Street. Appropriately, a pedestrian access to the Lion Walk centre passes through what was the inn's courtyard.

North of High Street is the most surprising, delightful and, for those who care for the conservation of historic towns, stimulating area of Colchester, the so-called Dutch Quarter – which contains three parallel ancient streets, East and West Stockwell Streets and Maidenburgh Street, together with connecting lanes. The name 'Dutch Quarter' was invented in Victorian times because, supposedly, the Flemish refugees settled there in the 16th century – though there is no positive evidence for this. The area was in decline in the early 20th century; the borough council bought many of the houses, intending to clear them as unfit. Fortunately the council was persuaded to restore the best of the old houses, and this was done in the 1950s. Many are 16th-century or earlier timber-framed buildings, some with gables and jetties, plastered over in the eastern English tradition. Private owners improved other old houses in the area. Finally, in the 1970s and early 1980s, cleared sites were filled with new housing, designed effectively in 'vernacular' styles, re-creating old street lines which had been broken, and bringing people back to live in the centre of the town. This is an outstanding example of the regeneration of a hitherto decaying but historic inner-town area – comparable to what has been done in the Colegate district of Norwich.

West Stockwell Street descends from the Town Hall, past restored Georgian and earlier houses; the view is embellished by a splendid tree growing out from the churchyard of the former St Martin's church, now a theatre store. A lane connects with East Stockwell Street, with a similar mixture of buildings, dominated this time by a former nonconformist chapel of *c.* 1830. St Helen's Lane leads on to Maidenburgh Street, equally picturesque. On the corner is the small restored St Helen's chapel, of dark flint, which overlaps the site of a semicircular Roman theatre, the foundations of which were excavated in 1981; parts of their line are marked out in the street. A

path leads on to the park surrounding the Castle.

This looks like no other English castle. It is the lower part of the original keep; all the outer defences, apart from traces of earthworks, have gone. The huge keep – on the Roman temple site, as already described – was sold to a local contractor in 1683; he demolished the top part for the sake of the materials, but fortunately left the rest. It later came into the possession of a lady who gave it to her son-in-law, Charles Gray, on his marriage. Gray was a keen antiquary; he restored and re-roofed part of the keep to house his library, and added the curious dome. The main part of the keep remained a shell until a new roof was constructed in the 1930s, primarily to protect the Roman base from the weather, but also providing a large area of covered space within the old shell. This, with new floors and galleries, now houses the museum, with its tremendous collection of prehistoric, Roman and later material, mostly from the vicinity. Despite the reduction from its original height, the keep is still very impressive outside, with its square corner turrets, and rounded projection near one corner – which originally continued upward and contained the chapel in the vanished upper storey. All is in rough stone with courses of reused Roman bricks, rather like the Roman town walls. Next to the castle is Hollytrees, the Georgian house where Charles Gray lived – now, like the castle he saved, a museum. The park around the castle was once the private garden of Hollytrees.

Hollytrees faces High Street, which continues, in name, for some distance eastwards – although the eastern end is very different from the busy main part. It has few shops; several substantial houses, Georgian and earlier, survive, though all are put to office or institutional uses. On the north side is Gate House, with a four-gabled front of 1680 (late for gables), with wide bay windows and plastering incised to look like stone. The Minories, opposite and further on, is a big house built in 1776 by a prosperous cloth maker, incorporating an older wing. It is now an imaginatively run art gallery, and keeps its domestic garden behind, with a Gothic summer house. Beyond the medieval St James' church, which stands inside the site of the town's east gate, High Street is continued downward by East Hill, with more interesting old houses – some are Georgianized timber-framed. The climax is at the crossing of the River Colne, where there is a tremendous former flour mill, built on the site of earlier mills in late Victorian times. It has been converted into a hotel, but keeps its outward form and dramatic skyline. Just beyond, a timber-framed building called the Siege House has holes in its woodwork which, it proclaims, were made by Roundhead bullets during the siege. East Street goes on for a long way further, with timber-framed and Georgian houses in variable condition.

Much of the best of historic Colchester is contained in the itinerary so far, but there is a great deal else to see, even if it is less concentrated. The ruins of St Botolph's Priory lie behind commercial buildings on the south-east corner of the town centre. This was dedicated to a Saxon saint of whom little is known; he probably lived in a monastery at Iken near Aldeburgh, and he became a popular patron of churches. Three in London dedicated to him stand outside the sites of City gates, Aldgate, Aldersgate and Bishopsgate, just as St Botolph's in Colchester lay outside the south-eastern gate there – but it is not known why the saint should have become associated with entrances to walled cities. (He is also the patron saint of the great church at Boston in Lincolnshire, which took its name from him – St Botolph's 'town'.) The church was rebuilt about 1100. The nave was retained after the Reformation as the chief parish church of Colchester, and must then have looked something like Waltham Abbey (page 158). Alas it was devastated in the 1648 siege and never restored. The ruin is impressive, built – again – of rough stone and reused Roman bricks, but this would not have been seen as the building was plastered over, with stone detailing in significant places. South of the ruin is the successor church built in 1837, with a tremendous neo-Norman west front in buff brick.

A narrow street, Short Wyre Street, leads west off the busy St Botolph's Street near the priory. This, with its continuation Eld Lane, runs inside and above the line of the Roman town wall – as can be dramatically seen if one goes down steps to the parking area below and looks back; the Roman wall survives, battered and patched, as a retaining wall, with the shops on the south side of Eld Lane built on top of it. Eld Lane passes the end of the 1970s Lion Walk shopping centre with its bright red brickwork, slate-coloured cladding and usually busy pedestrian alleys – following the architectural fashions of the time but fitting surprisingly well into what had been a back part of the historic town centre. Its immediate link with the past is the tall spire of the former Lion Walk Congregational Church of 1863 which, at first, it was intended to demolish but was retained after outcries by people who had been angered by the loss of St Nicholas' church spire a few years

Colchester, Dedham 131

before. It now rises in splendid contrast to the garish new buildings around, attached to the otherwise rebuilt church, now United Reformed. Next door is a Baptist church of 1833. These two churches symbolize the strong Protestant traditions of Colchester which date back to the time of the refugees.

Eld Lane continues in an engaging, small-scale way to an intensely picturesque corner of the town. Scheregate Steps, an alley of colourful plastered timber-framed buildings, descends steeply to the left, over and beyond the line of the Roman wall, while Trinity Street leads off to the right, between more colourful buildings, composing a view which has as its centrepiece the tower of Holy Trinity church and as its backcloth the Town Hall tower. The church has been excellently converted into a museum; the tower, probably of the early eleventh century, is the oldest standing building in the town other than what remains of the Roman walls. Like other early buildings it is of rough stone laced with reused Roman bricks. The small churchyard is a green oasis, with an entrance to the Lion Walk shopping area behind. To the west is the latest extension to Colchester's shopping facilities, Culver Square, with two department stores, built on what had for long been largely a cleared site. It is amazing how new development on this scale has been fitted into the ancient town centre without swamping it.

It is worth descending Scheregate Steps, then crossing two busy roads (the second by means of a subway) to St John's Green, an unexpected oasis like a village green – originally a fairground outside the gate of St John's Abbey. The abbey, one of two monasteries on this side of the town (the other was St Botolph's) was rebuilt as a house after the Reformation; this in turn was destroyed in the Civil War, leaving only the gateway, with a fine 15th-century facade of flushwork in flint and stone. The last abbot, John Beche, was hanged; the last owner of the house, Sir Charles Lucas, the Royalist commander during the siege, was shot after surrender.

Military buildings now extend over and beyond the site of St John's Abbey. One is of special interest, but it is difficult to find – the Garrison Church, at the junction of Military Road and Lisle Road. It is attractively boarded outside, with a broad pitched roof and round-headed windows – a prefabricated timber structure similar to others which were designed for erection in the Crimea. (Dubious legend has it that it was actually erected there, used as a hospital, and brought back to Colchester after the war ended.) According to a recent official publication, the designer was Isambard Kingdom Brunel – a major discovery. It has been altered inside, but the pews were by Augustus Pugin and came from the country church at West Tofts, Norfolk, which now stands within a military training area.

Dedham

Dedham is today a village; in its early Tudor heyday it was an important weaving town. The church, rebuilt from 1492, testifies to that. It is a 'wool' church with lofty arcades connected by stone shafts to the corbels of the roof; windows with slender and sinuous tracery patterns; and a splendid tower, completed c.1520. The tower has simple, octagonal corner buttresses which end in pinnacles – a pattern more characteristic of the middle Thames Valley than of East Anglia. Nevertheless the tower's design has been attributed, without confirmation, to John Wastell, later master mason of King's, Cambridge, the central tower of Canterbury cathedral, Saffron Walden church and much else – one of the great architects of the later Middle Ages.

The Dedham cloth trade flourished until the early 18th century, but by 1750, according to A. F. J. Brown in *Essex at Work, 1700–1815*, '. . . Dedham no longer wore the face of industry but was a fashionable centre with its gay life revolving around the "Sun", the "Marlborough" and the Assembly Room.' Both inns are still there, the latter now the Marlborough Head. The very fine house east of the church dates from that second heyday, with its pilasters and windows arched in red brick against a paler brick background. It housed the Grammar School, where John Constable was educated. A house of similar style but with a much narrower frontage, called Shermans, stands on the north side of the main street – where it begins to curve, past a splendid country-town sequence of buildings, to the west. Great House, at the far end of the street, was designed for his own occupation by Raymond Erith, the mid 20th-century Georgian architect and restorer of 10 Downing Street. A path leads past Southfields, south of the church, a picturesque quadrangle of timber-framed buildings which included the house and warehouses of a 16th-century cloth merchant. He probably stored the raw materials and the finished cloths there, but the actual weaving would, of course, have taken place in or near the weavers' own homes. It is unlikely that the timber-framing was originally all exposed; more probably it was plastered in the true East Anglian way.

North of the village is Dedham Mill by the Stour, the last of a succession of mills used for grinding corn

54 Shermans, Dedham, *c*.1730, is one of two remarkable early Georgian houses in Dedham with classical details brought out in rich red brick against paler brick wall surfaces. (Colour plate, page 116)

or fulling cloth for centuries – often for both at the same time. Nothing survives of the mill which Constable painted; the present one is late Victorian, recently converted into houses. The Stour was navigable up to Sudbury; much of the flour from this and other mills on its banks – like the Constables' at Flatford just downstream – would probably have gone by water, through Manningtree or Mistley, to London or elsewhere. (See colour illus. pp. 116–17).

Dunmow

There are two Dunmows, Great and Little. Little Dunmow is a small village with a superb fragment of a former priory church. Great Dunmow is an old market town. It had a Roman predecessor – and some of the approaching roads, notably Stane Street (A120) from east and west, show Roman straightness until they near the town, which has an irregular, un-Roman street pattern. The long, gently winding High Street forks into Stortford Road going west, and into the so-called Market Place northwards. Along Stortford Road are Georgian plastered fronts, mostly to older buildings, with bay and oriel windows. The Market Place is a short wide street, closed delightfully at its northern end

by a tall hipped-roofed house, on either side of which narrow streets continue. That to the left, Star Lane, descends to the Downs, an extensive many-branching green with a pond – providing an open, unconstrained rural ambience in contrast to the close-knit urbanity of the town centre. Half a mile north of the town proper is Church End, a distinct hamlet containing the parish church; it must have been the main settlement between the abandonment of the Roman town and the development of the later, medieval, town on the Roman site. The church is of town scale; 14th and 15th centuries – the fine tower is of the latter date, with square turrets set diagonally at the corners.

Halstead

Halstead was a medieval weaving town, but it came into real prominence when Samuel Courtauld developed the silk industry. Nevertheless its character is that of an old market town – the market charter granted by Henry III in 1250 still exists. The main street climbs diagonally; the dominant building is a wide red brick Georgian house with a Venetian window; there are other interesting facades with Georgian bows or lively Victorian polychrome. A restaurant incorporates part of a house for chantry priests, established by Lord Bourchier who died in 1400. Four generations of Bourchiers are commemorated in the parish church, which has a slender tower of 1848 – answering the spire of another church, Holy Trinity, half a mile away on the south-west outskirts of the town. The latter is a very good early work of the first Sir Gilbert Scott, in scholarly Early English style. But the gem of Halstead is the former Courtauld factory, converted after the firm left

55 The Old Mill, Halstead, spanning the River Colne, was from 1825 to the 1980s used by Courtaulds, a firm which began at nearby Bocking a few years before.

it a few years ago. Samuel Courtauld, having set up at Bocking (page 115), bought an existing flour mill in Halstead in 1825 and adapted it for throwing (spinning) silk. He installed steam power in 1828, which he soon applied to looms for weaving crape; according to J. Booker's *Essex and the Industrial Revolution* there were 240 looms there in 1840. The mill is three-storeyed and weatherboarded, and has long continuous windows on the lower two storeys. It is not clear how much pre-dates Courtauld and how much is due to his alterations. It is seen, delightfully, from the main street at the end of a stretch of the River Colne with, on the right, an attractive row of workers' cottages in 'Queen Anne' style, built by the firm early this century.

Harlow

Harlow is an old small market town and a post-war New Town. There was a Roman settlement, where the most spectacular known feature was a temple on a hillock, now within an industrial estate (Temple-fields) – nothing survives above ground, but the foundations have been thoroughly excavated. A market

existed by the twelfth century, and it was probably then that the present old town centre first developed; Market Street and Fore Street were for long separated by an islanded block of buildings, encroaching on the original market place. Recently this block has been partly demolished, restoring the old market area to something like its original extent, though part of the encroachment remains. Eastward, the old town straggles, like many places in Essex, into outlying settlements or hamlets – first Mulberry Green, near the remarkable medieval manor house, then Churchgate Street, almost a separate village but containing the parish church. This is vestigially Norman, but restored in 1871–5 under the inventive architect Henry Woodyer, who added a landmark spire. Old Harlow still has many timber-framed buildings, some wholely or partly weatherboarded.

Harlow was chosen as the site of one of the New Towns built round London after the Second World War, following the regional plan prepared by Sir Patrick Abercrombie in 1944. The idea was to contain London within the limits of continuous building reached in 1939 by the imposition of a sacrosanct green belt. People from London were to be rehoused in new towns beyond, which would have their own employment. The idea was simple, and it has materialized. The green belt (now much extended) is still being held against growing pressures, and Harlow, like several other new towns, is well-established. The master planner from the town's inauguration in 1947 was Sir Frederick Gibberd, who was an outstanding landscapist as well as an architect. He designed a new town centre on comparatively high ground, and planned housing areas in four main clusters separated by 'wedges' of open land mainly following the shallow valleys of the old countryside. Approaches to the town centre, especially from the east, were to be along these 'wedges', so that it was theoretically possible to arrive in the central area with its close-knit urban buildings

straight from open country, without realizing that one had passed near extensive housing areas (equivalent to the suburbs of most towns). It works to some extent.

The best parts of the new town are the oldest – old enough now to be considered 'historic'. The Mark Hall North neighbourhood is based on an old park, the memory of which survives in trees and open spaces. The ancient church of St Mary, Latton, which had been almost derelict, is a focal feature. Gibberd himself designed the housing in the areas called Mark Hall Moors and The Lawn, mainly in short terraces, informally arranged, grouped round old trees where they survived – very much in the manner of the inter-war garden cities, especially Welwyn. But looming in their midst, surrounded by trees and seen across lawns, is a nine-storey tower. It was described ominously when built in 1951 as a likely forerunner of many more 'tower blocks', following – though on a very tentative scale – the precepts of Le Corbusier. Nationally the prediction was all too true. But to their credit the Harlow authorities never built many tower blocks, preferring to concentrate on what most people wanted, two-storey houses with gardens. Housing nearby (Tany's Dell and The Chantry) was by the modernists Maxwell Fry and Jane Drew, quietly distinguished in its green setting. Further south, the housing area called Ladyshot (1954) was designed by F. R. S. Yorke, another pioneer architect of the inter-war years. Here the housing, essentially 'modernized Georgian' except for the single-pitch roofs, is more tightly and irregularly grouped than in the slightly earlier schemes, to very good effect. Alas, not all the subsequent housing in Harlow looks as good as these early examples.

Harwich

Harwich is on a peninsula between two estuaries – of the Orwell and the Stour. The town was probably founded by one of the Bigods, earls of Norfolk, in the early 13th century; it obtained a royal charter in 1319. It was particularly important during the wars of the 17th century; a small naval dockyard was founded in 1657, which continued as a private yard from the 18th century. Some of the best naval ships were built there during the Restoration period; later the yard specialized in barges which sailed up the Thames and East Anglian estuaries as well as crossing to the Continent. Harwich has been one of the principal passenger ports for Europe since the Great Eastern railway started its steamship services in 1863. At first these departed from the town proper, but in 1883 the company opened Parkeston Quay a little way up the Stour estuary – the

main port area today. There is still maritime activity in the town proper, but no passenger ships now leave from there. In Victorian times Harwich expanded west into Dovercourt, at first promoted as a small resort but now the most populous part of the larger town, containing the chief shops. The old town is now a backwater. Parts were very decayed after the Second World War, when some of the worst housing was demolished and replaced. But the very lack of commercial pressures on the old town, except on the waterfront, meant that a great deal of the Georgian and earlier fabric survived – though in variable condition. Since 1960 much has been done to conserve the old buildings; the local authority has bought several historic houses and improved them; others have been restored privately with the aid of grants. Gaps have been filled with new houses, keeping the old street pattern. There are still patches of decay, but, on the whole, Harwich is a remarkable example of an old town rescued from decline.

The old main streets run roughly parallel and end at the open quay at the tip of the peninsula. They are described in two itineraries: (1) from the Quay to the Lighthouse, via King's Quay Street, and (2) from the Lighthouse to the Quay, via Church Street, followed by (3) covering Dovercourt.

(1) Quay to Lighthouse, via King's Quay Street

The Quay is Harwich's nose. Through reclamation, the shoreline is some way further out than it was in the past, and the buildings fronting the Quay date from the last hundred and thirty years. The biggest is the one-time Great Eastern Hotel, built by the railway company in 1864 to serve passengers on their steamers; it lost its purpose after the latter moved to Parkeston and, after a period as the town hall, it is now converted into offices. On one side is the local branch of Trinity House, a distinguished building of 1952. On the other is the more modest and festive-looking Pier Hotel of 1875, and beyond that the weatherboarded and barge-boarded Angel. Together these make a memorable contrasting group. Round the corner to the east is the wharf on the site of the former dockyard. The twisty King's Quay Street skirts the wharf, and on its opposite side is a colourful series of buildings. First there is the former Globe, probably early 17th-century, gabled and deeply jettied; then, set back, the curving entrance into an alley called Castle Gate Street (recalling a small, long-vanished fortress), lined with restored Georgian houses; then there are more Georgian frontages, in plaster or brick – the whole forming an impressively conserved group. After that is a less interesting stretch until, past the crossing of Market Street, King's Quay Street becomes narrow and pedestrian. Here is one of Harwich's most treasured buildings, the Electric Palace cinema, built in 1911 and little altered since. It closed in 1956 but, after persistent efforts by preservation groups, it has been restored and once more shows films.

Beyond is St Nicholas, the parish church, rebuilt in 1822, outwardly in brick and artificial Coade stone. It is said to have a very impressive interior (usually locked), with plaster-cast vaulting on thin columns of cast iron – a very early example of an iron-framed building, dressed as a Gothic one. Past the church, King's Quay Street opens on to St Helen's Green – a greensward extending to the beach with a view across to the huge new installations of Felixstowe port.

Looking back from the shore, the spire is seen rising behind a row of houses of the Georgian seaside type, two of them with bold bow windows tiered through three storeys. Further along the green is a strange structure – a wooden shed with a projecting crane. This was the Treadwheel Crane, installed in the dockyard in about 1667; it remained in situ until 1932 when it was dismantled and re-erected here. The crane was worked by a large treadwheel with steps inside, preserved within the shed; the wheel was kept in motion by men treading the steps – this is a unique exhibit illustrating both social and technical history. It looks odd on the green, but makes a telling contrast with the huge container cranes of Felixstowe across the water.

Two former lighthouses rise beyond the green, both designed in 1818 by the engineer John Rennie. The smaller, the Low Lighthouse, is right by the shore, and is now a maritime museum open at restricted times (Sundays). The much more remarkable High Lighthouse is a slender, tapering tower, now converted into an extraordinary house of nine sides (see colour illus. p. 119).

(2) Lighthouse to Quay, via Church Street

The High Lighthouse stands near the site of the main gate to the town – Harwich was a walled town in the Middle Ages, though nothing survives of the walls. The wide West Street sweeps with a gentle curve to the Quay, past restored Georgian buildings and recent housing on the old alignment. More interesting is Church Street, which begins narrowly as it curves round to the church, then widens to pass the Guildhall, built in 1769 – like a grand town house with flat-fronted bay windows through three storeys. Further on is one of the areas which were decayed and have been renewed. Currents Lane, an alley to the west, was rebuilt on one side in 1973 with three-storey housing using white and dark cladding, single-pitch roofs and a broken alignment to form a courtyard – all architecturally 'dated' but fitting in well here. The next part of Church Street was being rebuilt at the time of writing. The final part of the street, beyond Hopkins Lane, is the most rewarding. Between here and the Quay maritime men of modest means but some social pretensions must have lived in Georgian times. The interesting group of buildings begins where a broad bay window projects over the street, followed by the best of the group, Register House (no. 42), in deep red brick, with a very fine Ionic doorcase; it was restored by the council in the 1960s. The next house is also Georgian, but was in need of restoration at the time of writing. Opposite is a pleasant succession of small brick-fronted houses,

56 **Church Street, Harwich**, one of many fascinating streets in this tight-knit medieval and Georgian town. The church was rebuilt in 1822, outwardly in brick and artificial Coade stone; it has an iron-framed interior with slender columns, dressed in Gothic detailing.

mostly with cornices, keystones and classical doorcases as if they were larger and grander.

Hopkins Lane leads into the parallel King's Head Street – even residents must confuse it with nearby King's Quay Street. Like Church Street, it has its most alluring group of buildings in its last stretch towards the Quay. This begins with a three-storeyed, double-jettied house, probably 17th century but with Georgian windows. Further on is no. 16b, with a fine Georgian front, recently restored, and finally, near the Quay, no. 21, a two-gabled, plastered timber-framed house with a jetty and Georgian windows. Mr L. T. Weaver, in *The Harwich Story* (1975), suggests that this house was probably the childhood home, and possibly the birthplace, of Christopher Jones, who moved to Rotherhithe, London, in 1611 and was the master of the Mayflower in her voyage of 1620. There is a documentary reference of 1609–10 to 'Xtopher Jones of Harwich, mr of the Mayflower of the same place', and there are other local references to the Mayflower before her famous voyage. The house could have been built in its original form by the later 16th century. (See also p. 114 for a Mayflower connection at Billericay.)

(3) Dovercourt

Dovercourt was the older rural parish within which the medieval town of Harwich grew, and has a partly Norman church on the western outskirts of the present built-up area. In 1845 John Bagshaw, owner of the Harwich shipyard and later the local M.P., started to develop a seaside resort just west of the old town of Harwich. He conveniently discovered a spring with supposed medicinal properties, built a small pump room (which does not survive), and promoted a plan for grand terraces along and off the seafront. Of these only one was built – Orwell Terrace, overlooking the pleasant Cliff Park Gardens, a fine and not fully appreciated terrace in the latter-day Regency tradition, with a taller end part, which contained assembly rooms overlooking the sea. Bagshaw died bankrupt in 1870.

Dovercourt matured around 1890/1900, and the town centre has a late Victorian or Edwardian atmosphere, with turrets on corner buildings, shops and banks under elaborate rooflines, and a statue of Queen Victoria looking along the approach road to the beach.

Hatfield Broad Oak

Hatfield Broad Oak was once a market town; the *Victoria County History* of Essex states that in the 14th century 'the market place was crowded with shops and stalls, and many artisans plied their trade in neighbouring streets'. The market ceased by *c.* 1830, and it is now a village with the form of an old small town that has not grown significantly. Two wide streets form a T; High Street narrows and twists out of sight, but the other street, called Cage End, is open-ended; one looks down it straight into country. The buildings are typically varied – plastered, occasionally weatherboarded, a few in Georgian brick; some are altered medieval, notably the many-gabled Town Farm in Cage End which was the manorial farmstead. The church consists of the 14th-century nave and aisles of a once bigger priory church which otherwise disappeared after the Reformation; it had two towers like Wymondham Abbey, but only the tall 15th-century western tower survives. Inside there are a lifelike series of heads in the corbels of the arcades, and impressive Georgian woodwork in the chancel. Nearby Hatfield Forest is a fragment of the old forests of Essex, and was saved by a benefactor who bought it and gave it to the National Trust in 1924. It had a famous oak (called the Doodle Oak), recently shown to have been about 800 years old when it died c. 1859; this was probably the 'Broad Oak' used in the parish's name to distinguish it from other Hatfields. An offshoot of the oak grows in the forest.

Horndon-on-the-Hill

Horndon is one of the smallest recognizable places in south Essex not yet caught in suburban sprawl. Yet at one time it was among the most important places in the district. It had a mint by the tenth century and a market by the 13th, where wool from sheep grazed on the Thameside flatlands was sold. After Tudor times the pastures were largely turned to cattle – which went to Romford market or direct to London. The early 16th-century Wool Hall is a monument to the last period of Horndon's importance as a market town. Restored a few years ago, it has an open ground storey with wooden arches and a timber-framed upper room – a type of structure that used to be common in market towns but of which there are now few in eastern England – the much grander Guildhall at Thaxted, the small octagonal Market Cross at Wymondham and the stone Guildhall at Peterborough are among the others. Horndon has a pleasant short main street; Hill House of 1728 opposite the Wool Hall has decorative brick sills, and the Bell inn has a traditional courtyard.

The church has a weatherboarded belfry, supported inside on a superb medieval timber framework with intersecting diagonal braces – very much in the Essex tradition. From the village the land drops to the riverside flatlands, where sheep and cattle have been replaced by refineries, docks and sprawling housing.

Maldon

Maldon's site is fairly dramatic, on a hill above the place where the rivers Chelmer and Blackwater merge and widen into the Blackwater estuary. The name means cross on a hill – suggesting that it was an early Christian centre. But its first recorded mention is as a defensive site; the Saxon King Edward the Elder stationed his forces there in 913 during his campaign against the Vikings, and three years later constructed an earthen fort or *burh*. This withstood a siege, and in 917 Edward went on to capture Colchester, freeing Essex from Viking rule. Seventy-four years later the Vikings returned, sailed up the estuary and defeated the Saxons in a skirmish which was commemorated as the Battle of Maldon in a poem written at the time. By the time of Domesday, Maldon was a fairly important town. It flourished as a market and port, especially in the 18th century when local produce, together with flour and malt, went by barge down the Blackwater, mostly destined for London. In 1797 the Chelmer Navigation was opened from Chelmsford to the Blackwater, skirting the town at Heybridge on its northern side. Commerce and industry then developed in this direction, especially after a branch railway (now closed) was opened in 1846.

Before the canal was opened, the main quays were at The Hythe, east of the town proper – an area now popular for pleasure boating, where restored sailing barges are moored, looking picturesque against the marsh-bound waters of the estuary. The Hythe was almost a separate village; its church, St Mary's, is of Norman origin with a low 17th-century tower topped by a Georgian cupola. The long High Street begins unimpressively near here and climbs steadily, becoming busier and gaining character, to the town centre at the top. The climax is the busy junction where Market Hill leads off to the right. Here is a strange building, the Plume Library, attached to a medieval tower which belonged to St Peter's church, the rest of which was replaced in c. 1700 by the brick-built library, housing a collection of several thousand books which had been bequeathed to his native town by Dr Plume, a scholar and archdeacon. They are preserved in their original bookcases on the upper floor – an early prototype of a public library. Beyond is the busiest and best part of the High Street. The buildings are tall and predominantly classical; the street is fairly narrow and there is a strong urban feeling in the best sense. The main landmark is the Moot Hall with an iron-columned loggia projecting over the pavement. This was originally a three-storeyed tower-like house built by Sir Robert D'Arcy, a local magnate, about 1435 and bought by the town council in 1576 for conversion to a town hall and court. It was

Opposite **Holy Trinity, Maldon,** a church of many parts, some very fine. The 13th century tower is triangular, fitting into the site available. The shingled pinnacles are unusual.

57 *Above* **High Street, Maldon** has a strong urban character, centred on the Moot Hall. (Colour plate, page 140)

altered in 1810 when the loggia was built, with balcony above, from which the election of M.P.s was proclaimed – Maldon was an old-established parliamentary borough. Across the street is a fine succession of buildings; nos. 54–6 have two handsome storeys in chequered brick above a bank and shop; no. 52 keeps a good doorcase between shop fronts; no. 40–2 has a long façade with central Venetian window and columned ground storey.

The next focal point is where narrow Silver Street meets High Street beside All Saints, the chief church of the town. The 13th-century tower is *triangular*, crowned by a spire with three oddly pointed turrets at the corners. The south aisle with large, mostly restored, windows facing the street is the finest part of the church; inside it has elaborately carved blank arches between and beneath the windows, and an arcade with slender columns in Purbeck marble from Dorset. The south chapel was added by Sir Robert D'Arcy, builder of what is now the Moot Hall, though its east window is older and reset. Silver Street is short, twisty and picturesque; it passes the Georgian-fronted Blue Boar, always the chief inn of the town, with much older parts behind. Down an alley behind the church is the Old

Vicarage, a timber-framed house originally with a central hall; the gabled wings are 15th-century.

The island block of buildings between High Street, Silver Street and Princes Street is the site of the town's original market place, encroached on early. The block looks outwardly Georgian and later, but there is a tell-tale overhang on the High Street frontage indicating a basically timber-framed structure. There were once other buildings on what is now open street in front of All Saints, hemming the church in until they were removed in the 18th century. High Street twists westward and ends at a complex road junction. What might have been a formless space is given character by distinctive buildings in dominant places, such as no. 3 with flat bow windows and a rusticated doorway, and also a pair of houses on an opposite corner, one with a Georgian front between wings under mansard roofs,

Overleaf left **The Moot Hall, Maldon** has a patchwork history. Originally part of the town house of the local D'Arcy family, it became the town hall in 1576 and was altered in 1810 when the loggia was built, with balconies from which the election of the M.P.s could be proclaimed – Maldon was an ancient parliamentary borough.

58 *Above*   **The Hythe, Maldon,** on the Blackwater estuary, where many old barges, which sailed up the Thames and the eastern estuaries, have been preserved and moored. The weatherboarding, very common round here, is traditionally of softwood imported from northern Europe.

the other with sunflower patterns in semicircular recesses over the windows. It is the frequency of buildings with such individuality that makes a walk round central Maldon so worthwhile.

Market Hill is the street leading north from the Plume Library. It is flat at first, then plunges steeply past another succession of Georgian houses in a long, curving, descending row, crosses the Chelmer and enters a highly industrialized area. Some of the older buildings here are handsome, such as the Victorian

Previous page, top   **Almshouses, Thaxted,** behind the church. The early 19th century gabled range adjoins an earlier thatched row, with the windmill in the background.

Previous page, bottom   **Watling Street, Thaxted** curves up from the Guildhall to the church. Clarance House, 1715, in brilliant brick, is the one substantial 18th century house in the town. (**66**) (map IX)

factory, with two gables and big round-headed windows, on the left. Down a turning is the former station, converted to a restaurant and bar. It was built grandly because, it is said, the vice-chairman of the railway company was prospective parliamentary candidate for Maldon and wanted to impress the town; he was elected. It is like a Jacobean mansion with Flemish gables, tall chimneys, and long arched loggia – recalling the stations at Stowmarket and Needham Market. Half a mile beyond is the former village of Heybridge, overwhelmed by commerce and traffic but retaining a delightful church, in a well-planted oasis-like churchyard. It is basically Norman, with original contorted ironwork on the south door, and the stump of what would have been a very broad tower, which either collapsed or was never built higher.

The canal reaches the estuary over a mile to the east, at Heybridge Basin – an entirely separate village which grew round the basin and lock, now an attractive place with pleasure boats, public houses and views over water and marshland, with the roofs and steeples of Maldon rising from on the hilltop in the distance.

Wivenhoe, an old small port with a few bold bow-windowed Georgian houses fronting the quay.

Manningtree and Mistley

Manningtree and Mistley are two small ports at the head of the spacious Stour estuary. The first is an important junction – 'for Harwich and the Continent' as the station signs grandiloquently say. Manningtree seems to have been established as a town and port about 1240, and Mistley about five centuries later. In Georgian times they were outlets for local produce, much of it brought by barge down the Stour, navigable from Sudbury. Grain and flour went to London, and sometimes to the Continent; from London in return came chalk and manure for fertilizing, from Newcastle coal, from the Baltic timber for both shipbuilders and house builders. Malt, made locally, became important.

The part of Manningtree that matters most is mainly the long High Street, more Georgian than not, together with South Street leading from the quay uphill.

59 Mistley Towers. These fantastic towers, designed by Robert Adam, 1776, were added to a church, since demolished, by Richard Rigby, local landowner, who promoted Mistley successfully as a port.

Coming from the west, one of the first prominent buildings is the old Corn Exchange with its Ionic entrance, built in 1865 (just before the agricultural slump), now the museum. By the South Street intersection is an islanded Georgian house; beyond that High Street is first wide, then narrows further east – with a series of Georgian fronts on the right, mostly in deep red brick, many having simple white Doric doorcases. With their differing heights and scales they make a fine irregular rhythm. At the far end, the street bends sharply in front of a house with a handsome porch reached up steps. (A particularly unimpressive house on the south side, with almost the only gable in the street, stands on the site of the Anglican church, built as a chapelry in 1616, altered in the 19th century and demolished in 1965 as unsafe; the congregation has merged with that of Mistley.)

South Street is Georgian in a lower key; it climbs to a charming green fronted by houses mainly in buff brick, then twists and continues to the Methodist church of 1807 with a complex classical front crowned

with a domed turret; in its prominence it is a good substitute for the lost Anglican church.

It is a short walk along the waterfront, past a park, from Manningtree into Mistley. The first buildings in Mistley are the most extraordinary – two baroque towers, rising to rounded cupolas, set in a churchyard. They were added in 1776 to an earlier, plain, church (of 1735) by the architect Robert Adam, at the behest of Richard Rigby, landowner and entrepreneur. The main part of the church was demolished in 1870 when another was built elsewhere.

All Mistley is strange. The older village had been small and scattered; the present town was founded as a port by the elder Richard Rigby, who died in 1730, and promoted further by his son of the same name. The father made a fortune from the South Sea Bubble, which he was astute enough to retain; the son became, in 1768, Paymaster to His Majesty's Forces, a post which could be very remunerative; Norman Scarfe, in his *Shell Guide* to Essex, quotes a saying that he died 'leaving over half a million in public money'. He also intended to promote Mistley as a resort; Robert Adam drew plans for baths and other buildings, but these were never carried out. The Rigbys lived in Mistley Hall about a mile inland, long since demolished.

It is not always clear when the various parts of Georgian Mistley were built, and by which Rigby. The central square has an ornamental pool – an early feature, with a plaster swan in the middle. Behind, and backing on to the river, is a small classical building which contained the port offices. Facing this is the Thorn Hotel, and westwards a street of simple classical houses ends dramatically at the towers, seen at a sharp angle. Southward a short street opens on to a green, bordered by more simple houses. The quayside, where ships were built of Baltic timber in the Rigbys' days, is still busy, but its character is now very different. The malting trade steadily became dominant, as breweries in London and elsewhere increased their demand. In 1893 a consortium of maltsters formed a single company. Over the next twenty years enormous maltings and warehouses were built, of four to eight storeys; a long range faces the quay; others are on rising ground behind. Built mainly of dark red brick within a gridwork of buff brick, they are tremendously impressive and do not overwhelm the domestic scale of Georgian Mistley as much as they might, as they have basically classical proportions and stand to one side of the older town. One can leave Mistley by the charming railway station, built of red and buff brick like the maltings (though it is earlier), and travel on the line to Harwich – familiar to ferry travellers – which skirts the surprisingly wide Stour estuary, with views across to the monumental buildings of the Royal Hospital School (1933) at Holbrook on the other side.

Newport

Newport is an exceptionally attractive street village. The name means new market (or place of trade; a *port* in early medieval times was not necessarily maritime), and it was mentioned in Domesday Book. The market ceased when a new one was set up in Saffron Walden in 1141 but seems to have been re-established later; certainly the town (as it then was) prospered from the 15th to early 18th centuries. Coming from the south the first striking building is Monk's Barn – an inappropriate name, for it is a splendid 15th-century house of 'Wealden' type (with central part recessed between jettied wings, all under continuous eaves); it has an original oriel window with a carving of the Virgin and angels on the sill. The street continues handsomely for some way, then narrows and bends; here lanes lead off left to an intricate area with two small greens, one called Elephant Green (after a former public house). This area must have contained the original market place, infilled by encroachment. The church, to the west, has a fine tower with octagonal turrets; it was rebuilt in 1858, but has so much local character (the turrets recall Cambridgeshire village churches and it

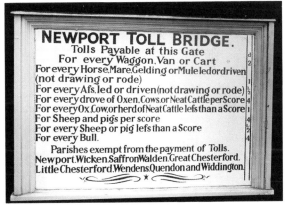

60 Notice of Tolls, Newport, indicating the nature of traffic a hundred and fifty years ago.

has an affinity with the tower at Great Dunmow) that it is difficult to believe that it was not a copy of a previous one. North of the openings to Elephant Green, the High Street descends impressively; the dominant building here is the former prison in Georgian buff brick, unaccountably large and handsome (presumably

61 Newport. This part of the old main street was cut off by the London to Cambridge railway from which these houses are landmarks.

it served a bigger area than Newport!). And this is not the end. The best part of Newport is to be found down a lane running off High Street beside the prison building, passing under a low railway bridge, and entering a stretch of street that was formerly part of High Street, but was cut off when the railway was formed in 1845. There is a long range of cottages, some weatherboarded, then two fine houses, one with a splendid rustic-classical facade of the 1690s with simple decorative pargetting and a shell-hooded door; the second is long and timber-framed with fine chimneys. These face the railway and are landmarks to travellers from Cambridge to London.

Rayleigh

A castle was built at Rayleigh soon after the Norman Conquest and was enlarged a few decades later. A huge earthen motte was thrown up on a natural promontory, and a flatter, lower area formed the outer bailey; a deep ditch surrounded the fortress. The castle was confiscated when its owner, Henry of Essex, was disgraced in *c.* 1165. After being used for a time as a royal stud, it was abandoned by about 1300. Massive earthworks remain but no buildings – the keep and most of the other structures were always of wood. The slopes are now tree-covered, with grassy spaces on the motte and elsewhere – the whole is well maintained in a half-wild state by its owner, the National Trust. Across the ditch, on the eastern side, is a splendidly restored windmill. Views from the motte are curtailed by trees, but would be largely over a sea of houses, for Rayleigh, a small town till the present century, is now part of the suburban sprawl based on Southend. There was already a market in 1227, and the town retains its attractive old shape, with a wide street narrowing and climbing to the church. Unfortunately most of the buildings along the now busy street are recent replacements, but some Georgian ones remain around the church – which is well placed on a bluff, with a tall tower, Tudor porch with decorative brickwork, and a pleasant overall texture of rough stonework and brick.

Rochford

Rochford is not the sort of town one expects to find in the hinterland of Southend, on the doorstep of an airport, and on one of the busiest commuter railways into London. It is an unspoiled country town, looking much as it must have done (though tidier) when it was the largest place in this corner of Essex, giving its name to Rochford Hundred. It is still the administrative centre of a wide area.

The town has a nice plan, with four streets meeting not quite regularly in the centre, and a roughly rectangular market place just to the west. This is set off by a big Georgian house and by a classical former Corn Exchange of 1866 by the Essex-based Frederick Chancellor, architect also of commercial buildings in London. West Street has restored weatherboarded cottages; there are others, slightly grander, in North Street. But the best street in Rochford is South Street, with what appears to be a nice succession of brick-fronted Georgian houses with doorcases on the east side; in fact part is neo-Georgian, thanks to careful recent rebuilding by the local council for its offices. Adjoining these is the Old House, very sensitively repaired and converted for council use with guidance from historic building experts. They revealed that the core of the structure is a 13th-century timber-framed hall, to which a northern wing was added soon after, and a south wing in the 14th-century. In the 16th century a brick chimneypiece, with Gothic decoration, was built to replace the open hearth, and in the 17th the hall was divided by an intermediate floor – as happened with almost all remaining open halls at about this time. Externally the house looks as it did after Georgian and Victorian alterations. Rochford church is west of the railway; it has a tall Tudor brick tower and walls in a medley of materials.

Romford

Romford is a historic town because of its market, founded in 1247 and now one of the biggest open markets in England. For long it was famous for cattle and corn. Now hundreds of stalls fill, on several days each week, the long market place, originally a widening of the highway but now sealed off from traffic. It serves the huge suburban areas which have enveloped Romford, but its vibrant atmosphere is like that of a market in a major country town. Romford is not notable for buildings and never was. The church, on the north side of the market place, was rebuilt in 1850 in rough Kentish ragstone with a spire; parts of the frontage of Ind Coope's brewery are of about the same date. In contrast is Havering-atte-Bower, two miles to the north, on the edge of the Green Belt and still a village. From the 11th to the 17th century there was a royal palace on the western side of the huge green; the Victorian church of flint and stone, by Basil Champneys, stands on the site of the chapel at the palace gate. The green might have become a market place if Havering had been on a main road, but the market was set up at Romford instead because of its position on the highway. The village stocks are preserved (though not used), and eastward there is a huge view over still green country with two Georgian houses; one, Bower House, by Flitcroft (1729), the other a curiosity – the Round House (actually elliptical), built in the 1790s. From 1465 till 1892 the area formed the Liberty of Havering, almost with the status of a sub-county, with its centre at Romford. When a new London borough was formed in 1965, covering an area larger than the old Liberty, it took the name Havering.

Saffron Walden

Even in East Anglia there are few towns with so much for the eye to enjoy as Saffron Walden. It is a busy place, the shopping centre of an affluent area – and first impressions can be disappointing if expectations are, rightly, high. The town sprawls a little to the south; the southern part of the main street, though handsome, is bitty in places; the main west–east traffic route, Hill Street, has little distinction. More even than most towns it should be explored entirely on foot. The narrow streets in the heart of the town provide a feast for those who like whole ranges of medieval to Jacobean timber-framed houses, variedly seasoned with Georgian and Victorian modifications or occasional rebuildings.

Walden means 'valley of the Welsh', or Celts, so named by the first Saxon settlers. After the Norman Conquest the manor was held by Geoffrey de Mandeville, earl of Essex and constable of the Tower of London, the first of a dynasty of powerful and ruthless barons who held many manors in Essex. His grandson, also Geoffrey, may have built the original castle in *c.*1140; he was involved in the civil wars of the time, frequently changing sides. In the 13th century, castle and town passed to the Bohuns, who had widespread estates across England and Wales. The castle lost its significance and fell into decay. But the town prospered.

Walden grew first along the ridge west of the castle, where the present church is. The original market, which was established by Geoffrey de Mandeville in 1141, may have been held to the west of the church. The

62 *Below*
Market Hill, Saffron Walden,
a street leading off the Market
Place, showing a typical
mixture of altered timber-
framed buildings and later brick
and stuccoed ones – though the
balcony over the shop is exotic
to Walden.

63 *Opposite*
**Myddelton Place, Saffron
Walden.** A 15th century
merchant's house, with carved
post and bracket on the jettied
corner, became a malting in the
18th century, hence the gantry.
Now it is a Youth Hostel.

Bohuns promoted the town further, granting it a charter, and encouraging
it to grow. They probably laid out a new large market place in the 13th
century, including the present small market square but also extending
southwards to the present Hill Street. The blocks of buildings called the
Rows represent encroachments on to a once larger space.

Walden had a share in the weaving industry, but its fame and prosperity
derived mainly from the saffron crocus, a small plant with a purple flower
which produced a deep yellow substance, valued as a flavouring, a medicine
and, especially, a dye. The plant had been introduced into Britain by the
Romans and grew wild in places after they left. (The Saxon place name which
became Croydon means 'valley of the saffron crocus'.) But its cultivation did
not begin again in England until the 14th century, and it is first recorded at
Walden in the 15th. The soil was specially suitable, and for about two
centuries the surrounding fields were intensively cultivated with this difficult
but very profitable crop. The name of the crop was added to that of the

64 The Old Sun Inn and the Wisbech Giant, Saffron Walden. This is an extraordinary amalgam of buildings, 14–15th centuries, plastered and pargetted in the 17th. The near gable depicts the legend of Tom Hickathrift, a carter who slew a giant, who had terrorized the Wisbech area, with the axle of his cart. Possibly carters from Wisbech lodged at the inn on their way to London, explaining why a Fenland legend should be depicted here.

town, and survived the local demise of the crop in the 18th century. By then the town's chief product was malt, made from local barley, mainly in small kilns, often behind the buildings which fronted the streets. Because there was no water transport, the malt industry did not develop in Saffron Walden as it did in Manningtree and Mistley, Ware, or nearby Bishop's Stortford, so there are no big Victorian maltings as there are in those towns.

The malting trade, and associated brewing, first brought fortune to the Gibsons, a Quaker family which, in its many ramifications, dominated the town in the 19th century. They founded a local bank in 1824 which became their chief business; eventually it became part of Barclays. Members of the Gibson family, at different times, helped to establish the local Natural History Society and Literary and Scientific Society; endowed schools, a

hospital and almshouses; founded a teachers' training college (fairly recently closed); and gave land for the Friends' School – still flourishing – when it moved from Croydon in 1879. They also left their mark on the Market Place. On one side is Barclays, formerly Gibson's, Bank of 1874, designed by Eden Nesfield with Jacobean-style windows and imposing entrance; on another is the Town Hall, with a Tudor-style gabled projection, added at the expense of a Gibson in 1876 to a much more reticent Georgian building. On the west side of the market place is the former Corn Exchange built in 1848 (*not* this time through the Gibsons) in a rumbustious classical style by William Tress, known as the architect of railway stations in the south of England (such as Battle). As at Sudbury, it has been converted into a library and meeting-place. Looking north-westwards across the market place there is a splendid view (best seen when the stalls are there, on Tuesdays and Saturdays), with the church spire soaring in the background.

South of the Market Place is the fascinating area known as the Rows, threaded by alleys between blocks of buildings with names like Mercers' Row and Butcher Row. They are successors to rows of market stalls which were allowed to become permanent and, with their small shops and other businesses, are now one of the most vital parts of the town. Other towns in East Anglia where comparable infilling has taken place are Diss and Holt in Norfolk, Bury St Edmunds in Suffolk, Braintree and many more.

On the corner of King Street and Cross Street is a very interesting group. Nos. 17–21 King Street were together a 15th-century hall house with gabled wings. As happened in so many other similar houses, the central hall was subdivided with a new floor in the 17th century, and it now has a Georgian-looking front. Each of the wings retains its medieval bargeboard, of the type so often imitated by the Victorians. The eastern wing always contained a shop in the ground floor, as is revealed round the corner in Cross Street. Here is a range of five arched openings, partly original though restored, four of which were 15th-century shop windows (the fifth was a door). At first they were unglazed and closed by shutters; now they have plate glass, while continuing their original function. Equally surprising is a range of similar but now blocked arches opposite; these too were shop windows.

Back to the Market Place; Market Hill provides an inviting exit from its north-west corner, passing more altered timber-framed houses. Round the corner in Church Street is the most spectacular sight in Saffron Walden apart from the church, a range of medieval buildings which were altered in the 17th century to form the Sun Inn – by which name they are still known, although the inn has long since closed; the range is now owned by the National Trust, under separate tenancies. Going along Church Street there are at first two wings with gables over jettied upper storeys, which date from the 17th century. Then there is a lower section, originally a hall and including a porch, then another gabled wing with a boldly projecting upper storey. This wing and the hall formed most of a 14th-century house of which the hall was, as elsewhere, subdivided in the 17th century. But the two-storeyed porch with its own small gable is an original feature. Further along the street is another former hall house, this time dating from the 15th century, with gabled wings on either side. The whole range, including the 14th- and

15th-century houses, was amalgamated in the 17th century and externally plastered and pargetted, providing the most spectacular surviving example of this traditional craft except for the Ancient House in Ipswich. There are representations in bold relief of flowers, birds, a dog, a date 1676 (presumably authentic), a stocking and, most remarkably, a depiction of Tom Hickathrift, a legendary Fenland carrier of prodigious strength who is said to have slain a giant, the terror of Wisbech, with the axle of his cart. The two figures stand out with a wheel in between, the giant brandishing his club, over the entrance to a yard into which waggons were probably driven. It is difficult to explain why a legend current in Wisbech should be depicted in Saffron Walden, many miles away. Possibly Walden was on a waggon route from Wisbech to London, and carters stayed at the inn.

A path leads from Church Street to the church – a building which seems to dominate the town in distant views, but which is intriguingly hidden behind small buildings at close quarters. The spire was built in 1832 to the design of Thomas Rickman, then working on the extension to St John's College, Cambridge; the lower part of the tower is older. One enters the church through the west door, so that the magnificence of the nave is immediately apparent. The body of the church was rebuilt c. 1470–1520; the master masons were Simon Clarke and John Wastell who were successively in charge of the building of King's chapel in Cambridge; Wastell, one of the greatest architects of the late Middle Ages, also designed the central tower at Canterbury and, probably, the nave of the present cathedral at Bury St Edmunds. The arcades – of stone from Northamptonshire which must have been hauled by road from the nearest quays at Cambridge – are lofty and have decorative treatment in the spandrels like those at Great St Mary's in Cambridge and at Lavenham. The clerestory is a glazed lantern which, of course, would have been filled with brilliant stained glass in the Middle Ages. The chancel is partly older and, like the rest of the church, was restored by Butterfield in Victorian times.

It is worth going to the site of the castle – not because the weatherworn flinty fragment that survives is impressive but because of the adjoining museum, founded as early as 1833 (one of the first in a small town anywhere) and excellent of its kind. Castle Street, north of castle and church, another of Walden's innumerable attractive streets, has a grassy bank on one side (probably connected, in some undetermined way, with the defences of the early town), and a long row of small houses on the other, dating variously from the 15th century to the 19th. At least two former 'Wealden' houses can be detected, with central inset portions, originally open halls, between jettied wings, all with continuous eaves. Such houses were specially characteristic of Kent and Sussex, hence the name, but are found elsewhere – as here.

If one can find the right narrow entrance (it is signposted) on the north side of Castle Street, one can walk into Bridge Street Gardens, a delightful largely formal garden, created in Victorian times by one of the Gibsons. There is an exit from it into Bridge Street, the northernmost street in the town and one of the most interesting. It begins, on the corner of Myddelton Place, with what is now the Youth Hostel, a well-restored 15th-century house with carved beams and brackets, some original mullioned windows, and an attractive former gantry added in the 18th century when it was used partly as a malting. Further north, on the corner of Freshwell Street (a charming street) is a house with a tall Georgian exterior, which reveals a brick Tudor chimney at its northern end. The Eight Bells opposite has an early 17th-century front with leaded casement windows. Further, on opposite sides of the street, are ranges of timber-framed buildings, each of which contains 15th-century 'Wealden' houses, variedly and, in most cases, attractively altered. Beyond these the town suddenly ends as it did in the Middle Ages; there has been no sprawl in this direction.

If one has followed this irregular but intensive itinerary one will have passed a collection of small to medium-sized timber-framed houses, variously modified and adapted, that has few parallels in England, as well as grander or later buildings. There is a great deal else to see in the town, though it is less concentrated. The long High Street, which begins at its north end as a continuation of Bridge Street, passes buildings of different dates mostly put to commercial uses, and ends as a wide and dignified street with some fine late Georgian and Victorian fronts – the part of the town centre which most people see first when approaching from the south, but not the most characteristic part. Parallel to the southern end of High Street is Gold Street, with Georgian and a few earlier fronts, framing a view of the church splendidly placed on its low ridge further to the north. On the outskirts is Audley End, on the site of Walden Abbey, founded by the Mandevilles.

Southend

Southend is not everybody's idea of a historic town. But it has the best 'Regency' seaside architecture on the eastern coasts. There was just a hamlet – the south end of Prittlewell – for most of the 18th century; the home of oystermen. A few visitors came for bathing after the middle of the century, but the resort really began in 1791, with the start of the present Royal Terrace, on the cliff to the west of the old hamlet. The Grand, later Royal hotel, at the end of the terrace, was opened in 1795; it contained the assembly room, centre of the new resort's social life. Princess Caroline, wife of the Prince of Wales, later Regent, stayed in the terrace for six weeks in 1804 – hence the title Royal for terrace and hotel. Both survive, though not long ago they looked very dilapidated. Now they are well conserved, thanks to the efforts of the Southend Society, founded in 1973, which persuaded the council to initiate the conservation scheme. The terrace has three-storeyed houses, partly of brick, partly stuccoed, given special charm by their balconies, continuous along the first floors but all different in detail; each has three arches in elaborate ironwork, or woodwork, supporting a verandah roof. It is doubtful if there is a

more impressive range of Regency balconies in England. They face the shallows and mudflats of the Thames estuary, but the cliffside in front was landscaped when the terrace was built, and elaborated in the 1820s as the Shrubbery, still maintained as a piece of sylvan landscape.

Southend did not develop much more for several decades. Growth came with the opening of the railway in 1856. The railway proprietors, including Sir Morton Peto, an engineering magnate who built railways all over the world and lived near Lowestoft, developed land adjoining the station from 1859 as an early example of a long-distance commuter suburb. The centrepiece, Prittlewell Square, faces the clifftop to the west of Royal Terrace. From it two roads lead diagonally into Cambridge Road, which runs parallel with the coast. Along these are 1860s houses of distinct charm, many with iron balconies over ground-floor bay windows. The nearby clifftop is a grassy promenade, splendidly maintained (Southend council has a deserved reputation for municipal gardening and park keeping), with the cliff sides kept half-wild as an extension to the original Shrubbery. A pert statue of Queen

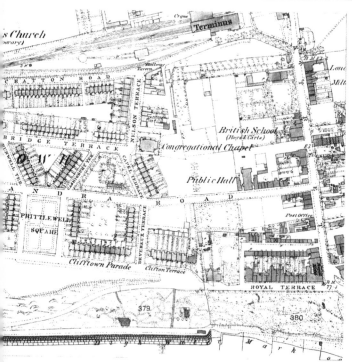

Map VIII, Southend in 1873. Seaside Southend began with the Royal Terrace in the 1790s, at the south-east corner of the map. After the railway came in 1856, the area round Prittlewell Square was laid out geometrically as an early commuter estate. The area largely survives as the historic core of a huge modern town.

The area described is only the old core of a huge sprawling resort and residential town, most of which was built in the early 20th century. It extends over several old parishes with their medieval churches and occasional historic houses. Little is left of the original village of Prittlewell except the church (the mother church of Southend), with a very fine tower of Kentish ragstone which, with its tall pinnacles, resembles those of Tenterden and Ashford in Kent, as well as Stoke-by-Nayland in Suffolk – the affinity with the last is not surprising since Stoke church was under the patronage of Prittlewell Priory, of which two well-preserved buildings remain in a park about half a mile from Prittlewell church. Of the other medieval churches in modern Southend the best is at Eastwood, almost at the end of the airport runway; this has a perky weather-boarded belfry and spire, characteristic of Essex, and *two* doors with exceptional 13th-century ironwork, one still the main door, the other unhinged, inside the church. Finally there is Southchurch Hall, a restored 14th-century hall house, now a museum, standing in a re-created moat within a well-maintained park.

Victoria and a war memorial by Lutyens provide landmarks, though the superbly ornate bandstand, illustrated in Essex Record Office's publication *Southend Past* was swept away in 1956.

Thaxted

Thaxted is more nearly medieval than almost any other town in East Anglia, except perhaps Lavenham. Its old street pattern is intact; its fabric is still substantially as it was in Tudor times, though much of it is outwardly – and nicely – Georgianized, and, above all, it is dominated by one of the grandest parish churches in England. In its heyday it was a centre of the cutlery trade, which seems to have begun in the 13th century, prospered in the 14th and was in decline in the late 15th; from then there was some weaving. There is no rational explanation for cutlery at Thaxted; iron ore would have had to have been brought from afar, and there was no navigable river anywhere near. Even if, as has been suggested, the local cutlers only added handles, sheaths and decorative work to knives and blades wrought elsewhere and brought here, these too would have been heavy to carry. But records indicate incontrovertibly that there were cutlers in Thaxted.

Any approach to Thaxted is bound to be dramatic, but the best is from the south. The town begins mod-estly with the narrow street called Mill End, which suddenly widens into Town Street – which on the map looks like the trunk of a tree with curving branches at the top. On the ground, the street is lined with varied, mainly plastered, houses, and broadens a little before branching. At the fork is the Guildhall, the focal feature of the town, built about 1400, with open-arched ground storey and two jettied storeys above, and a double-pitched roof which originally ended in gables. It was modified in 1714 when the gables were replaced by hips, and misguidedly restored in 1910 when the plaster applied in 1714 was stripped, the timbering on the first floor given an arched pattern which it did not previously have, and much else was done with good intentions. Thorough repair in 1975 was far more sensitive. This was the town's civic building, with marketing on the ground storey, and court and meeting rooms above. Almost certainly it was not built by a cutlers' guild as is often said; it seems that no such guild existed.

In Town Street there are two or three houses to note. The Recorder's House, a restaurant, is late 15th-century, double-jettied and now plastered. The plain house next door was the home of Gustav Holst from 1917 to 1925 where he composed much of his work – his resonant hymn tune for *I vow to thee my country . . . the service of my love* is called Thaxted. (Holst was English by birth and parentage, despite his name.) A

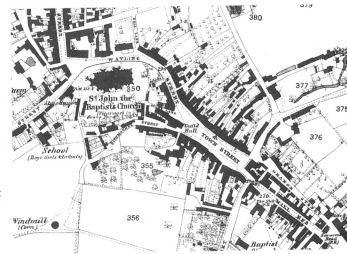

Map IX, Thaxted. Very much a late medieval plan, with the broad Town Street branching at the Guildhall (**67**) into three narrow streets where the market place, which originally came up to the churchyard, has been encroached on. To the south-east another wide space has been split into two narrow streets by an encroaching block. Note the garden plots behind the houses fronting the streets. The map is of 1878.

65 *Below* **Thaxted**, looking towards Clarance House (**66**), with the porch of the church on the right.

little further on, the house called Market Cross, facing the Guildhall, has a Georgianized jettied frontage but behind, quite unseen from the street, is a 14th-century hall. East of the Guildhall, the house called the Priory has a neo-Georgian front of 1938, but behind are a fine 15th-century roof and other features.

Three narrow thoroughfares branch beside the Guildhall and climb towards the church. Watling Street is the main one, curving first to the right and then sharply to the left. Stony Lane, narrow and cobbled, leads more directly up. Facing it is a range of three-storeyed timber-framed houses, the backs of which, even more romantically irregular, are seen from Fishmarket, the third of the hillside thoroughfares. Fishmarket curves and divides, and reaches an intricate area south of the church where there are groups of cottages, a windmill – open at times as a museum – and two ranges of almshouses, one gabled and barge-boarded, the other thatched (see colour illus. p. 141). Because of the dramatic contrast between the humble buildings in the foreground and the church, this is one of the most effective ways of approaching the latter.

Thaxted church is of two main periods, mid 14th century and c. 1510, with important parts built or altered intermediately. The most astonishing part, for Essex, is the tower and spire, originally built about 1485. It recalls Northamptonshire with its big double belfry lights, the flying buttresses at the base of the spire, and also the spire itself. The stone for the original spire, and indeed for the rest of the church, must have been brought overland from the quays at Cambridge – as remarkable as a long haul as that of iron or cutlery. (In fact the spire is a creditable rebuilding – after the original one was struck by lightning in 1814.) Inside the church is huge and spacious; the oldest parts are the finely moulded nave arcades of about 1340. About 1510 there was a major reconstruction, with new roof and clerestory to the nave, and new chancel aisles and arcades to a strangely rectilinear late Gothic pattern. Under the remarkable Reverend Conrad Noël, high churchman, Christian socialist, and vicar from 1910 to 1942, the interior was transformed. With few furnishings except in the chancel, whitewashed walls and stonework, and predominantly clear glass windows this is, paradoxically, a very Puritan interior. In the Middle Ages it would have been more ornate and more subdivided by screens; light would have been diffused through stained-glass windows. Colin Platt wrote in his *The Traveller's Guide to Medieval England*, 'This is

a church to linger in and savour … for the completely satisfying harmony of the whole. Its light and bareness are … Protestant … they have a Lutheran quality.' Yet it also has an atmosphere of Anglican high-church devotion.

North of the church is a meeting of streets, all pleasant, especially the long Newbiggin Street leading

66 *Left* **Clarance House, Thaxted**, 1715, an exceptional classical house of brick, in a largely timber-framed town.

67 Thaxted. The Guildhall, built *c*.1400, originally had two gables where there are now hips. Stony Lane, authentically cobbled, leads to the superb church. The spire, originally built *c*.1485, is the only old one of stone for miles. (Map IX)

northwards. One can return to the centre of the town down curving Watling Street, past the town's one 18th-century gem, the red brick Clarance House of 1715 (see colour illus. p. 141). Thaxted declined in Georgian times; in the Victorian period it lost population. Recently it defended itself, as strongly as it could, against threats of noise and pressures for development resulting from the all-too-close Stansted airport.

Waltham Abbey

Waltham is very surprising – only twelve miles from the centre of London, yet looking like an old market town, almost as if it were in the depths of East Anglia. It used to be called Waltham Holy Cross; this name and the town's fame arose from a particularly intricate legend. Two crucifixes were discovered in the place now called Montacute, in Somerset, in the early eleventh century. One was kept in the church there, the other (to simplify a little) was put into a cart harnessed to a team of oxen which would haul it, under divine guidance, to a specific place as soon as it were correctly named. Several places were mentioned without the oxen moving until 'Waltham' was uttered – a place where, as it happened, Tovi the lord of Montacute also possessed land. The cart proceeded, and after a long journey on which several miracles took place, it arrived at Waltham. Tovi built a church to contain the crucifix, which became an object of pilgrimage. One such pilgrim was Earl (later King) Harold who is said to have been miraculously cured of paralysis there; in 1060 he refounded the church on a grand scale with a college of priests. In 1066 his body was brought back from the battlefield at Hastings by his friend Edith Swan-neck (so the story continues) for burial at Waltham. At the time of Domesday the manor of Waltham was held by the bishopric of Durham; later it was in the possession of Henry I's queen Matilda, a great patron of churches. In 1177 Henry II, supposedly as part of his penance after the murder of Becket, replaced Harold's collegiate foundation by an Augustinian monastery. The eastern part of the older church was pulled down and a magnificent new abbey church built, the nave of the older church being retained, much as it stands today, as the parish church of the town.

At the Reformation, Henry VIII first intended to refound Waltham Abbey as a cathedral, as he did with the abbey churches at Peterborough and Gloucester. Unfortunately this did not happen, and the main part

68 **Waltham Abbey** remains a country town in feeling, on the outskirts of London. The post-Reformation tower, with top rebuilt later, was added to the preserved western part, superb internally, of the abbey otherwise destroyed after its dissolution.

of the church – which was as grand as Peterborough, Ely and the lost abbey church at Bury St Edmunds – was demolished, leaving only the older nave to continue as the parish church. Although far smaller than the main monastic church was, it is magnificent internally – but outside it shows the effects of vicissitudes. The monastic tower, east of the present church, was at first kept but collapsed in 1552, to be replaced by the present west tower – itself twice rebuilt in its upper part, the last time in 1905. The first impression of the building inside is unforgettable. Six Norman arches on either side, with alternate piers scored with diagonal patterns, make a magnificent composition which resembles that of Durham Cathedral on a smaller scale – and Durham had an interest in Waltham; so did Queen Matilda, who was associated with Dunfermline Abbey in Scotland, which also has piers resembling those in Waltham. There is no documentary evidence as to when the present church was built; clearly it is not Harold's church; equally clearly it was built before the refoundation as an abbey. Architectural style suggests a date *c.* 1100–20. From the 16th century there was just a blank wall at the east end, blocking the Norman arch which opened into the monastic church. In 1859–60 this was replaced by a Gothic east end designed by William Burges (architect for the remodelling of Cardiff Castle), containing exquisite stained glass by Edward Burne-Jones – one of his earliest and finest works. This Victorian east end matches the Norman nave in power and effect without overwhelming it, and

helps to make the whole unforgettable. In delicate contrast is the restored 14th-century south chapel, reached up steps.

The site of the rest of the abbey is a series of grassy spaces, with a few fragments of buildings, including part of the gatehouse and a bridge over a stream. Beyond is open country. A nicely curving street, with timber-framed houses, leads into the market place, which is best seen on Tuesdays and Saturdays (market days). The narrow Sun Street, now pedestrian, leads to the excellent museum in a partly 15th-century house.

Waltham Abbey is on the east side of the River Lea, which forms the boundary between Essex and Hertfordshire. The river is also, along this stretch, the barrier between countryside and country town on one side, and, on the other, suburbia, which extends up the Lea valley much further on the Hertfordshire side than on the Essex side, following the main roads and railway. If one crosses the river (which in fact has two or three interconnecting courses), one comes into dense suburbia at Waltham Cross – a place which takes its name not from the *Holy* Cross, already mentioned, but from the *Eleanor* Cross, one of the three roadside monuments that survive from the twelve set up along the route taken by the body of Queen Eleanor, wife of Edward I, on its journey from Nottinghamshire, where she died, to London. The Waltham Cross was in fact nearly all renewed in the 19th century, but the renewal was authentic – as can be seen by comparing old drawings – and part of the base is still original. Like the two other surviving Eleanor Crosses in Northamptonshire, it is an exquisite piece of Gothic design, and some people are stimulated by its utter incongruity in a redeveloped shopping centre.

Witham

Witham has two historic centres and a complicated history. First there was an earthen Iron Age fort. In 913 King Edward the Elder, campaigning against the Vikings, turned it again into a fortress – a *burh*. The Saxon village of Witham (pronounced Wittum) developed not within the *burh*, but outside it to the north-west. This original village is now called Chipping Hill because of the market once held there. Later the manor came into the hands of the Knights Templars – they built the superb barns at Temple Cressing two miles away. In about 1212 they founded a new town, originally called Wulvesford, about half a mile south-east of Chipping Hill, on the Roman road to Colchester and beyond, then growing in importance as a traffic route. This consisted of a single street – the present Newland Street – with sixty plots, mostly about eighteen feet wide and a hundred feet deep; these are typical sizes for medieval 'burgage plots'. The new town prospered and assumed the older name Witham; in Georgian times it flourished as a coaching stage. In 1843 the railway passed between Newland Street and Chipping Hill (though nearer to the latter) with a station on the site of the Saxon *burh*. Building soon linked the two parts, but Witham has grown fairly big only since the Second World War, partly through planned expansion, rehousing Londoners in new estates, with industries on the outskirts.

The dual origin of the town is still evident. Newland Street is now the main shopping street, but manages to retain some of its Georgian and older character. More remarkable is Chipping Hill which, enveloped now between the railway and spreading housing estates, survives as an enclave – looking like an unspoiled village. What had been the early market place is now

69 **Chipping Hill, Witham** was the original market place, until a new market was set up at Newland Street less than a mile away *c*. 1212. Now it looks like a village green, though well within the town. An altered medieval house, originally with central hall and gabled wings, stands in front of the 14th century church.

an irregular village green, with varied old houses, some timber-framed and plastered, most notably a former farmhouse at the top of the green, with the tower of Witham parish church beside it. The church is almost all 14th-century. Chipping Hill has survived through being a Conservation Area; many of the old houses have been sensitively restored, often with the encouragement of the local authorities.

Wivenhoe

Wivenhoe is an outport of Colchester, on the estuary of the Colne, but in Georgian times it had its own economy. As A. F. J. Brown points out in his *Essex at Work* there was a busy coastal trade, sending corn and other local produce to London and importing coal from the Tyne. Oysters were a speciality. Many of the vessels using the port were built in local yards, and pleasure-boat building developed in the 19th century. There was even a bath house which, with accompanying entertainments, attracted some visitors, but this was closed by 1800. Today it is a tight-knit town, the old part crammed between quay and railway, riverside yards and open marshland; there is a fascinating network of narrow streets and lanes, centred on the

church – itself a dull Victorian building, but with a Tudor tower capped by a nice cupola which is a crowning feature of Wivenhoe when viewed from across the estuary. Next to the church is a house with a remarkable 17th-century pargetted facade, showing typical Jacobean scrollwork against a geometrical background. The stretch of open quayside is short and busy; many of the buildings overlooking it have bold, almost semi-circular, Georgian bow windows. Wivenhoe now straggles a long way along its approach road–the only way in which it could have grown–but there is still a fine stretch of country between it and Colchester, pierced by the Corbusian towers of the University of Essex. (See colour illus. p. 143)

Cambridgeshire

Cambridge

70 The Round Church, Cambridge, one of four in the country. Although the top part is restoration of the 1840s, the lower part is, inside and out, fine Norman work, c.1130, preceding the beginnings of the university by a century.

Cambridge, like Oxford, was an important place long before the university developed – indeed its history goes back further than that of Oxford. There was a Roman town called *Durolipons* (not *Camboritum* as used to be thought) above the left (west) bank of the River Cam. It was well placed beside the lowest practicable crossing of the river before it flowed into the fen country. That the Romans built a bridge is indicated by the ending *-pons* to the Latin name. There was a bridge again by 875 when *Grantebrycg* is recorded – Granta was the original name of the river, still sometimes used. (The 'Gr' in the town's name was changed to 'C' by the 12th century, and the form *Cambrugge* occurs in the 14th, but Cam did not replace Granta as the usual name of the river until the 17th.)

The late Saxon town, which had a market and mint, was mainly centred on the Roman site, but also spread across the river into the area of the present city centre. By the 12th century the main part of Cambridge was, as now, on the right bank, although there was an important medieval castle (of which nothing survives except a mound) on the Roman site.

Medieval Cambridge throve on river trade, along the Cam and Ouse to the Wash. Merchandise was carried by water to and from the port of (King's) Lynn, especially in connection with the annual Sturbridge Fair, held on the town's eastern outskirts, which from the 14th century was one of the greatest trade marts of northern Europe, overshadowing the once more important fair at St Ives (page 193).

Young scholars settled in Cambridge from the early 13th century. Some had migrated from Oxford, which became a centre of learning slightly earlier. Teaching – which was at first given by clerks in holy orders – came to be organized on an increasingly formal basis. The university became a corporate body, awarding degrees and establishing its status in relation to the often hostile town authorities. At first the students lodged and were

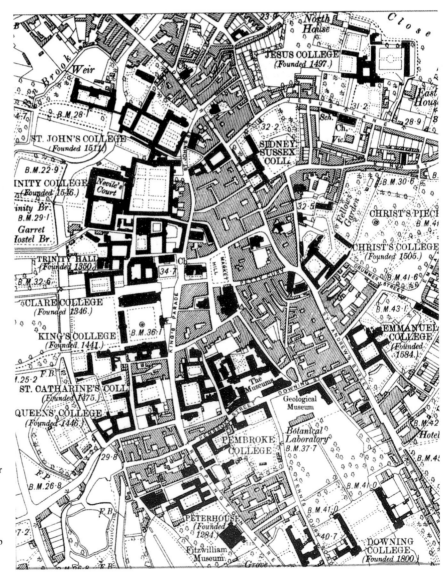

Map X, Cambridge. This map of 1901 shows the concentration of old colleges, with their courtyards of different sizes, between the river and the winding main street of the town, with the fairly small market place to the east and outlying colleges beyond. The bridge which gave the city its name, often rebuilt, is at the top of the map, and the original Roman site is further north.

taught in rented rooms, inns and hostels; some of the last became exclusively academic, presided over by masters – providing prototypes for formally constituted colleges.

The first college with a formal constitution was Peterhouse, founded by the bishop of Ely in 1280, initially for a master and six fellows (post-graduate academics); the undergraduates they taught continued to live in hostels, inns or other private accommodation. The next two colleges to be founded were Michaelhouse in 1324 and King's Hall in 1337 – both now superseded by Trinity College. Michaelhouse was for Benedictine monks (and so did not survive the Reformation), but King's Hall was the first college to house students as well as fellows – so setting the present pattern. Gradually, as more colleges were founded, with increasingly substantial buildings, the college system peculiar to Oxford and Cambridge evolved. By Tudor times every undergraduate had to belong to a college, even if he did not live in. From then to the present day varying proportions of undergraduates have lived in their colleges; others lodge outside, though obliged to maintain their connection, particularly by dining in hall. Until about a hundred years ago nearly all teaching was done in colleges, and the University was little more than a degree-granting and regulatory body. Only since the late 19th century, with the development of sciences and other specialized subjects, have the University and its faculties provided centralized teaching outside the colleges.

Medieval Cambridge was an informally planned town – more so than Oxford, which has a greater regularity in its street pattern. The colleges were founded and sited piecemeal. Many were built on the sites of houses, gardens or riverside yards bought by the founders and cleared; others took over older establishments. As most of the earlier colleges were built alongside or near the river, the town underwent a drastic transformation. Originally much of it had been oriented towards the waterside, where were numerous quays and wharfs. As these gave way gradually to college sites the river trade was concentrated further downstream, especially around the main bridge, and the town itself became more strongly focused on the central market place. True, colleges were founded on the eastern fringes of the town as well, but they did not form a continuous collegiate area like that which developed along the riverside from Queens' to St John's.

The typical college always has at least one courtyard or quadrangle (always called a *court* in Cambridge). The hall is always a prominent feature – just like the typical hall of a large medieval house, it has the high table at one end and the service rooms beyond the other end, with the screens passage (normally a through passageway) between the hall itself and the service rooms. The chapel and library may form parts of the buildings surrounding a court, otherwise these generally contain fellows' or undergraduates' rooms. Gatehouses are a Cambridge speciality; some late medieval and Tudor examples are particularly grand. Most colleges added further courts as they grew, though many have outlying buildings which are not related to any enclosed courtyard. Somewhere there is the residence of the head of the college, usually called the Master's Lodge, and most colleges maintain Fellows' Gardens for their senior members. The extent of college sites

Opposite
Queens' College, Cambridge. The Great Gate, *c*.1450, is the earliest of the type which became characteristic of Cambridge, the apparent defensive character being symbolic rather than of real necessity. Brick was used early in Cambridge because of the absence of fine stone quarries nearby.

varies enormously; some of the original sites are now densely built up; others are still park-like, while colleges bordering the river have their grassy, tree-shaded waterside spaces which collectively form the famous Backs.

Cambridge had no natural building materials close at hand except timber and clunch, a fairly hard variety of chalk, which does not last well when exposed; it was used for many of the first colleges. Brick came to be used very early; it was a normal local material in the 15th century. But one of the glories of Cambridge is the prominence of fine limestones – usually from Northamptonshire or neighbouring counties, brought along Fenland waterways. They vary in colour from buff to deep brown, often with reddish tints. White Portland stone was sometimes used in the 18th century. The older buildings of Cambridge show an enormous variety of colours and textures – in contrast to Oxford, where there were nearer supplies of stone and a greater consistency of materials.

Up to Georgian times most college buildings were modest to moderate in scale. King's chapel was the big exception, followed in the classical period by Wren's library at Trinity and Gibbs' building at King's. The great expansion of the 19th century resulted in many more buildings of large scale, as well as an even wider range of building materials and – as everywhere – a huge variety of styles. Some of the 19th-century architects produced works which are both prominent and congruent with Cambridge, notably Wilkins with his King's screen and the *second* George Gilbert Scott at Pembroke and elsewhere. Others, like Waterhouse, and the *first* Sir Gilbert Scott with St John's chapel, designed buildings which are impressive in themselves but out of accord with their surroundings. In the present century academic Cambridge has expanded even faster, particularly beyond the Backs, where the inter-war university library, by Sir Giles Gilbert Scott of the *third* generation, is the most prominent feature. Because space is limited, the following descriptions are confined to inner Cambridge and concentrate on the older college buildings. The city gets relatively little coverage in its own right except for those streets which are intertwined with the colleges. These limitations occur not because the author considers that later buildings, or Cambridge as a city, are not important, but because there is so much to say about the buildings and settings that make Cambridge unique.

There are two main itineraries and a shorter third section, which cover most of the older colleges:

(1) Peterhouse to Queens', King's, Clare and the Senate House
(2) Market Hill to Trinity, St John's and Magdalene
(3) Emmanuel and Christ's

(1) Peterhouse to Queens', King's, Clare and the Senate House

It is a good idea to approach central Cambridge from the south. Trumpington Street is, in large measure, an old street such as one might find in any sizeable historic town in East Anglia – slightly curving, with modest timber-framed and plastered houses interspersed with grander Georgian ones. In such a setting the Fitzwilliam Museum is grandly out of place with its metropolitan scale. It was built gradually from 1834, initially under the architect George Basevi, and continued after his death by C. R. Cockerell.

Opposite top
President's Lodge, Queens' College, Cambridge, *c.*1540, the only timber-framed college building in Cambridge, typical of the long-drawn transition from Gothic to Classical. Most colleges have Masters; Queens' has a President.

Opposite bottom
St John's College, Cambridge. The deep red brick building of 1670, tentatively classical, rises from the river, with the romantic Gothic 'Bridge of Sighs' crossing to the new buildings of *c.*1830.

Overleaf
Trinity Great Court, Cambridge. The Great Gate of *c.*1500, in brick and stone, gave entrance to the older King's Hall, which was absorbed into Henry VIII's Trinity College, founded in 1546. The fountain of 1601–15 is perfectly placed as the focus of this very large courtyard of varied Tudor and Jacobean buildings, standing serenely against a threatening sky.

The collections, particularly the paintings, are so splendid that it would be advisable for a first-time visitor to Cambridge to set time aside later to look at them, after he has seen something of the town. Essential Cambridge begins just beyond with Peterhouse, appropriately the oldest college. It was founded in 1280 by Hugh de Balsham, bishop of Ely, with a constitution based on that of Merton College, Oxford, founded six years before. The buildings are a microcosm of Cambridge architecture. The first was the hall of 1286. In the 15th century two more ranges were added, and the hall incorporated into a third, to form three sides of the courtyard that essentially exists today, though thoroughly transformed. Originally these buildings were of clunch and other rough stone. Their frontages to the courtyard were refaced in 1754 with Ketton stone from Rutland, with new sash windows and a pediment. Such classicization occurred in many of the surviving medieval courts in Georgian times. The hall was restored by the second George Gilbert Scott in 1870 – and it contains colourful details in tile, glass and wall decoration by William Morris's firm. To see what the buildings were originally like, one can go through the hall passage to look at the back, where some of the original stone and clunch is visible. The college chapel was built in 1628–32 when Matthew Wren, uncle of the great architect (and later bishop, successively, of Norwich and Ely) was master of Peterhouse. It is a building of great interest, blending later Gothic with classical details (as so many Cambridge buildings of around 1600 do), and stands in what was the open side of the courtyard, linked to the adjoining buildings by wings with open arches. On the street side, the chapel is the centrepiece of three very different buildings as one approaches from the south. First there is the gabled end of a red-brick library block, built in 1633, with an original oriel window, then the chapel with a twirly gable crowned by a pediment, and finally a chastely classical range, in Ketton stone, of 1738–42, designed by Sir James Burrough, master of Caius College and amateur architect, who was also responsible for refacing the courtyard. This mixture of periods, styles and building materials is utterly typical of a Cambridge college. Less typical is the location of the master's lodge – across the street, in a handsome town house which was built in 1701 and bought by the college in 1727.

Pembroke College, founded in 1347, is a little beyond Peterhouse. A visitor with limited time would be advised to pass it, noting the splendid street front to the chapel of 1663–5, one of the first two buildings designed by Christopher Wren (the other is the Sheldonian Theatre, Oxford); it was also financed by his uncle Matthew, then bishop of Ely. It was Cambridge's first piece of confident classical architecture and it must have startled when it was first built, standing in contrast to other recent Cambridge buildings which were lingeringly Gothic, or where classical elements were less surely handled. Otherwise, Pembroke is mainly interesting for its Victorian and Edwardian architecture. Part of its original small court remains, with buildings later refronted in stone, but two sides were pulled down in 1871–2 when the college was enlarged under the architect Alfred Waterhouse. He designed buildings such as Manchester Town Hall and the Natural History Museum in London which look splendid in their settings, but his ebullient Gothic is often out of place in a Cambridge college. Nevertheless his

71 *Opposite top*
Peterhouse, Cambridge.
This view summarizes much of Cambridge architecture; the brick library in the foreground of 1633; the Gothic-and-Classic chapel of 1632; the Georgian block, of 1742; behind that the steeple of the United Reformed church, 1874.

72 **Trumpington Street, Cambridge,** showing Georgian houses that might be in any country town, and the Pitt Building with its broad tower, built 1833 for the University Press.

library at Pembroke, with its municipal-looking clock tower, is an attractive landmark. It is worth going behind the college hall, past the 17th-century building named after Sir Robert Hitcham, owner for a time of Framlingham Castle in Suffolk, and benefactor there, into the beautiful college gardens, which are flanked by Victorian and Edwardian buildings much more amenable to Cambridge than Waterhouse's. Their culmination is the open-sided New Court of 1878 at a far corner of the college site, designed by the second George Gilbert Scott in a vigorous style using many motifs from local 17th-century buildings, all in nicely weathered stone. Nearer to the main college is an attractive little range with steep gables by the architect W. D. Caröe, who also designed the nearby splendid stone screen of 1907 facing Pembroke Street, almost Parisian in character with its five bold rounded arches and central grand entrance.

Besides the colleges, Trumpington Street passes three buildings with towers, which are landmarks along the curving street. One is the steeple of the United Reformed church of 1874, in a French Gothic style that is out of place in Cambridge. The second is the broad buff tower of the Pitt Building, built for the University Press in 1833, much more acceptable. The third, opposite, is the more modest tower of St Botolph's, one of the city's numerous old parish churches. Like several of the others it is flanked by a colourful row of cottage-scale buildings, and the churchyard is delightful.

Silver Street leads from opposite St Botolph's to Queens' College, one of the earliest brick-fronted groups of buildings in Britain. Its first founder, in 1446, was a rector of St Botolph's; two years later he obtained the patronage of Margaret of Anjou, queen to Henry VI; in 1465 there was further patronage from Elizabeth Woodville, queen to Edward IV – hence the plural possessive *Queens'* in the title. The main court dates from Margaret's time and survives essentially complete, with its original dark red brick, which however is only a facing over clunch, of which the core of the walls is built. The Great Gate is one of the first of those typically English gateways, with octagonal corner turrets, that became specially characteristic of Cambridge, though not peculiar to it – there are earlier examples at Battle Abbey and St Augustine's in Canterbury, and later ones into St James's Palace and Hampton Court. The hall passage leads through to Cloister Court – a great surprise. It has a brick arched cloister round three sides, with the only timber-framed college building in Cambridge, the President's Lodge of 1540, rising romantically in two storeys over the arches on the north side. (Most colleges have Masters, but Queens' has a President.) The building at the far end of the court backs on to the river, as is revealed if one goes through a passage on to the college's famous wooden bridge – originally built in 1749, last rebuilt in 1902. This is one of only two old college buildings actually abutting on to the river; the other is in St John's. In between are the Backs, described later. (See colour illus. pp. 162–4).

Back to Trumpington Street, and Corpus Christi College. The main court of 1823–7, opening from the street, is in rather uninspired Gothic, designed by William Wilkins – architect also of the National Gallery in London, the classical buildings of Downing College in Cambridge, and the Gothic screen

73 King's Parade, Cambridge. The screen of King's College, on the left (1828), matches but does not compete with King's College Chapel. In the background the classical Senate House of 1722–30 and Waterhouse's Gothic addition to Caius College, 1870.

to King's College. The chapel is opposite the gatehouse, and the college library is on the south side – famous for its collection of early medieval manuscripts which were rescued after the Dissolution of the Monasteries by Matthew Parker, who became archbishop of Canterbury after he had been master of Corpus Christi. Visually the best part of Corpus is the Old Court, reached through the hall passage – the original courtyard of the small college founded in 1352. Apart from the Old Court at Queens' it is the least altered medieval courtyard in Cambridge, with many of the original windows, and plastering over the rough stone walls (as there probably always was). An even older survival is the tower of St Benet's church rising beyond the buildings on the north side of the church. This tower is late Saxon and the oldest standing building in Cambridge (the rest of the church is later).

Corpus Christi College illustrates the modest beginnings of much of collegiate Cambridge, King's College its architectural climax. When Henry VI founded King's in 1441 he envisaged something fairly modest, and the college started with a small cramped courtyard, but within a few years he conceived a much grander college, round a very large courtyard with the chapel on the north side. King's College Chapel was started in 1446, but work ceased with Henry's deposition in 1461. It was resumed in 1477 for seven years, and again in 1508 to its structural completion in 1515 (the glass and furnishings came a little later). Nothing else was built round the intended courtyard until in 1723–30 James Gibbs designed a monumental classical block of white Portland stone, at right angles to the chapel. Then there was another hiatus, until William Wilkins completed the courtyard in 1824–8 with a screen to King's Parade (as the street beyond came to be known), and a range including a hall opposite the chapel. When these were completed the old cramped courtyard north of the chapel was vacated by the college.

King's Parade is one of the great townscapes of England, with a medley of country-town buildings on one side, the university Senate House and former library at the far end, and the screen of King's with the east end of the chapel on the left. Before the 1820s it was a narrow street; the buildings on the western side were demolished to allow it to be widened and Wilkins' screen erected. The screen is a masterpiece in this setting – it has a central gatehouse, slightly oriental in feeling, with a tall double-curved turret ending in a pinnacle, and a cluster of subsidiary spirelets, the whole successfully setting off, but not competing with, the view of the chapel from the street. It is a much more inspired work of Wilkins than his court at Corpus Christi.

The original master mason for King's chapel was Reginald Ely; he may have envisaged a larger version of the Lady Chapel in the place from which he took his name, with a fairly simple vault. But under Simon Clarke and, especially, John Wastell, master masons (that is, in effect, architects) in the second and third stages, the design was dramatically modified to include a fan vault – that peculiarly English invention of which major examples already existed, notably at Sherborne Abbey in Dorset. It is exceedingly fortunate that not only was King's chapel completed, together with its furnishings and stained glass, in the nick of time before the Reformation, but also that it remained largely undamaged during that convulsion. The strangest thing to happen to it occurred only a few years ago when a painting by Rubens, having been given to the college, was placed behind the altar, despite the fact that its colouring clashes with that of the window above. Perhaps the authorities will find a more suitable setting for the painting.

King's College has its bridge, a single span of 1819, from or near which is one of the most famous views in the world, that of the Backs. The Backs were originally what the name implies: the colleges faced the town and backed on to the river. As the colleges grew, and the waterside area was transformed through the closure of old wharfs and the drainage of boggy land, they took greater account of the potentialities of their sites. A late 17th-century map shows that the colleges already possessed fields on the other side of the river which they had landscaped, at least by planting avenues. Now the relationship of the riverside spaces to the colleges is like that of parks to country houses. The view from near King's bridge has three main elements. The classical Gibbs building of 1723–30 and the Gothic chapel together show that the effect of contrast between two buildings of totally different styles, forms and textures can be tremendous. In front of them immaculate lawns sweep down to the river. In the background Clare College, with its mixture of classical and Gothic elements, complements both the principal buildings.

The path over King's bridge leads to the all-too-busy highway which forms the western boundary of the Backs, Queen's Road. A little to the right are the exquisite back gates to the main part of Clare College. (Clare was the first old college to expand west of the Backs and Queen's Road, with the neo-Georgian Memorial Court of 1923–34, designed by the same architect, Sir Giles Gilbert Scott, as the later University Library which looms behind. A description of this area – 'New Cambridge', hugely expanded since the Second World War – would need several pages to do it justice.)

Clare College was first founded in 1326 and re-established in 1338 by Elizabeth de Burgh, the redoubtable lady of Clare Castle in Suffolk. The path from the college's back entrance leads through a beautiful iron screen of 1713 to the bridge – built in 1639 and the oldest on the Backs. The college itself was entirely rebuilt between 1638 and the early 18th century to form one of the most attractive courtyards in Cambridge, classical in most of its elements but, with its horizontal mullioned windows, still reminiscent of the Gothic past. The main gate, with its Renaissance detailing, is very different from earlier Cambridge gatehouses, but it has a fan vault inside the archway – surely one of the last to be constructed until the Gothic Revival. There is a similar, though slightly smaller, gateway leading directly from the bridge – indicating that the approach to the college from this direction was already considered important in the 17th century.

The front of Clare, under the shadow of the west end of King's chapel, is on the edge of the most densely built part of Cambridge, where the narrow Senate House Passage runs between the university Senate House and Caius College. Gonville and Caius College (the full title) was founded first in 1348 by Edmund Gonville and again in 1557 by Dr Caius – he Latinized his name from Keys but kept the old pronunciation. He symbolized the student's progress in four stages; first by a Gate of Humility which he built at the entrance to the college (unfortunately it has been resited), then by the Gate of Virtue between two courtyards, with a proud Renaissance display on one side, and a more modest return front symbolizing Wisdom, and finally by the Gate of Honour which opens on to Senate House Passage and is one of the most curious buildings in Cambridge, quite small, but covered with classical detailing. Caius Court, from which it leads, has simple Tudor-style ranges built of blocks of limestone, said to have come from dissolved abbeys including Ramsey (86). Gonville Court, the original courtyard, was re-fronted and sash-windowed in 1753 by Sir James Burrough, amateur architect and master of the college (page 168). In complete contrast, Tree Court was rebuilt under Waterhouse in 1868–70. As elsewhere his work is grand and romantic, but it is even more unsuitable here than it is in Pembroke College. His large block with tower and spire would be splendid as a town hall, but standing beside and rising above the classical Senate House when seen along King's Parade, it spoils the effect of one of Cambridge's finest architectural groups.

The Senate House is the university's formal centre, where degrees are conferred. It was built in 1722–30 to the design of James Gibbs, who combined discretion and assertiveness to just the right degree. Flanking it to the west are two other classical façades; one, dating from 1754–8, with Venetian windows, conceals the still partly medieval buildings of the Old Schools behind; the other, more assertive but set back, is the old university library of 1837–42 by C. R. Cockerell, with a big, deep, round-headed upper window. The final element in this informal group of buildings is Great St Mary's to the east – both the university church and the chief parish church of the town. The tower with its octagonal turrets was not finished till 1608; the body of the church was built *c.* 1480–1510. It has a late Gothic interior with flat roof on arched tie-beams, lantern clerestory and panelled arches, resembling the churches at Lavenham and Saffron Walden, though not quite so grand as either. It is possible that John Wastell, designer of the upper parts of King's chapel, was master mason here as at Saffron Walden.

(2) Market Hill to Trinity, St John's and Magdalene

Market Hill – as the market place is called, in East Anglian style – is the centre of Cambridge as a town. It originated in the early Middle Ages when it was, perhaps, about twice as big, including roughly the area of the present square and the site of the Guildhall and adjoining buildings to the south. Gradually, as elsewhere, there was piecemeal encroachment of permanent buildings where market stalls had been. Early 19th-century maps show an L-shaped space about half as big as the present one; there were groups of buildings on the western part of the present space, blocking Great St Mary's church from view. These were cleared later in the century, forming the market place we see today. The present neo-Georgian Guildhall replaced an older smaller one on the southern side of the square in 1936–7. On the opposite side is one of the few distinguished inter-war college buildings in Cambridge, a five-storied stone-faced block of 1934, by Murray Easton, containing rooms for Caius College over shops; the long horizontal windows with their mullions are typical of their period but at the same time reflect the Tudor tradition. Nearby Rose Crescent is an attractive alley, formed about 1830, which curves round to emerge dramatically into Trinity Street.

Trinity Street is a narrow, slightly sinuous thoroughfare of intense character, still dominated by tall Georgian frontages over shops, with one gabled 17th-century building and a Victorian Gothic fantasy on a corner. The street bends slightly to reveal one of Cambridge's most memorable urban scenes. The Great Gate of Trinity College is set back on the left, and beyond, past the projecting end of Trinity chapel, is the long facade of St John's College with its gatehouse, closing the view obliquely as the street bends again out of sight. Trees, happily placed beside the street, embellish the picture.

Trinity College was founded by Henry VIII in 1546, incorporating King's Hall, a royal foundation of the 14th century, and also the site of Michaelhouse which, as a monastic college, had just been suppressed. At first an irregular augmentation of the buildings from both older colleges, Trinity was transformed, as we see it today, by Thomas Neville who was master from 1593 to 1615. He created the Great Court, by demolishing some of the older

74 Gibbs Building, King's College, Cambridge, 1723–9, is named after its architect. It is a major landmark from the Backs, and contrasts, in its classical Portland stone purity, with the adjoining King's College Chapel.

buildings and erecting others to enclose the present very large, nearly rectangular courtyard. It is informal in the sense that there is no symmetry; the dominating landmarks, including three gates, the Great Hall and the fountain are placed irregularly, and the result is very satisfying. The Great Gate, stone-faced outside but partly of brick inside, was started in about 1490 for King's Hall; the older King Edward's Tower of about 1430 (another gatehouse) was resited by Neville on the north side of the court, balanced by a new Queen's Gate on the southern side. The Great Hall was completed in 1605; its style is lingering Gothic like that of the two-storeyed ranges Neville built on the southern and eastern sides of the court. The *clou* of the courtyard is the fountain, set in a splendid round-arched, Gothic-topped cage, placed not in the exact centre but just where a trained eye must have perceived that it would have the maximum effect in pulling together the diffuse elements of the Great Court (see colour illus. pp. 166–7).

After the ordered irregularity of the Great Court, the grand symmetry of Neville's Court – reached through the hall passage – comes as an impressive surprise. Neville built only the side ranges, shorter than they are now, with the present classical cloister arcades but also with gables over the top windows – the latter were replaced by balustrades in the 18th century. The climax of the court, and of Trinity, came with the building of Sir Christopher Wren's library in 1676–90. It is a confident classical building unlike anything seen before in Cambridge except for Wren's much more modest chapels at Pembroke and Emmanuel. The elevation from the court is deceptive. Wren

75 St John's College, Cambridge, founded 1511, has preserved complete its frontage of Tudor brick with diagonal patterns, and the finest of the characteristic Cambridge gateways with octagonal corner turrets.

had to build a very high room for the library itself; he raised its floor a few feet above ground level because of the risk of flooding, leaving a low, open-fronted ground storey. But he designed the facade on the Neville's Court side as if it had two storeys of about equal height, both to give it better classical proportions and to relate it satisfactorily to the rest of the court; this is why the arches to the ground storey are blocked at the top. But the tall windows of the upper floor dominate with their rounded tops, although the inserted mullions and transoms are a little disconcerting. The facade to the river is more straightforward and much more familiar, as it is a focal feature of the Backs.

One can walk along the far side of the river and enter St John's College from that direction, but the college makes more sense historically if one starts from the main gate. St John's, the second largest college, was founded in 1511 by Lady Margaret Beaufort, mother of Henry VII. Her driving force was John Fisher, who was chancellor of the university and bishop of Rochester (he was executed in 1535 and has been canonized by the Catholic Church). The gatehouse and flanking ranges, all of red brick, are parts of the original First Court of 1511–20; the gate is probably the finest in Cambridge, though similar to the one at Queens'; it is given added splendour by the heraldry brought out in colour and gilt (see colour illus. p. 164). First Court used to be small, with the chapel on the north side; the latter was unfortunately pulled down in 1863 to be replaced by the present chapel, designed by the first Sir Gilbert Scott. It is a fine building in itself, and the tower, based on that of Pershore Abbey near Worcester, is one of the most familiar skyline features of Cambridge, but it is quite out of character and scale with the college itself. More typical of Cambridge is the hall, enlarged, but this time sympathetically, by Scott; it retains its fine hammerbeam roof, probably made by Thomas Loveday, a carpenter from Sudbury. Through the hall passage into Second Court, almost as built in 1598–1602, in dark red brick, three-storeyed, with small gables over the top windows. It is dominated by a second gateway leading into Third Court, a simpler version of the main gate, with the same tall turrets. It seems nonsensical to have a gateway like this between two internal courts, but when it was built Third Court was not there; the gate led through to the riverside. Even so the gate is remarkable, for there were no Backs as we know them when it was built; one presumes that there was then a route to the college from the town bridge along the then very different riverside. Third Court is a delightful surprise. The library on the north side was built in 1624 with florid early Gothic windows – clearly early self-conscious 'Gothic Revival' rather than the simple Tudor-derived 'Gothic Survival' of the time. But the west and south ranges are not Gothic at all; they were built in 1669–71, with classical arches on the western side, and a curious baroque centrepiece. But they look very amateurish in their classicism compared with Wren's later Trinity library.

The passage from Third Court leads to the covered Bridge of Sighs, built in 1831 and now St John's best known feature, but, as this looks better from the side than within, it is a good idea to go over the college's older bridge (dating from 1709–12) and obtain the whole famous view – with the 17th-century brick buildings rising direct from the river, the Gothic Bridge of Sighs itself (looking little like its namesake behind the Doge's Palace in Venice), and, on the left, the theatrical New Court, built as a major extension of the college across the river in 1825–31, to the design of Thomas Rickman. 'Theatrical' is the word used because from the south it looks like a huge stage set rising behind the Backs, a formalized piece of romantic Gothic.

It is possible to walk through New Court, along a vaulted passage, passing the much admired Cripps building of 1963–7 spanning a tributary of the Cam, into Magdalene College's interesting Benson Court. This itinerary, however, assumes a return to the main gate of St John's, then along Bridge Street to Magdalene. The junction of St John's Street and Bridge Street is historically a focal point of the city. Here the ancient route coming south-east from the site of the original bridge forks; Bridge Street and its continuations lead on south-eastwards, while St John's Street, which soon becomes Trinity Street and then King's Parade, goes south. Unfortunately the old buildings which defined the junction on the south-west side were pulled down by St John's College between the wars and some very unsatisfactory ones substituted, though Scott's chapel tower, rising behind them,

does look impressive from this side. Opposite is the Round Church – one of only four in England still roofed; of the other three, one is in Northampton, another at Little Maplestead near Halstead, Essex, and the third is the Temple Church in London. It was misguidedly restored in 1841–3, from when the conical roof and clerestory date, but inside it is still, for the most part, magnificently Norman – the circle of eight cylindrical pillars, the round arches they support, and the gallery above are all original.

Bridge Street retains on one side a pleasant series of country-town buildings, some well restored, including a three-storeyed jettied house with Georgian oriel windows. The bridge over the Cam, the starting point of the city, has been replaced repeatedly, the last time by an unpretentious iron structure of 1823 – now called Magdalene Bridge after the college.

Magdalene College was founded in 1542, taking over the buildings of an older college which had housed student monks from four abbeys – Crowland in Lincolnshire, Ely, Ramsey and (Saffron) Walden. The founder was Lord Audley, ruthless Chancellor to Henry VIII and despoiler of monasteries; he took over Walden abbey and converted it into Audley End. The main court is still largely that of the 15th-century monastic college, of glowing brick, with original windows. The college's best-known building, the Pepys library, mainly 17th-century but partly older, is reached through the hall passage; Samuel Pepys bequeathed his library, which was installed in 1724 (he died in 1703). The college has extended across Magdalene Street in an interesting way. Along the far side of the street is a range of medieval to 17th-century timber-framed houses, many jettied, mostly plastered (as they should be). Several have small shops in the ground floors, but above the shops and in wings behind they have been converted into college rooms. In the 1950s the old yards and backland behind were partly cleared, discreet new buildings added, and an irregular court, Benson Court, formed with the pleasant backs of the buildings on Magdalene Street partly forming one side. Nearby Mallory Court had undergone much the same treatment between the wars. In complete but effective contrast is a block by Sir Edwin Lutyens, in heavy classical style tempered by colourful brick – not one of his masterpieces, but his only contribution to Cambridge.

76 **Trinity Lane, Cambridge,** is a medieval lane, with the backs of college rooms of the 1590s. Among the tall chimneys are the turrets of a gateway built at the same time, all in the lingering Gothic tradition.

(3) Emmanuel and Christ's

If the centre of Cambridge were the main shopping streets without the colleges, it would be a very dull city. Sidney Street has particularly insipid inter-war commercial building; its continuations St Andrew's and Regent Streets are not much better, and Petty Cury, once an attractive, though not spectacular, narrow street has recently been ruined by the uniform rebuilding of one side. Lloyds Bank, by Waterhouse, with a richly encrusted clock tower and strident façade of alternating brick and stone, is one of the few commercial buildings in the area that rise above mediocrity. (Waterhouse's style is specially appropriate for this type of building, even in Cambridge, but not always for additions to old colleges.) Two colleges, Christ's and Emmanuel, seem stranded in all this commercialism.

Emmanuel, founded in 1584, has always had a puritan or low-church ethos. It has a long facade with central Ionic columns supporting a pediment over the entrance – a classical variant of a Tudor gatehouse tower. Facing the entrance in First Court is one of Cambridge's most memorable architectural compositions – Wren's chapel with two flanking ranges, arcaded underneath. Wren designed it in 1666 (just after the completion of his chapel in Pembroke College); the former master of Emmanuel had become Dean of St Paul's, and Wren was already commissioned to alter the old cathedral before it was destroyed in the Great Fire. Emmanuel has a large site (that of the former Dominican friary) which has retained a park-like character. To the south, the so-called Old Court has a garden with a pool, backed by a brick building of 1663 and another of 1965–6. Eastward, reached through the colonnade beside the chapel, is a larger sweep of landscape, centred on an irregular pond remodelled in 1964 in the English informal tradition.

Christ's College is in the very heart of commercial Cambridge; its gateway with gilded heraldry competes successfully for attention. It was refounded by Lady Margaret Beaufort, who took over an older establishment, six years before her other foundation, St John's. Christ's main court retains many of the original buildings behind later stone refacings, mainly done in the 18th century. The hall was rebuilt in 1876–9 by the second George Gilbert Scott. The most striking architecture in Christ's is that of the Fellows' Building of 1640–3, free-standing behind the main court, using Renaissance elements with tentative vigour. It is instructive to go on to Third Court to see how the college has been enlarged over the last hundred years. First there was a block of 1888–9 which tried to repeat the Fellows' Building, with some modification. Then, the college having rejected, in the 1930s, designs for new buildings by Walter Gropius, which would have been in the world class as International Modern architecture, they commissioned, in the late 1940s, the leading traditional architect of the time, Sir Albert Richardson, who designed solid, institutional neo-Georgian blocks. And finally, in a second reaction, the college employed Sir Denys Lasdun (architect of the National Theatre) for New Court, built from 1966 in a romantic version of the then very fashionable 'ziggurat' style, each storey deeply recessed behind the one below. However interesting a building of such a shape looks in isolation, it can seldom group satisfactorily with others of more normal form. This is only one of many highly interesting and often provocative buildings in Cambridge from the 1950s to early 70s, both as additions to old colleges and on newly developed sites. It will be at least another fifty years before they can be objectively assessed.

Ely

The view from a train of Ely Cathedral rising at the top of a slight slope is the second finest obtainable on an English railway – surpassed only by that of Durham. Its story begins in 673 when Etheldreda, a princess of the East Anglian royal house, founded a monastery on an island surrounded by fen. (Audrey is a later form of Etheldreda's name.) It was a 'double monastery' of nuns and monks, living separately but both under the rule of the abbess. Such monasteries were fairly common in the early days of Christianity in Saxon England, and were generally ruled by women – the most famous was St Hilda of Whitby in Yorkshire, who was slightly older than Etheldreda and whom she almost certainly met. The Vikings destroyed the abbey in 870, but exactly a hundred years later it was refounded, this time under Benedictine rule, for men. Under Simeon, the first Norman abbot, who was brother of Walkelin, bishop of Winchester, where he had been prior, rebuilding on a tremendous scale began – reflecting both the wealth of the abbey and the importance of St Etheldreda's shrine as a place of pilgrimage. In 1109 it became the cathedral of a new diocese – as in other monastic cathedrals the bishop was titular abbot, with a prior under him who ran the monastery. By the end of the Middle Ages the bishops had judicial powers over the surrounding area – the Isle of Ely, much larger than the actual island on which the town stood – and their power there was almost as great as that of the bishops of Durham within their own county. The bishopric, and hence the cathedral, survived the Reformation although the monastery was dissolved; the last prior became first dean of the new establishment, and several monks became Anglican

canons. The bishop continued to hold judicial powers in the Isle until 1834.

Apart from the cathedral, Ely has never been much more than a fairly small market town, although for long there was busy river trade on the Ouse, part of the water highway from King's Lynn to Cambridge and elsewhere. Despite its location at a railway junction the town has hardly grown, till very recently.

Although the station is at some distance from the cathedral, this description begins there, as the approach

77 *Below* **The Gallery, Ely**. The Ely Porta, *c*.1400, on the right, was the 'back' entrance into the servicing area of the monastery. Between it and the cathedral are monastic buildings, converted after the Reformation for Anglican clergy, and now used by King's School.

78 *Opposite* **Ely Cathedral**. The Norman to Gothic west front has been assymetrical since the northern part collapsed in the 15th century. The tower once had a stone spire, replaced in the 14th century by the present octagonal top.

on foot from this direction is the most dramatic. One makes for Broad Street, a turning right off Station Road, and then for a footpath leading through a gap on the west side of that street. This enters a public park, with a stunning view north-west to the cathedral. In the foreground is a field, not part of the park, but roughly grazed by cattle, and scattered with trees, so providing an informal, genuinely rural, setting for the cathedral which now has few parallels (though the very different view of Salisbury across the water-meadows is comparable in this respect). The ground rises irregularly, so dramatizing the great bulk of the cathedral where it is visible between trees. There is an interplay of length and height – the effect of length emphasized by the even lines of the leaded roofs of nave and choir, that of height by the tremendous western tower and the unique octagonal lantern. This replaced a central crossing tower that collapsed in 1322. At that time there were in charge three men who had the calibre fit for the challenge – Bishop Hotham, Prior Crauden and, especially, Alan of Walsingham the sacrist – who was directly responsible for building operations. William Hurley, one of the greatest medieval carpenters, was appointed master craftsman for the building of the lantern – which above the internal arches is of wood.

The path emerges in the midst of King's School – an ancient foundation which has taken over many of the monastic buildings that had survived the Reformation, variously and picturesquely altered since. Among them is Prior Crauden's Chapel, an exquisite private chapel built just before the calamity that led to the construction of the octagon; it contains a superb mosaic floor. The buildings at the heart of the monastery, surrounding the cloister, have largely gone; there is now a space where the cloister was, which allows a tremendous close-up view of the cathedral. To the east are the extraordinary remains of the monastic infirmary, which has lost its main roof, but where the sites of the former aisles, behind the blocked arches, are occupied by later buildings – an arrangement paralleled at Peterborough (page 192).

The interior of the cathedral is likely, rightly, to take most of a visitor's time at Ely. To proceed down the nave with its Roman-style grandeur – more truly Roman in feeling than any other 'Romanesque' work in England – and then to enter the supremely Gothic space under the octagon is to experience one of the greatest thrills any building can provide. In contrast is the Lady Chapel, begun just before the octagon and finished after it was completed, more human and delicate in its rich details – brutally mutilated though some are through the fanaticism of a later age; all the statues were beheaded. And there is the stained glass museum in the spacious gallery of the nave.

After the cathedral, the town of Ely is very low-keyed. The best part is immediately outside the stupendous (though incomplete) west front – the irregular Palace Green with the former bishop's palace, of Tudor and later brick, on the south side and Georgian houses on the others. It narrows into a street and then opens again beside St Mary's, the town's parish church, which anywhere else would seem impressive, especially the Transitional Norman nave interior. St Mary's Street writhes back into the centre of the town, with more pleasant Georgian buildings – but Ely's Georgian heritage cannot compare with that of Wisbech. High Street is a narrow street north of the cathedral, much of its southern side taken by a range of medieval buildings, with two gates, which included the offices and stores used by the sacrist – they were indeed originally built by Alan of Walsingham at the time of the building of the Lady Chapel and octagon. The small market place is disappointing – it has crushingly inappropriate buildings of the 1960s. (The market place was originally much larger, occupying all the space between the present High and Market Streets, now a densely infilled area through which a few alleys thread.) High Street is continued by Fore Hill and Waterside, an attractively rehabilitated street descending with a curve to the river. What was for centuries a trading area is now devoted to pleasure boats, colourful and lively. A waterside path has been renamed *Quai d'Orsay* – because Ely has a relationship with the town of Orsay in France! In the background is The Maltings, a fine former brewery building of 1868 with interesting brick details, converted for public use in 1972. Nearby is the station.

Godmanchester

Godmanchester, across the river from Huntingdon, has its own peculiar quality. It was a Roman place – first a fort, then a town with walls enclosing an irregular hexagon. The Roman town declined, and the Saxon settlement assumed a different form – it was *God-mundcestre*; Godmund was the Saxon lord; the term *-cestre* was used by the Saxons for any place with Roman remains. The correct pronunciation is Godman-Chester, with emphasis on the first and third syllables, *not* God-Manchester.

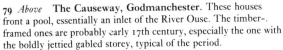

79 *Above* **The Causeway, Godmanchester**. These houses front a pool, essentially an inlet of the River Ouse. The timber-framed ones are probably early 17th century, especially the one with the boldly jettied gabled storey, typical of the period.

80 *Above right* **Godmanchester**. Along the curve of Post Street are a house with a mansard roof, common in the area, with local mottled tiles; a Georgianized jettied house; and, in the distance, the pedimented front of Island Hall, *c.*1750.

81 *Right* **Chinese Bridge, Godmanchester**, in a delectable place where a mill stream joins the River Ouse, originally built in 1827 but replaced twice in replica.

The approach from Huntingdon, across the ancient bridge over the Ouse (page 188), is impressive. Passing under the intrusive but very necessary bypass, and proceeding along a short grassy avenue, one enters the town suddenly, at the entrance to a fine street – called Post Street – which curves gently but invitingly out of sight. At first the buildings are modest Georgian or earlier, brick-built or plastered, with the local mottled tiles, but the scale suddenly heightens with a part-Victorian, part-Georgian house of three storeys in buff brick laced with red, on the outside of the curve. It is the beginning of a memorable group which culminates in Island Hall, a tall Georgian mansion, brick-built and stone-framed, set back from the street behind an iron screen. Why it is called Island Hall is revealed by turning to the right a little further on, and finding that behind the street is a side stream of the Ouse – an old millstream – which separates part of the house's garden as an island. A path runs alongside the millstream to reveal a scene which is the quintessence of Godmanchester. The main river and the millstream converge into a wide pool which extends to the Causeway, one of the town's main streets. Crossing the end of the

millstream where it enters the pool is the so-called Chinese Bridge, wooden, trellised and gracefully humped, originally built in 1827 but reconstructed twice in replica, the last time in 1960. This forms the centrepiece of views across the water to the town with the church spire rising behind. The bridge leads to a small space, beside an Elizabethan building which was formerly the grammar school, to the centre of the town at the meeting of its three main streets, Post Street, the Causeway and Cambridge Street. It is worth walking back along Post Street, since the view along it in this direction is as splendid as it was the other way. The pivotal building is a small white-plastered gabled house with oriel windows; the roofline of Island Hall rears behind and the street curves out of sight beyond. A path leads from Post Street to the church, with its

Gothic tower and spire dating from as late as 1623; the rest of the building is 13th to 15th centuries, with misericord seats in the chancel, carved to represent animals. Legend has it that they came from Ramsey Abbey after the Dissolution, but if the letters WS on one of them relate to William Stevens, vicar in 1470–81, they must be indigenous, though unusual features for a parish church.

Back to the hub of the town, and along the Causeway, running by the side of the pool, with glimpses, especially in winter, through trees across the water into the huge meadow which extends towards Huntingdon. A pleasant succession of buildings, some timber-framed, face the pool from across the street. The Causeway continues to an irregular road junction, from which West Street wanders to the right, beginning with a charming group of houses combining rusticity with country-town urbanity. First there is a thatched cottage, then a jettied plastered house with mottled tiles, and finally a Georgian brick facade with Venetian windows on both floors. The street then winds, 'giving ever-changing vistas of small cottages, large houses set in their own grounds and farm buildings', as the excellent *Godmanchester Town Trail* succinctly puts it. The climax is Farm Hall, on the edge of the town, a severe classical mansion of 1746, looking towards the river along an axial avenue, in the French manner.

This itinerary has covered most of the best of Godmanchester. But there is more for the intrepid explorer to see, although it is less concentrated. Back to the beginning of West Street; the street called Old Court Hall continues the Causeway southwards. It passes a striking succession of three detached timber-framed houses, gable-ended to the street, and then turns sharply left into London Street. This is not a specially interesting street but follows, in its further part, the line of the vanished wall of the Roman town on one of its six sides. Where London Road, coming in from the south, makes a T-junction with London Street was the entrance to the Roman town; a modern block of flats stands on the site of the gate – excavated before they were built. The street called Earning Street continues the line of the Roman town wall, making a bend where one of the angles of the hexagon was – a map in the booklet *Godmanchester*, by H. J. M. Green, makes this clear. Earning Street has three fine 17th-century timber-framed houses, of which at least the first, with a date 1625 over the door, was a farmhouse; it still has fine 18th-century brick barns and farm buildings adjoining. From the end of Earning Street, Cambridge Street leads back into the town.

Huntingdon

Huntingdon is 'written off' in many people's minds as a historic town because of its recent expansion, and the partial rebuilding of its centre. This is too drastic a judgement, for it is still very attractive in parts. Pleasantest of all is the market place, called Market Hill – a memorable triangular *piazza* with three of the town's chief buildings round it – the Town Hall, All Saints and what is now the Cromwell Museum. The Town Hall of 1745 and 1817, with a pedimented frontage, was the social and judicial centre of the Georgian county; there is an assembly room on the top floor and the county courts were held on the first floor. All Saints is a survivor of *sixteen* parish churches which once existed in the town, long since reduced to two. It was largely rebuilt in the 15th century – which is paradoxical, for the town's fortunes were then at their ebb. It is like a smaller version of the grand East Anglian churches of the period, well proportioned inside and with finely detailed roofs. The tower top was rebuilt after Civil War damage. Huntingdon was Oliver Cromwell's birthplace in 1599; he was great-grandson of Richard Williams, nephew of Thomas Cromwell, Henry VIII's minister and dissolver of monasteries. Richard obtained spoils from several, including Ramsey abbey (page 193) and Hinchingbrooke nunnery on the outskirts of the town. Richard changed his name to Cromwell after his famous uncle. Oliver Cromwell (would he have achieved as much as Oliver Williams?) attended the Grammar School, then housed in a building on a corner of Market Hill, which had been part of a hospital founded c. 1160 (the word then meant a place of refuge for poor people, including travellers, the sick, the disabled and the aged). The building was restored in Victorian times, but four blocked arches and a blocked doorway remain from Norman period; it is now the Cromwell Museum.

High Street leads off Market Hill in both directions. It is amazing to think that in 1931 the town's population was only four thousand, and that it consisted of not much more than the long High Street. It had been a Saxon *burh*, with a market and mint in the tenth century. The Normans built a castle to guard the crossing of the River Ouse; it was dismantled in 1173, never rebuilt; only grassy mounds survive. The town's heyday seems to have been in the 13th century when it was a flourishing trading centre and river port. At that

82 Market Hill, Huntingdon is a delightful urban space. The Town Hall of 1745 and 1817 has an Assembly Room as well as the old shire court. The War Memorial in front, one of the best in England, shows a bending soldier, by the sculptor Lady Katharine Scott, wife of the Antarctic explorer.

time the fair in neighbouring St Ives had international fame, and this may have initially benefited Huntingdon as the nearest substantial town. However St Ives soon developed into an important town of its own right, and was much better placed for river traffic than Huntingdon. This was especially so after weirs were built across the Ouse between Huntingdon and St Ives in *c.* 1270 (page 194). From then until river improvements were carried out in the 17th century, the Ouse was virtually unnavigable above St Ives, and this had a severe effect on Huntingdon's prosperity. By Tudor times it was little more than a village. Huntingdon revived in the 18th century, with the development of coaching and commercial traffic along the two old branches of the Great North Road, and with agricultural improvements in the country round – as plenty of Georgian houses testify today. It slumbered again in the 19th and early 20th centuries, and was shaken from its sleep only in the late 1950s and 60s when, under 'overspill' agreements (as they were called), Londoners were rehoused in a much expanded town, with concurrent development of industries. Now the population is over 15,000.

To provide for the new population the centre of the town, south-east of Market Hill, was reconstructed. The narrow winding course of High Street was retained, but the new buildings facing it are without exception nondescript, as is a 'precinct' leading off to the left. More successful is St Benedict's Place, on the opposite side. Luckily the further part of High Street, towards the river, is largely as it was. First there is the former Literary and Scientific Institute of 1840, staidly classical with Corinthian pilasters, and then a long red-brick Georgian range where the biggest house, with a pediment, was the home of Cowper the poet in 1765-7. Opposite is St Mary's church with a striking tower, low, massive and with complicated buttresses receding boldly to the top. The upper part collapsed in 1608 and was rebuilt, but most of the tower must be medieval, especially the lower part of the west front with its elaborate doorway and niches. Perhaps there was once a spire; the composition would make more sense if there had been, in the local tradition. The south arcade is fine work from the town's 13th-century heyday.

Castle Hill House is a severe, free-standing building of 1767 in buff brick – early for this material. It used to back on to the mounds which mark the castle site, which are now cut off by the ring road – a drastic but necessary intrusion into Huntingdon's townscape which has enabled traffic to come off the High Street and Market Hill. High Street passes more Georgian houses to meet the ring road again near the river – at least a new park has been created between road and river. Traffic still goes over the old bridge into God-

Above

Ramsey Abbey Gatehouse
The great abbey of Ramsey was
taken over at the reformation by
Richard Cromwell, ancestor of
Oliver. Most of the gatehouse,
*c.*1500, was, like the rest, pulled
down; the remains suggest
former splendour. (86)
(*see p. 193*)

Opposite

Kimbolton Church. The 13th
century spire, with its window-
like lucarnes, is one of many
splendid examples in the old
county of Huntingdonshire,
built of stone from neighbouring
Northamptonshire.

manchester, but a new footbridge has been built alongside, giving a good view of the old one. It was started in 1332 and without much doubt is one of the best-preserved medieval bridges in England. The first three arches were built by the Huntingdon authorities and are more elaborate, with their machicolation, than the other three which were built by the Godmanchester authorities. Beside the bridge is the impressive building originally erected in the 1850s as a flour mill, later used for textiles, then derelict for a time; now it is converted into flats. At the time of conversion a few years ago it had pleasant red tiles which contrasted well with the newly cleaned buff brick of the walls; since then they have either darkened or been replaced by different tiles, and the effect is not so good.

From here one can walk straight into Godmanchester (page 182), but there is one other part of Huntingdon to describe. The part of High Street north-west of Market Hill is largely unspoiled. The George hotel has a Victorian front – surprising for a coaching inn, but explained by its partial rebuilding after a fire in 1865. The courtyard survives, with its 17th-century first-floor gallery on the far side. High Street ends with informal Georgian grandeur. It broadens slightly beside Ferrar House, early 18th-century with an elliptical archway into a courtyard. It then narrows in two stages, each with a house punctuating the view. First there is Whitwell House of 1727 where a road forks to the left, and then Montagu House of about 1800 at the far end – actually standing beside the ring road. The name Montagu recalls the family of the Earls of Sandwich who bought Hinchingbrooke House from the Cromwell family in 1627 and lived there for three centuries – the house, on the southern outskirts of the town, is now a school.

Kimbolton

Kimbolton, now a village but in the Middle Ages a prosperous market town, would, if it were in the Cotswolds and all built of stone, be widely publicized as a picturesque place. But because it is in a back part of Huntingdonshire it is little known except to local

83 *Below* **Kimbolton Castle**, remodelled by Vanbrugh, 1714, with a screen by Robert Adam, closes the wide main street of this delightful town.

people, and to lorry drivers trying to negotiate its sharp bends. When there are no lorries the views along High Street, towards or away from the 18th-century castle, make almost perfect townscapes. The first castle was built about 1200, when a market charter was granted and, presumably, the town laid out on its regular plan. The castle was transformed into a Tudor house, where Katherine of Aragon died in 1536 (she was buried at Peterborough, page 189), and altered in the 17th

century by the Montagu family who were Earls of Manchester from 1626 (the title was taken from Godmanchester nearby). The fourth earl employed Sir John Vanbrugh, assisted by Nicholas Hawksmoor, to remodel the castle; their work was finished by 1714; five years later the earl became Duke of Manchester. Since 1950 it has been occupied by Kimbolton School, an old foundation moved from elsewhere. Its grandest front faces south-east; what we see from the town is the battlemented roofline and, in front of it, a classical screen with central arch and prominent wings, designed by Robert Adam. The effect of the *château* apparently turning its back on the town, but with an imposing entrance at the end of the main street, is very French in feeling. But the street is not axial to the castle entrance, as it would be if Kimbolton were an 18th-century estate village. Instead it is a notable example of a medieval planned town, with a wide High Street which accommodated a market (this ceased last century), and a narrow back street – East Street – on one side. Most of the frontages are Georgian, with many variations in roofline; several of the houses are older behind the facades. Looking from the castle, the church spire appears beyond the buildings on the right; it is a nice example of the Midland type, with three tiers of lucarnes (window-like openings piercing the spire). East Street has a succession of simple houses which are nearly as attractive as those in High Street; a many-paned Georgian shop front closes the view. The perplexing bends into and out of the town date from its original laying-out when the nature of traffic was very different. Luckily a new road is being built which will take off the lorry traffic – bound between the Midlands and the east coast – before very long.

March

March is a curious town. Its market was established in 1670 – it is held in an irregular market place with Georgian buildings and a tall-towered late Victorian town hall, beside a crossing of the river rather mysteriously called the Old Nene. In the Middle Ages this was an important part of the Fenland navigation system, but it must be an artificial cut – a river would not have flowed naturally through the low clayey island, surrounded by fens, on which the town stands. Because the fens on either side have sunk through being drained, the course of the river through the clay has been lowered from time to time, and now it has steep banks thickly grown with greenery, to good effect. North of the river the town is mainly Victorian – it grew northwards towards the station which was an important junction with, eventually, a huge marshalling yard nearby. Now there is simply one through line.

On the southern edge of the town, where the first settlement was, is the church of St Wendreda, famous for its roof. The saint was a Saxon of whom little is known, but she may have been associated with the East Anglian royal family at the time of St Etheldreda of Ely. According to early accounts, her remains were taken first to Ely and then to Canterbury, and then returned in 1343 to March where she had lived (this complicated history is described in the church guide). The church was then small; it was gradually enlarged and its crowning glory added in the late 15th or early 16th century – the double hammerbeam roof with its host of angels attached to the ends of the beams, to the corbels supporting them, and to the structural members high in the apex of the roof.

Peterborough

Peterborough has in succession been a monastic town, an Anglican cathedral city, a railway centre and a thrusting New City. The first and greatest of these phases started in 657 when Peada, king of *Middle* Anglia, a shadowy district between Mercia and East Anglia, founded one of the first monasteries. It was sacked by the Vikings in 870 and refounded a hundred years later. Fire destroyed the monastery in 1116, after which the church was rebuilt largely as we see it today. The first town was east of the abbey, but Martin, abbot in 1135–55, laid out a new town to the west, with a market place outside the monastery gate and streets leading in three directions – the plan that survives today. The first bridge over the River Nene was built in 1308 – it was probably the early absence of a bridge which led to the Great North Road being established further west, passing through Stamford and leaving Peterborough out on a limb.

The abbey church became the cathedral of a new diocese in 1541. Katherine of Aragon, whose repudiation by Henry VIII led to the severance of the English church from Rome, was buried there after she died at

84 *Above* **Peterborough**. The Guildhall, 1671, is one of the best examples of a 'town house' with open ground floor. Behind is the parish church, 1402–7; the building to the left was built by an insurance company, 1964–6.

85 *Opposite* **Peterborough Cathedral**. The west front is a magnificent muddle, thanks to successive changes of mind by designers, *c*.1180–1400, and a further clash of scale when the relatively small porch was added in the 15th century. But inside the cathedral has splendid unity.

Kimbolton in 1536 (page 188); it has been suggested that this led Henry to save the church by making it a cathedral. But the relative smoothness of the local transition from the Roman Catholic to the Anglican church is indicated by the fact that John Chambers, the last abbot, became the first bishop, and that the former prior of a monastery in Northampton became the first Anglican dean. In 1587 Mary Queen of Scots, beheaded at Fotheringhay not far away, was buried in the cathedral – but twenty-five years later James I arranged for her body to be re-interred at Westminster. Katherine's tomb was smashed by Roundheads in 1643.

In Georgian times Peterborough was the smallest English cathedral city – smaller than Ely was then. It developed with the railways, particularly the Great Northern, which reached the city from King's Cross in 1850 and continued to Edinburgh. A suburb of railwaymen's houses grew to the north. Later in the century large brickworks were opened on the claylands of Fletton, south of the city. Engineering and other industries grew in the 20th century. Then in 1967 came the designation of Peterborough as a 'New Town'. At that time it was thought that the country's population would increase hugely, and Peterborough was considered to be one of the best places to accommodate some of the extra population, including many who would move out of London. On the whole the 'New Town' development has been done wisely and well. Many of the housing areas are attractive – they were built late enough to benefit from the reaction against high-rise flats, and are mostly two-storeyed. The existing city centre – which outside the cathedral close was no showplace but moderately pleasant – was adapted and enlarged, rather than redeveloped; on the whole this has been done effectively – even to the extent of fitting a huge new covered shopping centre within the old framework. The most questionable thing to happen in the city centre occurred in 1965 – before the 'New Town' designation – when the open market was banished from its ancient site to nearby backland (since developed as a covered market). The old market place was freed of traffic (this itself was a good thing) and

then prettified, with unsuitable trees (birches) planted. It was renamed Cathedral Square – although separated from the cathedral by the all-important precinctual gate. No longer is there the dramatic contrast there once was between the bustle of the city centre (at least on market days) and the quiet of the cathedral close, separated by the gateway.

Despite the prettification and the loss of the stalls, the former market place still looks good. The centre-piece is the so-called Guildhall – really a very fine example of the traditional small-town market house, built of golden stone from nearby Northamptonshire in 1671, with classical upper storey, roofed in stone slabs, standing over an open-arched ground floor. Next to it, in informal relationship, is the parish church of St John, built in 1402–7 with a pinnacled tower. Looking from under the Guildhall, the view is focused on the precinctual gate, the top of the cathedral west front rearing behind. On each side is a bank, one in white Portland stone, the other, more elaborate, in local golden stone. The seeming symbolism of the banks standing outside the cathedral gate was perhaps not intentional. There is a third bank on an opposite corner, where Bridge Street leads south from the square. Bridge Street was widened in 1928 when the neo-classical Town Hall was built on the eastern side – in pleasant brick with a stone portico, seen impressively along the street, into which it projects. Unfortunately this effect has been blurred by excessive planting and regimented seats along a straight axis – a more open and informal arrangement would have been better.

Through the precinctual gate and into the rarefied world of the Close – with the magnificent architectural hotchpotch of the west front of the cathedral. There are three huge arched recesses, of which the central one is worryingly narrower than the others, under a busy skyline of spires, gables and pinnacles which was never completed to the symmetrical pattern intended – one of the two central turrets is missing. The effect was the result of more than one change of mind in the early 13th century, at the last stage of the rebuilding of the church which had started after the fire of 1116. To add to the visual disorder, a delicate but under-scaled porch was added in the late 14th century in the lower part of the central arch. All this makes the impact of the interior all the more dramatic. Instead of con-fusion there is unity, for, apart from the west end, the long-drawn process of reconstruction after 1116 resulted in a building of surprising consistency of style. This is the most complete large Norman interior in England – more so than Norwich. Even the flat wooden roof of the nave, recently repainted, is original (the aisles are stone-vaulted). But that is not all – there is another great surprise. The last abbot but one added to the east end the so-called New Building with an exquisite fan vault. The disappointing feature of the cathedral is the central tower. Rebuilt in the 14th century, it was kept cautiously low. It had to be rebuilt again in the 1880s because of structural faults, under the great architect J. L. Pearson. He submitted a design for a new taller tower with a spire that would have rivalled Salisbury. Either for financial or antiquarian reasons – probably both – this was not accepted, and a replica of the old tower was built. Of all the might-have-been building works that were never realized, this one ought to be regretted more than most. If the spire had been built, and were seen soaring over the city near and far, the effect would have been electric.

The abbey precinct became the cathedral close after the Reformation. Some monastic buildings were adapted, others rebuilt, mainly as clerics' houses; others were demolished or allowed to fall to ruin. It has the quintessential form and atmosphere of the English close, not so large or as interesting as that at Norwich but with many similarities. Inside the gate from the market place there is on the right a range of mainly Victorian Gothic buildings, centred on the medieval Abbey Gate which led to the abbot's house – which, largely rebuilt in the 19th century, is now the bishop's palace. The gate has two original statues which Pevsner, in his *Buildings of England* series, says are 'deserving to be better known than they are'. The green space of the close sweeps round the north side of the cathedral, first with a row of Georgian houses on the left (needing their glazing bars restored to give the proper effect), then a projecting Tudor gateway which led to the prior's house (the prior was deputy to the abbot), largely rebuilt in Victorian times. Fortunately this and other houses enveloping the cathedral retain their big bosky gardens, giving the further part of the close a feeling of semi-wild seclusion – immensely valuable in the heart of a large modern city. The public path winds round the end of the cathedral into a fascinating area where bits of monastic buildings have been adapted and altered – especially the former infirmary whose main roof has gone, leaving blocked arches on either side of what has become an open passageway, much as at Ely (page 182). Paths wind on between old buildings and walls of near-local limestone; a gateway leads into the cloister – which has lost its covered walks but remains a secluded space.

Returning to the city centre, the final architectural drama is that of the huge Queensgate shopping centre, built on backland behind the old streets, with bits of new frontage between the older buildings. As an example of fitting large-scale new development into an old town centre it is a remarkable achievement. If only the old open market could be returned to its proper place, Peterborough would acquire something of the character of Norwich. The contrast between the bustle of the city and the quiet of the close would be fully restored.

Ramsey

Ramsey feels strangely remote even today, and must have seemed much more so before the Fens were drained. Its abbey was founded in 969 by (St) Oswald, bishop of Worcester, one of the churchmen who sought to revive Christianity after the devastations of the Vikings – Ely and Peterborough were both refounded at about the same time. Ramsey grew nearly as rich as both; it had the shrine of St Felix, first bishop of East Anglia, and also that of St Ivo, associated with St Ives (page 194). But it never became a major pilgrimage centre because of its situation on a remote peninsula almost surrounded by fen, without the advantage of a nearby river which made Ely relatively accessible. After the Dissolution the site was taken by Richard Williams, a nephew of Thomas Cromwell, Henry VIII's minister. He changed his name to Cromwell; Oliver was his great-grandson (page 184).

The interest of the little town is concentrated near the site of the abbey. A school occupies the mainly Victorian mansion which incorporates part of the medieval Lady Chapel. Part of the Tudor abbey gateway survives, facing Abbey Green, a neat rectangular village-like green, with ornate estate cottages on two sides – built by the Fellowes family, later Lords de Ramsey, the Victorian squires (see colour illus. p. 186). At the corner is the parish church which, apart from the 17th-century tower, is a complete, impressive building of the late 12th century, originally the *hospitium* or guest house. It is amazingly substantial for this use – which seems to have been given up early, as the building became the townspeople's church well before the Reformation. Beyond the church is another green, Church Green, with Georgian and Victorian houses. This was really the easternmost end of the

86 **Abbey Green, Ramsey** was the space outside the abbey; the remains of the gatehouse are in the background. The church, with a 17th century tower, was converted from the 12th century *hospitium* or guest house. (See colour plate, page 186)

original very long market place which, before most of it was encroached on, occupied the whole space between High Street and the narrow street called Little Whyte. Round the corner is Great Whyte, now a wide street. Until just over a hundred years ago a watercourse ran down the centre of this street. This was a lode, or navigable channel, cut from the Old Nene river about two miles away, along which goods supplying abbey and town could be brought. On the southern outskirts of the town is Bury, a settlement which preceded Ramsey. Its church has a strange and striking 13th-century tower with tall thin lancets in the belfry and west front.

St Ives

St Ives derives its attraction, and in the past drew its prosperity, from the River Ouse. Its fair, founded in 1110 and held annually after Easter, was in the 13th century one of the most important trade marts in Europe. Merchants came from Flanders, the Rhineland and northern France, bringing fine cloth (in the days before the English weaving industry developed significantly), and other valuable goods for sale; Henry III bought material for his wardrobe there. The goods came up the Ouse by boat – presumably through Wisbech at first, then through King's Lynn after the river was diverted to enter the Wash there (page 199). In the 14th century the fair ceased to be of international significance, but St Ives continued to prosper as an

important local market town and river port.

The name is that of St Ivo who, according to one of the most outlandish of early legends, was a bishop from Persia who somehow found his way to Huntingdonshire in the early days of Christianity. He was associated with a village then called Slepe – a name meaning muddy or slippery, presumably relating to a ford across the Ouse. When Ramsey Abbey was founded in 969 it was endowed with the lordship of Slepe, and promoted the cult of the saint. When a skeleton was dug up at Slepe the abbot pronounced it that of St Ivo; it was taken to Ramsey and enshrined there as an object of veneration (page 193). A small priory was built over the site of the grave at Slepe, and by about 1100 a wooden bridge crossed the river nearby, putting the village – which by then was coming to be known as St Ives – on an important route from the south into Fenland. An abbot of Ramsey founded the fair. The village grew into a town, at first enveloping and then encroaching on to the fairground, and in 1290 a weekly market was established. The abbey further increased the commercial prosperity of St Ives – from which it derived great benefit through rents and tolls – by blocking navigation further up the river. About 1270 the abbot built a weir across the river on his land at Hemingford Abbots, upstream from St Ives, and persuaded Reginald de Grey, lord of neighbouring Hemingford Grey, to do the same. Ostensibly these were to harness water for driving mills, but their real purpose was to prevent vessels getting up to Huntingdon, hitherto a river port (page 185), so making St Ives the effective head of navigation on the Ouse. The river link with King's Lynn remained important for many centuries.

St Ives has grown fivefold since 1951 when its population was scarcely over three thousand, but the new building has been entirely northward; the old town, with its busy shopping streets and (on Mondays and Fridays) open markets, remains lively and attractive.

The town is now bypassed and the medieval bridge, hitherto the main point of entry from the south, now takes only essential servicing traffic and, of course, pedestrians – there are car parks across the river. The bridge was built in 1415–26 on the site of the older wooden structure; four of the arches are original but the two southern ones were rebuilt after they had been destroyed as a defensive measure in the Civil War. The great feature is the chapel, half-way across on the eastern side, one of only three in England to survive in this position (the other two are in Yorkshire). The chapel contained an altar dedicated to St Leger (who was a French bishop tortured while being held hostage), where travellers were expected to pray and leave an offering – so funding the bridge. The chapel is at roadway level; below it (but above water level) are two rooms where lived the priest-warden. It was put to various uses after the Reformation, and in 1736 two upper storeys were added, making it look like a tower; for a time it was a public house. It became derelict, and in 1929 was bought by benefactors who restored it after demolishing the upper storeys. The balcony attached to the lower floor, projecting over the river, is on the site of a privy which must have been extremely convenient for both the priest-wardens and later the customers of the pub, in the days before sanitation.

From the bridge there is a lovely view up-river, with extensive meadows stretching to the left and, towards the right, a tree-grown island with the parish church spire rising behind. Down-river the view is dominated by a tall – and elegant – mid-Victorian building with classical detailing, built as a flour mill. The bridge itself is best seen from the short Quay to the east – it is difficult to appreciate that most of the river vessels would have moored on this short stretch. Bridge Street leads north from the bridge. By the river is a 17th-century house with four jettied gables, outwardly one of the oldest buildings in the town, though earlier ones survive behind later facades. Along the street on the left is a nice succession of early Georgian upper storeys above modern shop fronts, many in deep red brick. Bridge Street forms the stem of a 'T' with Crown Street, which runs parallel with the river, with a similar variety of Georgian and later fronts. In either direction Crown Street opens, after a short distance, into a wider street or space, and this helps to explain how the town developed. Originally the fairground must have extended from the line of Crown Street to the river, and for some distance along the river front on either side of the bridge. Gradually buildings encroached until most of the river frontage was occupied, and Bridge and Crown Streets covered the central part of the fairground. All that was left, eventually, of the fairground was the still spacious Market Hill to the east and the wide Broadway to the west. Market Hill has the rough-and-tumble character of a working market place (stalls are there Mondays and Fridays) and is none the worse for that. There are many individually good buildings, and in the middle is a statue of Cromwell – he moved from Huntingdon to near St Ives in 1631, and in 1636 moved on to Ely. Appropriately, beside him is the Free Church, built in 1863 by the owner of the flour mill across the river, with a tall and powerful spire which – deliberately – competes with the Anglican spire at the opposite end of the town. The church has been successfully subdivided; the worship area is now the top part of the original interior, where the thin Gothic ironwork of the supports and elaborate woodwork of the roof are seen to good effect. The alley beside the church leads to the Quay.

Going westwards, Crown Street opens into Broadway, the most elegant street in town. There is a succession of classical fronts of different heights, predominantly in buff brick, on the south side of the street, backing on to the river. The buildings on the north side are more modest, and many have passageways through to courtyards, some of which have been converted for shopping. The parish church with its spire beckons in the distance, but well before it is reached the buildings on the south side end and the street, now called The Waits, opens on to the river – or more exactly a side stream of the Ouse, from which it is separated by the tree-grown island seen from the bridge. Nearby is the interesting Norris Museum, founded by a local historian.

Finally there is the church. It has a particularly beautiful spire rising from a tall and slenderly proportioned tower. It is not certain how far the present spire resembles the original one, since it was rebuilt in 1723 after a storm, again in 1879 and finally in 1924 after an early aeroplane had flown into it. The spacious, essentially 15th century interior has an ornate screen and elaborate organ designed by Sir Ninian Comper early this century. Overlooking the churchyard is a Georgian house with broad canted bay windows, built of brick of the particularly attractive local pinky buff colour (seen also, for instance, in the centre of the nearby village of Bluntisham), set off with red brick dressings.

St Neots

St Neots has three special things – the market place, the church and the river. The town grew beside a priory said to have been founded *c.* 972. By some means the remains of Neot, a holy Cornishman who had lived on the edge of Bodmin Moor, found their way here and were placed in a shrine in the monastery where they were venerated. The Vikings sacked the priory in 1010, but it was refounded in 1081 as a dependency of Bec, the great abbey in Normandy. The big rectangular market place was probably laid out in the twelfth century to the south of the monastery, and a bridge built across the River Ouse. The priory has vanished, but the market place is very much there, full of stalls on Thursday and cars on other days. Its character is set by the Georgian buildings on the southern side, mainly in buff brick; the most striking has a broad frontage with pediment and elliptical archway; this was the Bull Inn when St Neots was a stage on a loop off the Great North Road – which runs on the other side of the river. Other buildings on this side of the market place also have arches leading into yards which originally extended back to the Brook, a tributary of the Ouse. Later buildings now block these yards from the water, but Brook Street, reached from the south-east corner of the market place, runs alongside the stream, now accommodating pleasure boats. Past Brook House of *c.* 1700 is the magnificent church – not the priory

church, which was on a different site, but the parish church. Most of the building was finished by 1486; the tower, started about then, was completed by 1535. It recalls the great towers of Somerset, with its complicated buttresses, each having a pinnacle of its own at the belfry stage, its tall belfry lights and its square corner turrets, each ending with a cluster of small pinnacles and a spirelet. There are interesting roofs to nave and aisles, with openwork brackets, figures of angels, and a menagerie of animals, birds and mythical creatures on cornices, beams and bosses. Near the church a bridge crosses the Brook into Eynesbury – originally a Saxon settlement which preceded priory and town, but for long a suburb with village character. The narrow main street bends past various interesting buildings, not all in the best condition, to the church which looks modest compared with that of St Neots. Paths and lanes lead westward from Eynesbury to the Ouse, or to sidewaters separated from the main river by islands. The river is more accessible on its western side, reached over the bridge from the market place, where a park and meadows stretch in both directions.

Thorney

Thorney is a place of much charm, quite unlike anywhere else in the Fens. A settlement of solitary monks was set up about 670, which developed into an ordinary monastery; it was sacked by the Vikings and refounded in 972 at the same time as the abbey at Peterborough. At the Dissolution the lands passed to the earl of Bedford, appropriator also of monastic lands at Woburn and at Tavistock in Devon. A later earl headed the Bedford Level Corporation which organized the drainage of the central part of the Fens; the Dutchman Cornelius Vermuyden was appointed in 1631 to carry out the work, completed after the Civil War – hence the names Old and New Bedford River for the straight parallel watercourses which Vermuyden formed (well to the south-east of Thorney) to take the waters of the Ouse and other rivers. The earls took over the abbot's house at Thorney and rebuilt it; the oldest part is Elizabethan, but the main part is a small but distinguished classical work of 1660. The village, or town, seems to have disintegrated after the Dissolution; the abbey church fell to ruin, but the western part was repaired in 1638 to serve the now revived community. It has an extraordinary west front – the central part of

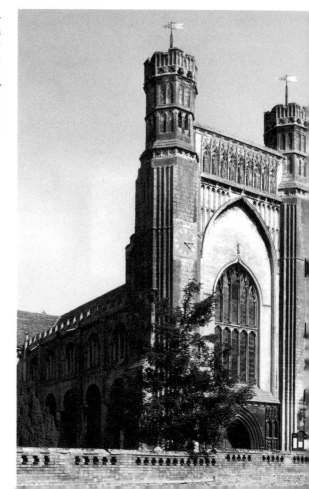

89 Thorney Abbey (St Mary and St Botolph) Part of the extraordinary west front of the abbey church, converted 1638 into the parish church.

the original front – Norman but altered in the 15th century, with tall corner turrets and a single huge recessed arch, like one of the three great arches of Peterborough cathedral. The west window, doorway and other detailing are 'Gothic Survival' of the time of the restoration. The Norman arches of the arcades are blocked to form the side walls of the church. For a time the church was also used for services in French – a number of refugees originally from France had settled in Thorney and drained some of the marshes in the late 16th century; there were still people who spoke the language when the church re-opened. South of the church is an attractive rectangular green said to have been formed from the abbey cloister (though it is rather far from the church, which a cloister should adjoin); the oldest building facing it is a two-gabled 17th-century house in stone. Along the nearby street is a range of simple Georgian brick houses – obviously Bedford estate houses of the period. More remarkable is the very long series of Victorian estate cottages along the street leading east, mostly neo-Tudor in brick and stone. At the far end they form contrived picturesque groups, reminiscent of inter-war garden cities, or some of the more enlightened public housing of the 1950s to 70s. The Victorian dukes (the earldom of Bedford became a dukedom in 1694) also provided florid Gothic

90 *Top* **Thorney Abbey** was taken over by the Russells, later Dukes of Bedford, at the Dissolution. The classical house of 1660 now bears the name.

91 *Above* **Thorney**. One of many fancy Victorian buildings, in rather rough local brick, built by the Duke of Bedford when Thorney was transformed into a large model estate village.

buildings, including a school, among the older houses in the village centre. Thorney is probably a village rather than a town, but it is near enough to town size to justify inclusion in this book.

Whittlesey

Whittlesey is an unexpectedly attractive town, in an unpromising part of Fenland, dominated by one of the finest spires in England. There is an astonishing variety of old building materials around the market place. One early 17th-century house just beyond the south-east corner is in rough limestone with stone slates, as if it were near Stamford, a few miles to the west. Other buildings are in Georgian brick, reddish on the present Post Office, buff on a house near the north-east corner, with distinctive 'Venetian' doorway and window above; the bank on the north-western corner is of red brick with stone dressings. Prominent on the west side is a white plastered house with thatched roof, a rare survival in the Fens. The central feature of the square, pulling together the disparate buildings, is the Market Cross, with stone columns supporting a pyramid roof of stone slates. Soaring above the buildings to the south is the superlative steeple. Norman Scarfe in his *Shell Guide* to Cambridgeshire calls it 'one of the most perfectly designed towers and spires in Christendom', a pardonable exaggeration. He likens it to steeples in Northamptonshire, whence came the stone. In his eulogy, Mr Scarfe describes how the buttresses, squared up to the belfry stage, are given a diagonal profile at the last stage, suggesting the form of an octagon; perhaps a reminiscence of the west tower of Ely – although Thorney Abbey, not Ely, was the patron of the church. The rest of the church is not as grand as the spire, and the churchyard has been needlessly turned into a lawn by the removal of the tombstones. Surprisingly, there is a second medieval church, St Andrew's, with pleasant houses around it, and a winding fenland drain with the character of a canal nearby.

92 **Market Place, Whittlesey** is surrounded by buildings of varied styles and materials; the dynamic spire, with its flying buttresses and pinnacles, is one of the finest in England. The broad Market Cross has a roof of stone slabs from the Stamford area, well to the west.

Wisbech

Wisbech has a quality of its own. The view from the bridge along the Brinks, where two irregular rows of mainly Georgian houses face each other across the deep-banked, tidal River Nene, has no parallel in England. Nearby, in contrast, there is formal Georgian town-planning on the site of the vanished castle. The first castle, which became a stronghold of the bishops of Ely, was built in Norman times beside a wide estuary which formerly opened into the Wash. Until the 13th century this was the outlet for several rivers converging from the west and south – the Nene, the Ouse, the Cam and others, the lower courses of which, meandering over the partly undrained Fens, were completely different from those of today. At some time in the 13th century the Wisbech estuary became silted, and the water of the combined rivers were diverted eastward a few miles south of the town, eventually to enter the Wash below King's Lynn. Lynn benefited hugely from this diversion because it provided navigable links with the hinterland, but Wisbech, for a time, was left with a blocked estuary and no inland navigation. Its fortunes improved from about 1480, when Bishop Morton of Ely constructed a new course for the River Nene – Morton's Leam – from Peterborough eastwards, probably linking with an existing small stream and forming the basis for the present course of the Nene through Wisbech to the Wash. This brought a limited amount of waterborne trade back to Wisbech, but for long it was small compared with that of Lynn.

Following the Fenland reclamations of the 17th century, Wisbech developed into a very prosperous market town for the surrounding area, much of it newly drained and highly fertile. Navigation improved in stages, and by the early 19th century Wisbech was a busy port with coastal trade – corn went out; coal, timber and other goods came in. The port trade was affected by, but survived, the coming of the railways, which favoured March and Peterborough but left Wisbech on branch lines. Now it has no passenger railway but remains a busy, seemingly remote and self-sufficient town which it is a pleasure to visit. (See colour illustration pp. 2–3)

Starting at the bridge and going along the incomparable North Brink – the row of buildings along the northern side of the embanked river – the first landmark is the Town Hall with a classical front in stone (Wisbech is mostly a brick town), built in 1811 as the Corn Exchange by Joseph Medworth, the successful developer of much of late Georgian Wisbech. Two Victorian banks on the downstream side are worthy companions; a third, upstream, is neo-Georgian of 1928 with red-brick columns; one of the joint architects was Munro Cautley, the Ipswich architect famous for his book on Suffolk churches. Beyond is a lovely succession of Georgian buildings in varied materials; one is stuccoed, the next is in red brick; then there is a brick pair with Regency bow windows. Farther on, past a house with wistaria, is a warehouse making a pleasant contrast, in dun brick with a roof of red pantiles, conspicuous because its slope is parallel with the frontage. No. 12 has an 18th-century front with later iron balcony. No. 14, with a fine stone doorcase, provides a foretaste to Peckover House, the showpiece of the town and property of the National Trust. Unlike the other buildings on the Brink it is set back behind a small forecourt, emphasizing the dignity of the classical doorway of stone in an otherwise straightforward

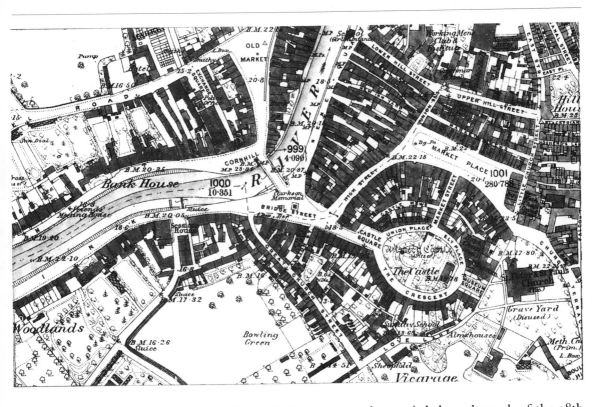

Opposite
St Peter and St Paul, Wisbech, a building of many periods, with a splendid tower of *c.*1520 built of stone from Northamptonshire brought along the river.

Above **Map XI, Wisbech.** The striking oval of Georgian houses (93) was built on the site of the castle. The Market Place developed to the north of the castle ditch, with the church (colour plate, page 67) to the east. The Brinks (pages 2/3) are to the west, with houses facing the winding river; 'Bank House' is now Peckover House, a property of the National Trust. The map is of 1889.

brick front. It was built in 1727 and occupied through much of the 18th century by the Southwell family; the interior has rich and lovely details dating from various times during their occupancy. The house was bought in 1777 by Jonathan Peckover, a Quaker who had moved to Wisbech three years before, starting as a shopkeeper and becoming, like so many Quaker traders of the time, a banker. He founded, with members of other families including the Gurneys of Norwich, a local bank which for a long time operated in a wing of the house (since demolished). Behind the house is an unexpectedly large garden with fine old trees, extending behind several of the houses further along the Brink. Beyond Peckover House is a Quaker meeting house, built in 1854 by Algernon Peckover, a member of the family who was a watercolour artist as well as architect. He also designed the next group of gabled houses which, although at odds with the prevalent Georgian style of the Brinks, provide an effective focal feature seen from the bridge.

Standing in front of Peckover House, one looks across the river, with its steep grassy banks and exposed mud when the tide is out, to the succession of buildings on South Brink, only slightly less eventful than those on the north side. What is now the Grammar School occupies the grandest house on the south side, with a late Georgian front in yellow brick – in contrast to the motley reds and browns traditional to the area. Further back towards the bridge is an early Georgian pair of houses with a central pediment (added later) over a passageway, with the two doorways oddly on either side; in the eastern one, no. 8, was born in 1838 Octavia Hill, daughter of another local banker (less successful than the Peckovers), who became a protagonist for better-managed housing for the poor, and was one of the founders of the National Trust. The climax of the view along the South Brink is formed by a Gothic memorial enclosing a statue to Samuel Clarkson, son of the headmaster of the Grammar School, who was an associate of Wilberforce in the abolition of slavery; he died in 1846 and the monument was erected thirty-five years later – one of the last designs of the great Sir Gilbert Scott.

Clarkson lived in one of three gabled 17th-century houses, among the oldest in the town, in nearby York Row, which leads to the area developed in late Georgian times on the site of the castle. The medieval and Tudor buildings were demolished during the Commonwealth by John Thurloe, a government official under Cromwell, and replaced by a classical mansion. At the Restoration the property reverted to the bishop of Ely, but it was bought in 1797 by Joseph Medworth, a native of Wisbech who had been a speculative builder in south London. He surrounded Thurloe's house with an oval of town houses called, in different parts, The Crescent, Ely Place and Union Place, providing a memorable piece of formal town-planning reminiscent, on a country-town scale, of Bath. The houses are three-storeyed of the standard London Georgian type, but in colourful local brick with white doorcases. On the south side – The Crescent – the centrepiece is a grander taller house with a pediment, dating from 1808. On the north side – in Ely Place – the unity has been broken by a new library, following the roofline but otherwise different in style. The whole must have been magnificent while Thurloe's grand house stood, but unfortunately Medworth pulled it down in 1815 and replaced it with the surprisingly undistinguished house called The Castle, set back behind Thurloe's remaining gateposts. But it provides a centrepiece for Museum Square, which is flanked by the classical Wisbech Museum, built in 1846 to house an institution founded the eleven years before – one of the earliest outside London and the university towns, though preceded at Saffron Walden. The Peckovers were patrons.

Museum Square opens in front of the parish church, providing contrasts between classical and Gothic, in brick and stone, with background landscape. The tower, built just before the Reformation, is very fine, especially the elaborate parapet, but the belfry lights are, visually, too small. The rest of the building is extremely confusing, with work from the Norman to Tudor periods. It cannot compare with some of the magnificent churches around, as at Walsoken (now a suburb), West Walton, Leverington and Elm.

Away from the highlights of the Brinks and the Castle quarter, Wisbech is of intermittent interest. The elongated market place developed outside the castle ditch; it has atmosphere on market days (Thursdays and Saturdays) but the buildings are mostly unimpressive except at the western end, where the Rose and Crown hotel has a classical front and a delightful courtyard, with timberwork and brick of the 17th and 18th centuries. Alleys lead through to Nene Quay, a riverside road. Thirty years ago there was a splendid row of warehouses on the opposite side of the river, which reminded writers such as Arthur Oswald (in *Old Towns Revisited*, 1952) of Hanseatic towns; now, after long-drawn decay and damage after flooding, only one survives intact, an austere five-storeyed building of 1820. Another, smaller but similar, rises above the lower buildings on the Nene Quay side.

93 *Opposite*
Union Place, Wisbech is part of the classical development started *c.*1800 on the site of the vanished castle; the developer was Thomas Medworth, previously a speculative builder in south London. (Map XI).

94 Elgood's Brewery, Wisbech, a remarkable industrial building of 1795, at the far end of the North Brink.

Back over the bridge for a final architectural stimulant – in the triangular Old Market behind the beginning of the North Brink. This was mentioned by the present name in 1221 – implying that the newer, and present, market place had already come into existence. The Old Market continued as a place of trade, and it has a collection of Georgian brick houses, some splendid, although the 'Gothick' Octagon Chapel, which was the focal feature, was demolished against local opposition in 1952; its loss continues to be regretted. Now a public lavatory is the focal feature. The Italianate Barclays Bank, close to the bridge, was built in 1878 for Gurney, Birkbeck, Peckover and Buxton's bank, moved here from the wing of Peckover House. This is an appropriate place to end a tour of this highly individual town.

Bibliography

The bibliography is divided between the four present counties, with a short list of general books at the end. The publications range from full-scale books to booklets, folders, leaflets and town trails which, in the opinion of the author, help significantly towards the understanding of the history and buildings of particular towns. Not all, however, are in print. The author acknowledges his debt to these publications – considerable in many cases – in providing information about the various towns.

Each county list is headed by books from three general series, indicated by the initials (DC), (ME) and (BE):

(DC) *The Darwen County History Series* (Phillimore); general history of each county, with coverage of some towns in considerable detail

(ME) *The Making of the English Landscape series* (Hodder & Stoughton); history of the landscape, with considerable coverage of towns

(BE) *The Buildings of England series* (Penguin); covering the interesting buildings in each town and village, by Sir Nikolaus Pevsner.

Norfolk

A History of Norfolk (DC), Susanna Wade Martins, 1984

The Norfolk Landscape (ME), D. Dymond, 1985

North-East Norfolk and Norwich; North-West and South Norfolk (BE), N. Pevsner, 1962

Norfolk from the air, D. A. Edwards and P. Wade Martins, Norfolk Museums Service, 1987 – air photographs, including several of towns

A History of Thetford, A. Crosby, 1986, Phillimore

Publications on Norwich: *Norwich the growth of a city*, B. Green and R. M. R. Young, 1981; *The Norwich Blackfriars*, H. Sutermeister, 1977; *Norwich Houses before 1700*, R. Smith and A. Carter. Booklets on *Elm Hill* and *King Street*; also *Heritage Trail*

Norfolk Museums Service Information Sheets on *Flint*; *The Pilgrimage to Walsingham*; *The Norwich School* (of painters); *Norwich Castle*; *Thomas Paine*; *The Ancient House, Thetford*, etc.

Medieval Archaeology (periodical), vol. VI, 1962, has detailed articles on King's Lynn history and buildings by E. M. Carus-Wilson and W. A. Pantin

Portrait of a Village: Castle Rising, booklet by C. S. Dence, 1980

Cley, P. Brooks; *Cromer*, C. Crawford Holden; *Holt*, P. Brooks; *Great Yarmouth*, C. Lewis; booklets by

Poppyland Publishing, Cromer

King's Lynn Preservation Trust – folder with leaflets on historic buildings

Hingham in History; The Heyday of their Strength (emigration from Hingham to USA); booklets by M. E. Lonsdale

Other booklets, leaflets and folders containing town walks and trails: *Aylsham, A Guided Walk; A Cromer Walk; A stroll round Diss; Holt Town Walks; Looking at Lynn; Walsingham; Wells Town Trail; A Walk round Old Wymondham*

Suffolk

A History of Suffolk (DC), D. Dymond & P. Northeast, 1985

The Suffolk Landscape (ME), N. Scarfe, 1972

Suffolk (BE), N. Pevsner, revised 1974

The Suffolk we live in, P. Fincham, 1976/86, Barbara Hopkinson Books, Norwich

The Suffolk Guide, N. Scarfe, 1988 (based on earlier Shell Guide), Alastair Press, Bury St Edmunds

Suffolk Churches, Munro Cautley, 1937, new edition with supplements 1982, Boydell Press, Woodbridge

Hadleigh through the ages, W. A. B. Jones, 1977; *Ipswich through the ages*, L. J. Redstone, 1948 and reprints; *Long Melford through the ages*, B. L. Wall, 1986; *Sudbury through the ages*, B. L. Wall; all published by East Anglian Magazine, Ipswich

Ipswich, town on the Orwell, R. Malster, 1982; *Lowestoft, east coast port*, R. Malster, 1982, Terence Dalton, Lavenham

Bury St Edmunds, Alec Clifton-Taylor, offprint by Alastair Press, Bury St Edmunds from *Another Six English Towns* (1984 BBC)

Aldeburgh; Dunwich; Southwold; Walberswick; The Suffolk Shoreline; all booklets by J. & S. Bacon, Segment Publications

Woodbridge, A Short History and Guide, booklet by C. & M. Weaver, 1976/85

Lavenham and the Cloth Industry, folder, National Trust

The Suffolk Preservation Society has published folders of detailed walks in certain towns: *Exploring Beccles; About Hadleigh; A walk round Lavenham; Along Melford; Southwold; Concerning Thorpeness*

Other booklets, leaflets and folders containing town walks or trails: *A Walk around Bungay; Bury St Edmunds Sketchbook*, by K. Pilling; *A Short Look at Sudbury; Welcome to Thorpeness*

Essex

A History of Essex (DC), A. C. Edwards, 1958/85

Essex (BE), N. Pevsner, revised 1965

Historic Towns in Essex, An Archaeological Study, 1983, Essex County Council

Essex at Work, 1700–1815, A. F. J. Brown, 1969, Essex County Council

Essex and the Industrial Revolution, J. Booker, 1974, Essex County Council

Resist the Invader, the Story of Essex Forts and Castles, P. R. Gifford, 1982, Essex Libraries

Essex Markets and Fairs, booklet by W. Walker, 1981, Essex Record Office

Historic Building Studies no. 1, D. F. Stenning and M. C. Wadhams, 1986, Essex County Council (timber-framed buildings)

Essex County Council has published several illustrated booklets on different themes, many relating to towns, including *Towns of Essex; Essex and the Sea; Medieval Essex; Elizabethan Essex; Stuart Essex; Georgian Essex; Victorian Essex; The Visual Arts in Essex; Essex Homes; Essex Monasteries; Medieval Essex Churches; The Face of Essex*

Maldon, J. R. Smith, 1971, booklet by Essex County Council

Roman Colchester, 1980, Colchester Borough Council

Colchester, G. Martin, 1959, Benham, Colchester

History of Braintree and Bocking, W. F. Quin, 1981, Lavenham Press

Saffron Walden to AD 1300, S. R. Bassett, 1982, Council for British Archaeology

Six More English Towns, Alec Clifton-Taylor, 1981/5, BBC, includes chapter on Saffron Walden

The Harwich Story, L. T. Weaver, 1975; *A Walk round Old Harwich*, 1973, The Harwich Society

A History of Prittlewell (Southend), W. Pollitt, 1951; *The Rise of Southend*, W. Pollitt, 1957; also two leaflets, *Southend – a seaside holiday, 1750–1950* and *Southend's Heritage – Georgian and Victorian Terraces*

A Short Historical Guide to Thaxted, M. Arman, 1980; *Thaxted Guildhall*, M. Arman and J. Boutwood, booklets

King Harold's Town (Waltham Abbey), J. Camp and D. Dean, 1975; *A Walk round Waltham Abbey*, K. N. Bascombe, 1974, booklets

Colchester, official guide, good on history and buildings, includes town walk

Other booklets and leaflets: *Billericay Town Trail; Discovering Bradford Street* (Bocking); *Coggeshall, a Town Walk; Halstead, the Town Story; The Town of Maldon*

Cambridgeshire & Huntingdonshire

A History of Cambridgeshire (DC), B. Galloway, 1983

A History of Huntingdonshire (DC), M. Wickes, 1985

The Cambridgeshire Landscape (ME), C. Taylor, 1973

The Bedfordshire and Huntingdonshire Landscape (ME), P. Bigmore, 1979

Cambridgeshire (BE), N. Pevsner, revised 1970

Bedfordshire, Huntingdon and Peterborough (BE), N. Pevsner, 1968

Cambridgeshire, Norman Scarfe, 1983; Faber (Shell Guide)

The Changing Fenland, H. C. Darby, 1983, Cambridge U.P.

The Fenland, A. Parker and D. Pye, 1976, David & Charles

The Book of Huntingdon, C. Dunn, 1977, Barracuda Books

St Ives in Huntingdonshire, B. Little and H. Werba, 1974, Adams & Dart

Peterborough, H. F. Tebbs, 1979, Oleander Press, Cambridge

Clay That Burns, R. Hillier, 1981, London Brick Company (history of Fletton brick industry)

The Isle of Ely, booklet by T. Bevis, 1985

More than 1000 Years of March, booklet by T. Bevis, 1984

Roman Cambridgeshire, D. M. Browne; *Anglo-Saxon Cambridgeshire*, A. Taylor; *Medieval Cambridgeshire*, H. C. Darby, Oleander Press, Cambridge

Godmanchester, H. J. M. Green, 1977, Oleander Press; Cambridge

Wisbech, official guide, good on history and buildings, includes town walk

Town Trails of *Godmanchester; Huntingdon; Ramsey; St Ives; St Neots*; folders by Huntingdonshire District Council

Ely Town Trail; Peterborough Town Trail

(*Old Towns Revisited*, published by Country Life, 1952, has outstanding article on Wisbech by Arthur Oswald)

General

East Anglian Landscapes, J. Ravensdale and R. Muir, 1984, Michael Joseph

Coastal Resorts of East Anglia, M. Rouse, 1982, Terence Dalton, Lavenham – detailed history

The River Stour, R. Edwards, 1982, Terence Dalton, Lavenham

The Traveller's Guide to Medieval England, C. Platt, 1985, Secker & Warburg – covers several places

Historic Towns, ed. M. D. Lobel, 1974, Scolar Press – covers Cambridge and Norwich, with very good historical maps.

Index

The black and white photographs are shown in the Index in bold type under plate numbers.